THE OTHER SIDE

OF SILENCE

THE

OTHER

SIDE

of Silence

A MEMOIR OF EXILE, IRAN, &
THE GLOBAL WOMEN'S MOVEMENT

Mahnaz Afkhami

The University of North Carolina Press
CHAPEL HILL

This book was published with the assistance of the Greensboro Women's Fund
of the University of North Carolina Press.

Founding Contributors: Linda Arnold Carlisle, Sally Schindel Cone,
Anne Faircloth, Bonnie McElveen Hunter, Linda Bullard Jennings, Janice J. Kerley
(in honor of Margaret Supplee Smith), Nancy Rouzer May, and Betty Hughes Nichols.

Naghmeh Zarbafian, "I'm Not Invisible," in Mahnaz Afkhami and Haleh Vaziri,
Claiming Our Rights: A Manual for Women's Human Rights Education in Muslim Societies
(Bethesda, Md.: Sisterhood Is Global Institute, 1996). Reprinted by permission.

Manufactured in the United States of America

The University of North Carolina Press has been a member
of the Green Press Initiative since 2003.

Frontispiece portrait of the author courtesy of the Women's Learning Partnership.

Cover photo: Mahnaz Afkhami at the Preparatory Committee
for the First UN Women's Conference in Mexico, 1975. Courtesy of the author.

Library of Congress Cataloging-in-Publication Data
Names: Afkhami, Mahnaz, author.
Title: The other side of silence : a memoir of exile, Iran,
and the global women's movement / Mahnaz Afkhami.
Description: Chapel Hill : The University of North Carolina Press, [2022] |
Includes bibliographic references and index.
Identifiers: LCCN 2022015123 | ISBN 9781469669991 (cloth) | ISBN 9781469670003 (ebook)
Subjects: LCSH: Afkhami, Mahnaz. | Women political activists—Iran—Biography. |
Women political activists—United States—Biography. | Political activists—Iran—
Biography. | Political activists—United States—Biography. |
Women's rights. | Feminism. | LCGFT: Autobiographies.
Classification: LCC DS316.9.A336 A3 2022 | DDC 305.420955092 [B]—dc23/eng/20220429
LC record available at https://lccn.loc.gov/2022015123

To my husband, Gholam Reza, a true feminist

Contents

— Part II —

Author's Note

F OR THOSE OF US who work with the activists and leaders of the women's movements in the Global South, the scarcity of documentation or archival collections about the work of the majority of the women of the world is a constant barrier to research and learning. To address this, Women's Learning Partnership (WLP) has been conducting a series of oral history interviews that are now held at the British Library as well as available on WLP's Learning Center. At WLP, we have had the support of the Library of Congress, the National Archives, and other institutions dedicated to this cause. My own loss of documents and material about the work of the Women's Organization of Iran, as well as the loss of my personal correspondence, photos, and writings, has created in me a passion for saving historical records and making them accessible.

WLP is creating a new website (http://mahnazafkhami.com/archives-2/) that will serve as a repository for all the materials referenced in this book and beyond. This will include a wide range of original legal and historical documents and correspondence from my time as minister for women's affairs and secretary general of the Women's Organization of Iran. Included are materials relating to the 1975 UN World Conference on Women, including the contract with the United Nations to set up the International Research and Training Institute for the Advancement of Women (INSTRAW) and the Economic and Social Commission for Asia and the Pacific (ESCAP) centers in Tehran, as well as the draft World Plan of Action prepared by the Iranian delegation; legal documents on family legislation and civic support for professional women in Iran; scans of publications and research conducted by the Women's Organization of Iran; and photos and videos from Iran prior to the Islamic Revolution. These files are not widely available; in fact, the majority of them do not exist elsewhere and are at risk of being lost if they are not preserved. Having lost many personal documents, as well as archives of the women's movement in Iran, as a result of the Revolution, I have made it one of my life's missions to ensure that this does not happen again.

In writing about my conversations with friends and colleagues, I have referred to my diaries of the last forty years and to forty hours of recorded conversations in the early 1980s with Professor Shahla Haeri of Boston University. I have been mindful of the possible ramifications for individuals and their families, whether they live in Iran or abroad, using fictional names as needed.

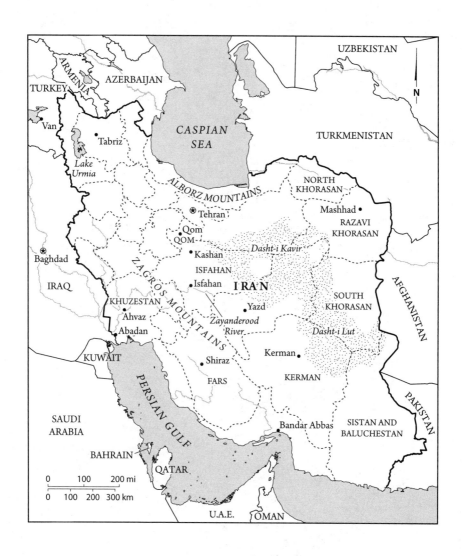

THE OTHER SIDE
OF SILENCE

Prologue

EARLY IN THE MORNING of November 27, 1978, I was awakened in my Manhattan hotel room by a ringing telephone. Calls at odd hours weren't unusual; I had traveled internationally for years, first as secretary general of the Women's Organization of Iran (WOI), then as Iran's first minister for women's affairs, and now in my second turn as WOI secretary general. Back home in Tehran, my husband, Gholam, knew that if he needed to speak with me, the time difference and my full schedule meant he needed to call before I left for a day of meetings. This time I had been in New York for nearly two months, leading the negotiations with the UN legal team to draft an agreement between the government of Iran and the United Nations to set up the UN International Research and Training Institute for the Advancement of Women (INSTRAW). The institute was to be based in Tehran, and it represented both the culmination of the work my colleagues and I had been doing on behalf of women's rights in our country, as well as recognition that Iran was becoming a progressive force for women not just in the Middle East but in the world.

But this phone call was different; I wasn't expecting it since I had recently spoken with Gholam to tell him my work had been finished in New York and I was about to return to Iran. Who could be calling at this hour, and why? Had something happened to our teenage son, Babak?

When I heard Gholam's voice, I braced myself for his news. It was not about Babak's safety at all. It was about mine.

"I had a conversation with the queen and mentioned that you planned to return to Iran in a few days," he began. "She said, 'It would be better if she continues her work in New York.'"

Confused, I asked him, "Shall I delay my trip this Sunday?"

"She knows your work is complete," Gholam said. Then he paused. "She is trying to say that things are out of control. You might very well be arrested at the airport."

"So it will not be next Sunday—or perhaps any Sunday?"

"It's hard to say," he replied.

I put the receiver down and sat on the bed, looking at my half-packed suitcase, trying to grasp the ramifications of what I had just heard. The daily demonstrations, strikes, arson, and destruction reported from Iran, especially the recent arrest of several members of the cabinet, including Prime Minister Hoveyda, indicated the shah's near-abdication of power. His choice of a military government with no intention of using the armed forces to stop the violence was obviously a contradiction in terms. The queen was simply trying to send a message that they were helpless to provide protection. She had known that the UN Secretariat had suggested that I lead INSTRAW and that the Iranian cabinet had decided that this was an excellent idea, although if I traveled back to Iran and there was pressure to arrest me to appease the revolutionaries, this would be made impossible by my UN credentials. I realized that the queen was trying to save my life.

Six weeks later the royal family would leave Iran for Cairo.

THAT MORNING in the hotel room, unaware of just how precarious my safety would become even in exile, I made myself a cup of coffee and began to watch the Reuters news bulletin, waiting for news from Iran, as I had done constantly in recent weeks. The news was even more concerning than usual and, for the first time, I was terrified for my country. But so far away from the violence and upheaval, what should I do? I thought I might begin with my plan for that day—what I had planned before Gholam's call. I would deal with the larger issues later. I remembered that I had planned to buy a winter coat that day. I came to New York in October with one suitcase and clothes to last me two weeks. The trip had taken a month longer, and it was cold now. Where should I shop and what kind of coat would I buy? Up to a few hours ago, I was the secretary general of the Women's Organization of Iran, negotiating with the United Nations on establishing a new institution in Tehran. I would be going back home. I knew exactly what I needed. But now all of that would no longer apply. Who was I now? What kind of life would I lead and what kind of coat would that life require? I realized I would need more time—as it turned out, nearly a decade—before I would begin to have an answer, and more time after that to be able to see that life and its work in full form.

THIS BOOK is the story of my life in Iran, a country in the grip of an intense struggle between tradition and modernity, and in the United States, where I have lived in exile—a condition that allows me to belong to both my countries and to neither—looking at both as an outsider, but seeing each from within. It is also the story of how the experience of Iran helped me to continue my life's passion in exile: to find the ways and means of helping to change the structure of human relations, which is not only the foundation of inequality between men and women, but also the precursor of war and violence in our world.

I was born in Iran and have lived most of my life in the United States. I attended high school and university in the United States and returned to Iran to teach English literature at the National University of Iran. I became minister for women's affairs in Iran and went on to lead international women's organizations in the United States. My total immersion in these two cultures and love for them has taught me how to bridge East and West when working with women.

As I look back on my life in the two countries, I am often reminded of the obvious differences and surprising similarities between the two cultures. Iranians are nearly certain that almost all that has happened to them in recent memory is the result of machinations by other, stronger, largely Western forces. Americans think that they have a mission to guide the rest of the world and lead them to salvation, in spite of often dubious results. Both are flawed in dealing with history. Iran is attached to the glories of its ancient past in ways that are akin to psychological impairment. Hardly a day passes that one does not hear, in one context or another, a reference to something that happened or may have happened millennia ago. America, with a much shorter and more accessible history, refers to its origin and "the founding fathers"—what they may or may not have said and what they meant is an ever-present part of the national discussion. Iranians revere the *Shahnameh*—the *Book of Kings*—the national epic, and quote from it by heart. Americans refer to the Constitution as if it were a sacred book, revered and everlasting. Iran has clerics who have taken up the task of interpreting what the religious holy book of Islam means. In the United States, nine men and women have the lifetime function of deciphering the Constitution and what its framers had in mind when they wrote it. Neither country considers that society has evolved over the centuries or that parts of the wisdom expressed to guide people ages ago may no longer apply.

Telling these stories of my life in Iran and in the United States has been a challenge. On the one hand, because I have participated in or witnessed crucial and life-changing moments in Iran's history from a unique vantage point—working with grassroots women in farms, factories, and schools, as well as working in the government and on legislation—I feel a debt to the women of the country to tell the story of what I have experienced. Since the story of women is intertwined with history, I feel a sense of anguish and uncertainty as I write—not about the truth or validity of what I have seen and heard but about my right as a woman to speak to history, especially since the history of Iran's revolution is even now, over forty years after its unravelling, so controversial and divisive.

In his autobiographical poem "Song of Myself," in *Leaves of Grass*, Walt Whitman writes, "I celebrate myself, and sing myself, and what I assume you shall assume." Should I, a woman, dare say this? Even though I am certain of the story I have to tell and the course of action that the story leads to, I am not certain of my own right to tell that story and to derive a conclusion. I know hundreds of wise women whose words have shaped my view of things, but among them there is not one—indeed there cannot be one—who believes like Whitman in her own right to speak boldly and decisively to history. They don't because their view of their own authority has been shaped by the same culture that shaped the poet's certainty and entitlement. But through thousands of conversations with women from all walks of life, I have learned that the telling of a life story by a woman, in her own way, through her own choices and assignment of values, is an alternate and valuable way of learning, teaching, and knowing.

In dialogue with women across Iran I learned that women's aspirations are the same across differences of religion, lifestyle, and economic and political circumstance. The women I spoke with also shared basic limitations and boundaries embedded in the culture of patriarchy that shaped and continues to shape every aspect of their existence. I learned that rights and freedoms will only be tangible to people if they are communicated with reference to culture and values. These experiences helped me understand and believe that rights are universal, but that contextualized implementation—understanding and incorporating local values and cultures into how we work with women—was the only way to create a truly global movement and lasting change.

At the turn of the twenty-first century, with the support of women leaders I had come to befriend, respect, and work with while in exile, I founded the Women's Learning Partnership (WLP), an international women's organization that was initiated by women from the Global South—an organization made possible by the communications revolution that offered the possibility of ongoing contact across the world, regardless of the existing infrastructure in each country, and with little cost. Through our ongoing communication my colleagues and I learned that not only every aspect of our lives but also our destiny is interconnected. This includes the objects we use or consume, the diseases we suffer from, the state of the air, water, and earth around us—in short, politics, economics, religion, art, and culture. I also realized that the value system that determines women's lives is essentially the same across the world, even if on the surface it looks different. Our subjugation takes many shapes, but the framework of the social structure is frighteningly similar. I worked together with my colleagues across four continents, in thirty languages, and as we shared our road map for self-realization and change, we were shocked repeatedly by wars that erupted without cause or justification, destroyed vast areas of our partner countries, killed millions, displaced people, and brought economic and political disruptions—and seemed to benefit only a small portion of the world's population.

It has become clear that movement building and mobilization that focused on a single issue, no matter how needed and justified that issue is, does not result in the global and holistic change necessary to create the world we seek. Women, the 50 percent of the population who have not been part of the system of decision-making that has caused such incredible destruction and violence, can and will make a difference. We have only to raise our glance from the part of our being that has been the primary focus of the other half of the population—that is, the sexual and childbearing part—to see the entire vista of human experience and create a vision that will allow us to shape a world of peace and security for all. The feminist struggle is the longest fight for achieving justice and equality that the world has ever seen—and it is the feminist movement that will lead us there.

In the words of Rumi, "Beyond all talk of right doing and wrong doing, there is a field. I will meet you there"—on the other side of silence.

PART I

Chapter 1

The Women of Kerman

A LTHOUGH I SPENT ONLY my first eleven years in the small desert city of Kerman where I was born, its light and scorched landscape still pervade my memories. I need only to close my eyes to feel the heat of blinding sunlight on my lids, see the thick gray-green leaves of pistachio trees, and hear the trickling of water—a symbol of sacred beauty.

It was not unusual for our extended family of grandparents, parents, children, aunts, uncles, and cousins to drive out in a jeep caravan across the desert to an oasis miles away where we threw down carpets next to a narrow stream we called *pahnab* (ironically, "wide waters"). There we drank wine and a variety of fruit drinks and sang melodies to the sound of Iran's most popular stringed instrument, the *tar*. On those evenings we felt no contradiction between being proud descendants of Shaykhi Muslim religious leaders and drinking, singing, and dancing together on a desert outing.

The women in my father's family, my aunts and cousins, owned land in their own right and retained that ownership after marriage. They managed their property, handled the workers, dealt with agricultural issues, bought what was needed, and sold what they grew on their land. This area of Iran was still patriarchal and rather feudal, and class in this case trumped gender.

My father's mother, Shah Jan,[1] a descendant of a Qajar prince who had ruled the province of Kerman, was the unquestioned authority in a large household that was spread over several buildings. The *andaroon* (inner house) was where we lived as a family, while the *birouni* (outer house) was where the men entertained, and where my grandfather, Mokhtar-ul-Molk, conducted business and dealt with the concerns of the villagers who came to deliver goods, provide reports, or share their troubles. Every morning the household members came to Shah Jan in the andaroon to offer their salutations and receive guidance, whether requested, desired, or not. My grandmother spoke softly as she puffed on her hookah, with her printed chador around her shoulders and a white scarf carefully pinned under her chin, showing her parted gray hair.[2] From this command center she presided over the household and made decisions that affected the lives of many in the villages.

My maternal grandmother, Tooba Naficy, also came from a respected family, but the Naficys were not landowners. They were intellectuals, interested in books and learning; a cousin had been chosen as tutor by Reza Shah for his son, the crown prince. Tooba was a restless young woman who read any book within reach, from *The Sermons of Sheikh Mohammad* to *A Thousand and One Nights*. She was also beautiful, and at eighteen she married a distant cousin. Her curiosity then led her to the Baha'i faith, and when she converted, her husband's family forced him to divorce her. Tooba moved to her own house and was allowed custody of her daughter on one condition: that she not raise her as a Baha'i. Although she passed on her values and love of learning to my mother, Ferdows, and later to us children, she did not promote her religion. Tooba set up her tailoring business at her house in Kerman, where she brought up my mother and trained and employed many young women who worked for her in the rooms around the small courtyard. In her life as a convert and a single working mother, Tooba was decades ahead of her time.

These formative role models—one an aristocrat who presided over a large household, the other a rebel who forged her own path—had an incredible impact on my view of what a woman could do. Their quite different ways of gaining and exercising independence and power remain with me to this day.

MY MOST vivid childhood memories center around the stories that my brother Hamid, who was three years younger than me, and I were told every evening by Naneh Fatemeh, our powerful nanny. The keeper of folk tales, she passed her knowledge on to us with a sense of duty.

Naneh had a double chin and always tied her white headscarf under the first one. On summer nights she would lift her headscarf and wipe the perspiration from her chins. Her hennaed hair was reddish where the white hair had been and black in other sections. She wore black cotton pants under her printed chintz dress and tied a tiny Quran sewn into a piece of gold and turquoise brocade in the corner of her long headscarf. As she told us stories, her white-flowered cotton chador would fall to her shoulders and gather in her lap. I loved her deep, low voice and her aroma of rose water and tobacco. Although she didn't smoke, she spent the early evening hours by my grandmother's hookah, and the smell hung about her all the time.

Naneh was the keeper of myths and traditions. She instilled in me my first notion of how the world is ordered. She told me at a very early age that those who dealt with carpets dealt with money. They were merchants. They were called *aqa*, or "mister." A whole other category of people, among whom my family had a rather prominent position, dealt with land and its produce. They were called *khan*. The third category of people were workers, who were called *adama*—literally, human beings. Naneh was a member of this last category. I later learned to appreciate the subtle value system implied by this categorization.

Every evening Naneh would come to our bedroom and sit between our two mattresses on the carpet that bore the likeness of Nasr al-din Shah, the storied Qajar king. She would lean against the wall, her legs crossed over the late shah's moustache, and begin her tales. One of our favorites was the story of Amir Arsalan, the bravest hero of all time, and Farokhlaqa, the most beautiful of all maidens. Night after night she described in detail how Amir Arsalan fought monsters and the jinn and the *divs*, and how he endured great hardship and danger to earn the hand of Farokhlaqa. At the outset she reviewed what she had told us the night before, and at the end of each storytelling hour she gave us a preview of the coming night's tale.

"Our betters, the jinn, surround us," Naneh whispered one night. "They can take any shape they want. They can look just like Asghar the gardener or Nassi the cat. They can talk in any voice and no one can tell them from the person or the thing they want to impersonate. They can come alone or in pairs or groups. They sometimes make you do *terrible* things." Naneh stopped and stared into the dark through the half-open window. She pulled her headscarf lower over her hennaed hair.

"*Anything?*" I asked in a hushed voice.

"Anything," she repeated absent-mindedly. "There is only one way to tell if someone approaching is a real person or a jinn," Naneh intoned. "By looking at their feet. The jinn can look exactly like someone you know, be dressed in clothes you have just seen on them, or wrapped in a chador you have tugged at a minute before. But they have hooves instead of feet. They can appear or disappear as quickly as you bat an eyelash. They are around us often when we cannot see them. Their little ones are very mischievous and always hang around humans. One of the most dangerous things you can do is to step on a baby jinn or pour water over them. That's why you must always say 'Besmellah-e-Rahman-e-Rahim!' ['In the name of God, the Merciful, the Compassionate'], before pouring water on the ground. The jinn cannot withstand the name of God. They will disappear then, whether they are in their visible or their invisible form.

"Another terrible thing the jinn often do is they impersonate someone you know and trust, then in the guise of that person, lead you into terrible danger. Why, only last week Fati, the maid, was just emerging from the bath—that's another thing you must know, the jinn love dark, damp places like the bath—when she saw her mother and aunt coming toward her. She told them she had delivered Khanom's tray and bath things and was on her way home.[3] Her mother and aunt told her to go with them on an errand. She followed them—silly girl—without checking out their feet. She walked along, chattering as she always does, until suddenly she found herself in the wilderness in the dark and the two jinn impersonating her mother and aunt were suddenly gone! She ran terrified back to town and fell breathless at the door of the house, where Asghar found her. Anything could have happened to her! And to think all she needed to do was to check the feet and whisper her 'Besmellah,' as she had been told to do so many times."

Every Thursday afternoon my mother went to the bath with her sister-in-law. My cousin Narges (who was two years older than me), my younger brother Hamid, and I often tagged along. We grumbled and complained about going to the bath, but actually, though we would never admit it, we rather enjoyed the outing. Nosrat, my mother's favorite bath attendant, was a vigorous woman with a keen sense of her own expertise who took her work very seriously. She held my head up with one hand and with the other she rubbed the mixture of moistened *katira* powder and raw egg into my hair, pouring warm water from a copper bowl over my head in one long, gushing stream, making me gasp for breath. I rubbed off the katira swiftly with the back of my hand, closing my eyes for no more than a second—I was not about to take any chances. And my caution paid off: in all those Thursday afternoon sessions at the bath, I managed to avoid encounters with the jinn altogether.

My mother and the other women of the family sat in a circle, each on an overturned copper tray. During our weekly visits, it was arranged that the bath was closed to the general public, although we were often joined by other female members of my father's clan, the Ebrahimis. The family felt free to gossip and exchange information without worrying that strangers would overhear them. There were few secrets in Kerman though, as Nosrat relayed much of what she heard to other customers. Near the end of the bath time, between the hard rubdown and the last stage—soaping the body with soft mittens followed by a quick dip in the heated pool—the conversation generally became more intense. At this point bowls of watermelons and trays of pomegranates, split open to reveal ruby-red seeds sprinkled with angelica, were brought in and served with sweets and scented sherbets.

One Thursday, after the bath, we were resting in Shah Jan's sitting room upstairs when we heard great thumping sounds from the first-floor pantry room. The sound, like a large, soft object hitting the ground, came in regular, measured intervals. Grandmother sent Naneh to investigate. On returning, Naneh whispered something in her ear. It was not until the following week in the bath that I overheard the cause of the thumping: Asghar the gardener, who had been charged with seducing the maid Fati, had refused to accept responsibility. He had been told that he must marry the girl, and he was trying to kill himself by hurling himself into the air and dropping to the floor. The suicide attempt was unsuccessful on all counts—he survived, grandmother strongly suggested that he marry Fati, and he did. Asghar and Fati had twin boys and became pillars of the household.

Through the ritual of the bath, by the time I was old enough to go to school I had absorbed a great deal of information and misinformation about the rites of passage and sexual lives of women.

Islam was an important part of our family's life. We didn't observe all of the religious practices, but there was an underlying current of belief in all of our daily affairs. Yet people thought nothing of our attending a local Zoroastrian school. It was a good school, so that's where Hamid and I were sent. The atmosphere in school was congenial. Every morning we all prayed to "God, the compassionate, kind, and forgiving."

There were books around in the house, and we were encouraged to read and have opinions. But the only books available belonged to adults—translations of Ernest Hemingway's *The Old Man and the Sea*, Leo Tolstoy's *War and Peace*, Margaret Mitchell's *Gone with the Wind*. I read these and everything else I could find. Sometimes this included scraps of newspapers in which some purchases were wrapped and which I read, searching frantically, generally unsuccessfully, for the next page.

My father, Majid, was the youngest of four siblings, and by the time he finished high school, it had become fashionable for young men to be sent abroad to attend university. So he was sent off with a few friends to the Sorbonne in Paris and returned ten years later, a modern young man, very much in synch with European culture. He was fun-loving and urbane and became the darling of his family. Soon after his return, he met my mother, Ferdows, at the home of a relative in Tehran, where she had moved to complete her education. My mother was one of the first three women in Iran to attend university. She fell in love with the French-educated young aristocrat and left university to marry him and live in Kerman in the Ebrahimi compound. As the son of a leading Shaykhi Khan, my father found it a bit difficult at first to marry and bring to his family's great house the beautiful daughter of a Baha'i single mother—especially since, like her mother, she had planned to be an educated and independent woman, a desire that eventually led to her dissatisfaction with her life and marriage.

Both of my parents put a high priority on education. Neither made a distinction between my brother and me or expressed a different vision of what girls should aspire to. In fact, they expected me to become a doctor. I don't remember any talk of my staying home and becoming a housewife. It was always assumed that after I received my medical degree I would work. This was unusual in Iran at this time, and my father may have been influenced by my mother's dissatisfaction over her own choices.

My sister, Farah, was born on November 5, 1948. To us children, our parents appeared to be happy, holding a position of leadership in the community. We were surrounded by many affectionate people, young and old, most of whom were our relations. I felt secure and certain that nothing bad could happen to me or those I loved. But later, when I grew up and discussed this time with my mother, she confided that the feudal lifestyle was not to her liking. She had wanted to study and yearned to be connected to a wider world.

My carefree childhood was abruptly upended at the age of eleven when my parents separated. We three children moved with Mother and Grandmother to a small house in Tehran, leaving behind a supportive extended family that had helped us feel rooted with a strong sense of belonging. In my home in Kerman, everyone's role had been quite clear. Everything had its place and function. I had my own specific spot in the universe, and it was quite a comfortable one.

Several of my older cousins had gone to the United States, and they wrote to my mother about their exciting experiences, giving her a sense of the tantalizing new possibilities that life might hold for her there. A year after moving us to Tehran, she was ready to go off to America to continue her studies. She promised that once she had settled in, she would bring us over. In the meantime, we stayed in Tehran with my grandmother. Over the next three years, Mother first brought me, then my sister, and finally my brother, to America.

I don't remember much about that time in Tehran. Later, after the Revolution, Mother gave me the letters I had written to her during this period. I sound like a preachy kid who is playing parent to her own mother, urging her to enjoy herself, find a partner, not to sacrifice her life for us. There is nothing in my letters about the challenges of a new school and new environment—nothing about the claustrophobic space in Grandmother's two-bedroom apartment that accommodated Grandmother, her tailoring workshop, and the three of us children. And Mother didn't share with us the exhaustion, insecurity, and fear she felt working the nightshift in a cannery near San Francisco to support herself through college. In a little less than a year, I would join my mother in America and experience for myself the anxiety that comes with being uprooted and the struggle it takes to rebuild a life, and one's self, in a new place.

Chapter 2

Coming to America

T HE CAR CAME TO take me to Tehran's Mehrabad airport at 4:00 a.m. on September 17, 1955. My grandmother, Tooba Naficy, checked my bags, passport, and ticket. Once again she asked if I had everything. She put some curdled cream on a piece of wafer-thin bread, added orange blossom jam, rolled it into a small morsel, and, ignoring my objections, put it in my mouth. My stomach felt queasy, partly because of lack of sleep, partly because of my fear of leaving home on such a long journey. I kept thinking of my mother at the end of the long flights that would take me to California, but her figure shrank in my imagination. Grandmother held my shoulder with her left hand and with the finger of her right wrote a prayer on my forehead. Then, always true to her promise to support our Muslim upbringing, she held a Quran above my head at the doorway and made me pass under it three times. After the last time, when I stood across the threshold on the other side of the doorway, I bent over and kissed the holy book. She then threw a bowl of water on the floor behind my retreating back, to ward off evil spirits. I turned back for a last look. Hamid, my brother, was up now, rubbing his eyes and squinting at the dark hallway. He waved, looking glum. I wished I could talk with Farah, my sister, one more time. But she was fast asleep—hadn't even awakened when I kissed her goodbye. I did that with more vigor than necessary, hoping she would wake up. But she drew her legs into her chest, mumbled something, her eyes closed.

Because I was just fourteen, I was to travel in the care of a friend of the family. Mr. Alai would be with me all the way to New York. From there until I reached my mother in San Francisco I would be on my own. I was happy that I was not alone as I flew over the ocean. Somehow, I thought if something happened over the black waters, it would be good to have a companion. I thought I could deal alone with whatever happened on land. Mr. Alai had traveled to America before and had answered my grandmother's many questions about conditions there, especially about availability of various food items. She seemed particularly concerned about fruits, especially watermelons. He reassured her that there were plenty of watermelons in America. Mr. Alai showed me the airsick bags "just in case," he said. He also showed me how to place my pillow next to my face and bend sideways to lean onto it to sleep. But I was wide awake the entire time, while he in turn used the airsick bag and dozed off, his face crushed into the little pillow. The journey seemed endless. Changing planes in New York did not quite register in my memory.

When I saw her at the airport in San Francisco, my mother looked very different to me. Perhaps I had forgotten her face and had reconstructed her looks in my mind. But she was paler and chubbier than I had pictured her. Her hair, long and wavy in Iran, was now short and very curly in the humid air. She wore a fluffy, short-sleeved sweater that made her breasts stand out. Her straight black skirt had picked up some of the bluish lint from the sweater. Her face did not seem as beautiful to me. But people turned around as we moved by—I suppose she was still beautiful, only in a different way. She kept hugging me and asking if I was happy to be in America, and I was not certain what to say. The last leg of the trip had seemed interminable to me. I still heard the humming of the engines in my ears. I could not answer her as she or I would have liked.

As we walked up the narrow staircase and down a small hallway to Mother's apartment, I saw Marilyn, her roommate, who hugged me and spoke in quick bursts of English as she led me in. She had the whitest skin I had ever seen, and freckles. She had very blue eyes, reddish-blonde hair, and a nice smile, in spite of slightly protruding front teeth. I couldn't understand a word she was saying. Then she left in a great hurry and quickly returned, carrying a box that she handed to me with a big grin and another outburst of English. Mother told me it was a gift for me and said I should open it and thank her in English. "You know how to say that?" she asked me in Persian. I opened the box and saw a white short-sleeved angora sweater and a small red scarf. The whole ritual of colorfully wrapped boxes tied with ribbons containing things bought in a store and given to others was new to me. I was too numb from my long trip to feel much beyond a dazed incomprehension. My lack of emotion seemed to bother Mother, and I felt guilty that I was not happier.

Marilyn walked around me talking excitedly, repeating a word that I did not understand but which I sensed must be important. Mother explained to me that Marilyn thought it would be much easier if I picked an American name that my future friends and classmates could pronounce. She wondered if I would let her call me Leah: it was a name she loved. My mother had asked her to be my godmother—that gave her the right to choose my American name, didn't it? Suddenly I had a whole new life and a new name. I remained "Leah" for the next ten years, until I returned to Iran.

Mother asked me to put on my new sweater and tied the red scarf around my neck, then we went into the kitchen to eat dinner. The idea of eating in the kitchen, even though this did not look like a real kitchen—there were no huge copper pots, no coal-burning stoves, no brick countertops—seemed odd. But sitting at the red Formica table in the small kitchen, I felt no particular emotion. The girl who would have reacted to the sudden changes was no longer there; the one called Leah, wearing a new white sweater and red scarf, was as yet an empty vessel.

The next day Mother left early for university, carrying a large book and some notebooks under her arm. She told me her friend would come for me later to take me to buy a school uniform. I was to attend a Catholic school called Mission Dolores. A few days later, wearing my new uniform, I was taken to a large building with wide, wood-paneled halls and classrooms with high ceilings and tall windows. I felt uncomfortable in my new plaid skirt and navy blazer and oxfords. The other girls had smooth, hairless legs. They had long straight hair, turned into a curl at the end, and bangs on their foreheads. My hair had turned frizzy in the humid climate of my new home. No one paid any particular attention to me. I was shown which room to go to and learned how to find my way around from class to class. But I understood nothing that went on during classes. I could not figure out anything in my big impressive textbooks. Even drawings and photographs looked strange. In a class on home economics we were given a project that involved designing furniture for a home and pasting colored pieces of paper in the shape of various objects and furnishings. I had no experience with this type of work. Our handicraft sessions in Iran had involved sewing tiny flowers on hand towels and handkerchiefs with delicate silk threads in a rainbow of colors. I tried to look over the work of others to find out what was to be done. I suppose part of the difficulty lay in my joining the class in midsemester.

My new schoolmates were not cruel or hostile—they treated me with total indifference. The sisters also, not knowing, I suppose, how to deal with me, ignored me throughout the school day. I sat in class not comprehending what went on and thinking my own thoughts about the process and the participants. In the morning we went to the chapel. There were words spoken and songs sung. Then everyone knelt down and opened their mouths and wafers were placed on their tongues. I stuck out my tongue but the girl next to me quickly said, "No!" and some phrases with the word *hell* (which sounds like the word for cardamoms in Persian). The wafer tasted nothing like "hell."

My stay at Mission Dolores did not last long. It was soon decided that in order to learn English and become fully Americanized, I should live with an American family. At Christmastime, Mother, Marilyn, and I took the train to Seattle, where I was to be left with Marilyn's parents, the Goodwins, to attend her old high school and learn to be an American. There was no question or discussion about it. Everyone had to become American, and the sooner one went about it the better. Mother and Marilyn stayed for a few days, then I was left with the Goodwins, who asked me to call them Mom and Dad. They, like everyone else, called me Leah. They were a gentle, middle-aged, middle-class American couple living in a small white house with three bedrooms, one of which became my room. They were determined to help me learn English as fast as possible. At dinner I would not be given a saltshaker or the bread unless I pronounced the word passably well. I learned to do my share of the work around the house, and I became familiar with the rituals of American holidays. Seattle was a rainy city. It took me a while to learn how to prepare for the weather—there were times when I had to shake the rain out of my shoes, recalling mornings at my childhood home near the desert when I was told by Naneh to shake my shoes before putting them on because "there was no telling when a scorpion might be hiding there."

I was registered at Roosevelt High School, a uniformly white, overwhelmingly Protestant, public school where few had even seen a foreigner, let alone an Iranian. Guided by my advisor, Alice Miller, my fellow students took a great interest in me and participated vigorously in my Americanization. The girls were kind and seemed to find me intriguing. They took me to basketball games and slumber parties and taught me the rituals of dating—information that for me at this point was akin to a study in cultural anthropology. Going out alone with a boy sounded strange and pointless to me. As my

Americanization continued, I walked the halls at school being Jane Eyre—alone, self-contained, hanging on to the idea that whatever I became, I would be a good person. A stranger in a strange land, I learned not to acknowledge fear, so that it would not exist. I graduated from Roosevelt High School, exemplifying the school's motto: "What I am to be I am now becoming." Mahnaz and Leah had found a way to coexist—one or the other getting the upper hand, as circumstance required. In my later work I saw this feeling of multiple identities in others, especially in the growing number of women who were suddenly forced into exile and deeply exposed to very different circumstances and cultures.

THE LONG list of courses I had taken in Iran persuaded my advisor at Roosevelt that I required only a few courses in American history, civics, and English literature to graduate. Thus at the age of sixteen I joined my mother in San Francisco and prepared to enroll at San Francisco State College (now San Francisco State University). My view of Mother had by this point evolved from adoration to resentment. Although my father had had an affair, giving her a legitimate reason to leave, and although her passion for education and independence was a model for me, I saw her as the cause of my separation from my grounded, happy, secure childhood, and I resented her for it. She tried to tell me how miserable she had been, but I resented her even more for burdening me with added grief while I searched for reassurance. She tried harder, coloring in more detail, some suspiciously vivid, in her narrative of misery, recollecting her life in Kerman. But I remembered only the warmth and happiness there and needed to hang on to my memories. The more she tried to seek my acceptance, the more I withdrew into myself. I wanted the relationship to be about *me* and about what I was experiencing in a turbulent and uncertain life, not about her hopes and disappointments. Neither one of us was able to give the other the approval and support each of us needed. Yet instinctively I admired her choices, and her brave refusal to settle for anything less than independence and freedom.

The apartment my mother and I shared with two young students faced Golden Gate Park. Every weekend she would prepare a feast of rice and various meats, vegetables, and herb sauces and invite a few of our friends and relatives who were attending the University of California. They joined us, bringing a large bottle of Gallo wine for a low-cost entertainment, followed by the inevitable morning headaches. Sometimes, very late at night, we would drive to the beach to walk on the sand and talk and laugh. Our outings usually ended with breakfast at a diner.

Gholam Reza Afkhami, a regular at these Persian dinners, was a sophisticated, charming young man who was about to graduate from the University of California at Berkeley. Five years older than me, he had read the major philosophers and listened to Bach and Mozart. What impressed me most was the dignity with which he carried himself. Before long, we fell in love. He came to San Francisco nearly every weekend, and Mother did not object to our outings together. But the regular commuting from Berkeley soon affected our studies. In those days, living together was not an option, and in retrospect our decision to marry at that time seems to have been largely influenced by the traffic. Mother was fond of Gholam Reza and was happy that I loved him. She helped us prepare letters to my father and to Gholam Reza's parents asking for their permission to marry. Mother's literary skills notwithstanding, they were angered and disappointed by our decision. They pictured us as two poor, uneducated young people—I was seventeen and he, twenty-two—struggling in a strange land. Their response was almost identical: "If this was the goal, you could've married right here in Iran. You didn't have to go all the way to America." After a few weeks of listening morosely to Nat King Cole sing, "They try to tell us we're too young" and discussing our limited options, we decided to get married anyway and to work our way through college. Mother organized a wedding party for our close friends and family, as well as the Iranian consul general in San Francisco, Majid Rahnema, who became a good friend in later years when he was a delegate and I an advisor at the Iranian UN delegation and more so when he became minister of higher education.

Gholam Reza's attempts to find part-time employment with a bit of autonomy brought types of jobs that were antithetical to his temperament. In a time-tested American tradition, he tried selling cutlery, Fuller brushes, and encyclopedias door-to-door. We kidded him about his lack of salesmanship when he told us how hard he tried to convince an older woman, seemingly of limited means but ready to buy a set of encyclopedias, that she really didn't need such an expensive set of books. Unfortunately, his best customer—sometimes his only customer—was my mother. In two months, much to my mother's relief, he graduated and took a position as a teaching assistant at the university.

INSPIRED BY my mother and in tune with my rapid Americanization, I wanted to be independent. I refused support from my father, who had reluctantly come to accept the fact of our marriage. He offered support in our adolescence but we each chose to work for our living as we became young adults. In 1958, at the age of seventeen, with no useable skills, I decided I would work to support my education. I began searching for clerical positions advertised in the newspaper but quickly realized I didn't have much of a chance, given my limited English and poor typing skills. One day I put on my best dress—a navy shirtwaist with a white collar—found my white cotton gloves, and took the bus to Market Street, one of San Francisco's busiest thoroughfares. I wavered a bit about whether I should cross the street but decided to begin with the side I was on. I walked into each store, smiled broadly, and said to the first person I came across, "I'm looking for a job." At most places I was told there was no position available. A few asked about my previous work experience, and when told I had none said they would not hire anyone without experience. On my twelfth attempt, my smile a little worn, my feet hurting, my white gloves damp and dirty, I walked into a variety store, where a young girl at the counter told me to go to the personnel department on the second floor. Seeing the exhaustion and anxiety in my face, she said, "They're still hiring. I started myself just yesterday." Half an hour later I was back on Market Street, the proud possessor of a new job at $1.25 an hour. My spirits dampened considerably on Monday when I met my supervisor Rose, a short, Italian American woman with a profusion of shiny black hair piled up on top of her head, who had shaved her eyebrows only to draw new ones in a perfect semicircle above her deep-set black eyes. Rose insisted on calling me by an Italianized version of "Ebrahimi," my maiden name: "Abernini, get a move on," she would say.

I was assigned to the notions counter, which held hundreds of small items— pins, needles, screws, beads, and a large variety of objects whose name and function were a mystery to me. I was surprised that so many people not only knew about these things and their use, but came in prepared to buy them. Rose taught me how to ring up an item once a customer had chosen it, how to return their change, put the item in a bag, smile, and thank the customer. Then, as soon as possible, I was to replace the item from the storage below the counter. There were always choices to be made—should I deal with the next customer immediately and *then* replace the item, or should I replace the item first and then ring up the next purchase? If I took the next customer, Rose complained that I should've replaced the stock. If I did just that, she complained that I was keeping the customers waiting. "This here store's no fancy college, Abernini—will you get a move on?" I found Rose's attitude less devastating when I learned that her problem was not with my performance alone. She just didn't like "fancy college girls" who seemed not to really need a job and would likely quit at the first sign of difficulty. I needed to prove to Rose and to myself that I could deal with the pressures of the real world.

After almost a year at the Kress Variety Store, one Thursday evening when I punched my timecard and picked up my pay envelope, I was told that I would not be needed anymore. I was more relieved than upset. I had stood my ground yet would finally be free of the notions counter and of Rose. Before I had a chance to begin looking for another job, I was called back and told that a new position had opened up. Rose seemed almost pleased to see me again. I suppose the idea of having to "break in" another college girl made working with me almost palatable.

During a slow moment Rose said, "Abernini, you know why you were laid off?"

"No," I replied.

"That figures," she said. Knowing Rose by now, I waited for her to choose whether she would go on. "You were laid off because they didn't want to give you a paid vacation or increase your pay. If you're fired and start all over again, they don't have to."

"What can I do about it, Rose?"

"*You*, nothing, but a working girl would go to the union. *They'd* do something about it. Now, d'ya suppose you can handle the counter while I go for my break?"

Rose didn't believe in using too many words or mulling over an event for long. Her tone told me that she considered this conversation finished. I waited for my break and asked another full-time worker about the union. The next union meeting day I walked several blocks down Market Street to a narrow, half-opened steel doorway and climbed up a few flights of stairs to a large hall lined with metal folding chairs, where members of Local 1100 were meeting. At the end of the usual agenda, the sturdy looking, gray-clad woman who seemed to be in charge asked if there was any other business. I raised my hand. Everyone turned to look at me. I remembered Rose and braced myself for whatever was in store. They listened quietly to my brief explanation. The gray-clad woman said, "We'll take care of that for you. Give me your name and address on a piece of paper." I took the note to her after the meeting. She patted me on the back and said "You'll get what's coming to you, honey. We take care of our girls." I was ecstatic. Not only I was reassured of getting my due, but I was finally one of "our girls."

In a few days, the store manager, a big, balding man in a white shirt with a loosened tie hanging about his neck, who had never before exchanged a word with any of us, stopped by the notions counter. He talked about a "misunderstanding" about my vacation pay and said it would be cleared up by my next paycheck. He then said, "We've taken care of the little issue we had, so is everything okay?" I said, "Yes, everything is fine, thank you." He said, "From now on, if you have any problems, you just come to me." I think it was then that

Rose began calling me "Leah." For the next few months the manager would stop by periodically and ask me again, "Is everything okay?"

Rose taught me to persevere and to speak up for my rights. Local 1100 gave me an unshakable belief in the power of working with others and taught me that when women band together, they can protect one another from injustices large and small. This was a lesson that would stay with me long after I left the notions counter and was in a position to make my own way in the world.

MOTHER HAD moved to Monterey after finishing her studies in linguistics and taken a job as curriculum developer at the Defense Language Institute (DLI). Gholam Reza and I decided to work for a couple of years, to save for our graduate school costs. Learning from Mother that there were vacancies at DLI, we both applied and were accepted. In September 1961, we moved to Monterey, where Gholam taught Persian and I was a research assistant at DLI. For over two years we lived in adjoining condominiums with Mother and my siblings, Hamid and Farah.

For some time Gholam Reza and I had wanted to visit Iran, but we were also influenced by the spirit of the time and were wary of what we might face in our home country. In the past several years, a growing number of Iranian students had been provided subsidies by the Iranian government to study in the West. Eventually there were 60,000 Iranian students in the United States alone, and as they finished their studies and returned, we heard about the changes taking place in Iran and the possibilities for meaningful careers in the now fast-developing country. At the same time, the revolutionary spirit of the 1960s reflected in the feminist, civil rights, and anti–Vietnam War movements and the unrest in the universities was reflected in the Iranian community in the United States. In Iran, the Soviet-inspired Tudeh Party's network of organizers and propagandists greatly influenced the intellectuals. Iran was a major target of interest for the Soviet Union, and the 1,200-mile border the two countries shared facilitated infiltration. Access to the Persian Gulf and Iran's oil were powerful incentives for the Soviets to destabilize the country. Their propaganda was relentless and powerful, magnifying every need and every flaw in society. It rarely referred to conditions in neighboring countries or in the developing world in general. But it magnified any fault in Iran's infrastructure or inequality in its educational or health systems.

In the fall of 1963, when I was three months pregnant with our son, Babak, Gholam and I traveled to Iran to see for ourselves what life was like there. At passport control the agent looked at my passport and smiled. "Mrs. Mahnaz Afkhami, welcome home," he said. This sealed the deal for me. After eight

years, a stranger pronounced the "h" in my first name and the "kh" in the last
and had no doubt in his mind that I was home.

Iran indeed had changed since I had left for America, and now the change
was gaining momentum. With the resumption of oil production in 1954, the
economy had begun to move, slowly at first and faster by the time we had
returned. Life had become socially and culturally more vibrant. The shah's
White Revolution of 1963, announced a few months before we arrived in Tehran
and later approved in a national referendum, included a six-point program
of social changes including land reform, workers' profit sharing in corporate
earnings, nationalization of forests and pastures, sale of state-owned enterprises to the public, extension of voting rights to women, and formation of
the health and education corps. Gholam and I, along with the majority of
Iranians, welcomed these reforms, but the clerics did not—they understood
that land reform would weaken their economic base by giving farmers ownership of the land, reducing the power of major landowners who donated
land to the religious establishment as their preferred acts of charitable giving.
Even more threatening, they felt that giving women the right to vote would
enable women to enter the public space, which would undermine the clerics'
concept of societal organization founded on women's role as secondary in the
family and society.

Women participated in the election for the first time that year, and six were
elected to the Majlis (parliament) and two were appointed to the Senate. Later,
in April 1967, a few months before we would return to Iran after finishing our
education, the Majlis would pass the first Family Protection Law, which gave
equal rights to divorce to women, increased the minimum age of marriage
to fifteen, and limited polygamy. That August, a constitutional amendment
would allow the queen to become the regent in the event of the shah's death
and prior to their son's twentieth birthday. The same year Farrokhroo Parsa
was appointed minister of education, the first woman to be a member of Iran's
cabinet. Change was in the air and the future, especially for women, seemed
promising.

Arriving back in New York on November 22, 1963, the man at customs said,
"I guess you haven't heard yet: President Kennedy was shot." Gholam Reza and
I looked at each other, thinking it must be a sick joke. We looked at the people
around us and the somber slowness—as if no one had a place they must be
or something they must do—told us it was true. The next few days showed
me once again what I loved about America. Yes, the crazy streaks of violence
were there, but the way the society responded to tragedy and came together
in civility and unity was a unique experience. I thought of Hemingway's words

"grace under pressure" and felt proud. I realized I loved both countries, but I would go back to Iran because I was needed there. In America, I would be just another professor. In Iran, I would be a role model and one with knowledge of a language, literature, and culture much needed in the country's interaction with the world.

IN MARCH 1964, Babak was born in a beautiful place. The rooms at the Carmel hospital had ocean views, the menu included wine, and they kept every new mother for four days. The baby arrived two weeks early, so I had worked until the day I gave birth and would start work again in two weeks. The nanny we hired was no Naneh Fatemeh, but she was reliable and organized. She was fully in charge from 7:30 a.m. when we left for work, as well as during our forty-five-minute lunch break when we came home and each cuddled and held the baby between bites of sandwiches, until the end of our workday at 4:45 p.m.

Over the next ten months, Gholam and I would begin graduate school and prepare ourselves to return to Iran. Our friend Ahmad Ghoreishi had just completed his PhD and was teaching at the University of Colorado in Boulder. In 1965 he arranged a teaching assistantship for Gholam while he worked on his PhD. I would complete my master's within a year while holding my first professional position at the journal *Abstracts of English Studies*. We would each support the other when it was needed. There was not much theoretical discussion—we simply acted on the belief that love involves helping each other to reach the full realization of our goals and capabilities.

On our arrival in Boulder, Ahmad took us to our student apartment down a hill and across a stream from the school buildings. Next door lived another couple who had a child the same age as Babak. Schuyler was a blonde boy with nearly white eyelashes. In the afternoons the moms took turns sitting by the sandbox and studying while the boys played. I was soon assistant editor of *Abstracts of English Studies*, a job that involved a substantial amount of work and familiarity with the use of enormous computers that filled an entire room, but fortunately were quite easy to use. I carried Babak on my back the whole day. I was lucky he was a well-behaved, quiet baby. At home, where I did a lot of reading and writing, I worked at the kitchen table while he played on the floor, usually with no major issues. One of a few painful incidents was when, as a toddler, he opened the refrigerator door and knocked a carton of eggs onto the floor. He watched with great interest and amusement as I tried to clear the mess.

As it would happen often in my life, during the first year in Colorado I ended up in the hospital twice for bouts of high fever and headache that were the result of exhaustion. Much later in the 1980s I found the symptoms were exacerbated by a genetic condition called sickle cell anemia, the only treatment for which is a lot of sleep and no stress, both of which would be hard to come by in my chosen lifestyle. In my family, my mother and I were the only ones who had this condition. My mother told me, "Some days when I get out of bed in the morning, my greatest desire is to dive right back in." I have thought of her and smiled with sympathy many mornings.

One day, following a challenging year of working, studying, and caring for a toddler, I opened our mailbox and took out a card and read, "Congratulations! You got the only A on the master's comprehensive examination!" I danced around with Babak in my arms. This meant so much because of my love for and awe of the English language and literature and because of the circumstances under which I had achieved this result.

While Gholam was finishing his PhD, I was also typing 300 pages of his dissertation. At the time, without computers, every typing mistake required a new page and retyping. It was one of the most exhausting and uninteresting tasks of my life. The notions counter at Kress's was exciting in comparison. My master's dissertation on Edward FitzGerald's translation of *The Rubaiyat of Omar Khayyam* was seriously considered for publication by the University of Colorado Press. My advisor counseled me to expand it and use it as the basis for my PhD dissertation. But by this time in our lives, Gholam was eager to go back to Iran and I thought there would always be a chance for me to come back and complete my work, not knowing the course of events that would take me away from teaching altogether.

Chapter 3

Return to Iran

I N THE SUMMER OF 1967 Gholam and I returned to Iran with three-year old Babak. As we waited to clear customs and receive our luggage, we could see familiar faces through the glass partition waving and sending kisses, while the children pressed up against the glass. Babak, who had spent his first years in a quiet, subdued environment, hardly seeing strangers other than the occasional dinner guest, was shocked by the crowd circling around him, eager to touch his arm, kiss his cheek, and ruffle his hair. He looked at me with a pained expression, and, seeing no hope of rescue, shut his big brown eyes and did not open them until we were in the car. For the next few months, until we found a place of our own, we were to stay at my mother-in-law's house, situated in the middle of Gholam's ancestral compound in Tehran.

Those months were not easy. The household was run on an entirely different clock than what we had been used to. Meal times were hours behind our usual schedule, and people dropped in at any time and stayed for any number of meals. After lunch on Fridays, pillows and sheets were brought out to the terrace and those who had stayed for lunch would then take a siesta.

Conversations were random and often conducted simultaneously. People poked good-natured fun at one another and laughed wholeheartedly. The objects of the merriment sometimes took offense, but there was no lasting damage. Card games went on late into the night, necessitating preparations for large dinners and endless service of tea, sweets, and fruit.

The greatest change in the new life for me was the lack of any specific plan or activity in the gatherings. In America people got together to celebrate an occasion or engage in a game or a sport or conversation. In Iran people got together to be together. A more shocking difference was lack of the concept of "privacy," for which there is no word in Persian. I had been puzzled in the United States by the guarded and selective interaction and exchange of information between family and friends. But the no-holds-barred attitude in Iran was equally troubling. I thought how wonderful it would be if we could manage a way of sharing inclusive of aspects of the two cultures—more intimacy and sharing combined with some choice of boundaries.

Babak's schedule was in shambles. Everyone had theories about what he should eat, how he should be treated, and when he should sleep. In America, he would beg for "a few more minutes" at bedtime and would be put to bed after a short reprieve. In Tehran, however, he was delighted to find that he could delay his bedtime indefinitely by sitting on his grandmother's knee and putting an arm around her neck. It was good to see how happy he seemed receiving so much warmth and attention.

I went to bed each night exhausted by the simple proximity of so many people over such an extended period of time. This was summer, and I was half-sure that life would soon become normal again—I looked forward to the beginning of kindergarten for Babak and work for me.

I HADN'T expected that getting a job would be quite so easy. A week after calling the office of the dean of the School of Literature and Humanities at the new National University of Iran, I found myself on the main campus in Evin, nestled at the foot of the majestic, snow-capped Alborz Mountains, for an appointment with the dean, Ra'di Azarakhshi. Our conversation over a cup of Turkish coffee was brief and congenial. The dean began by asking me about literature in the United States in the eighteenth century: "Was there literature in America at that time—after the revolution?" I paused, since I had often wondered whether Jonathan Edwards's *Sinners in the Hands of an Angry God*—passionate as it was—could really be considered literature. I recalled the imagery of "the God that holds you over the pit of hell, much as one holds a spider or some loathsome insect over the fire, abhors you, and is dreadfully provoked. His wrath towards you burns like fire; he looks upon you as worthy of nothing else, but to be cast into the fire." But I stoutly defended the idea that America did indeed have a literature of its own in the eighteenth century, which must have made an impression on the dean. I was to start in September. Salary was not mentioned. My specialization in English literature was of little interest to him, since Iranians with advanced degrees in that field from universities in the United States or Great Britain were difficult to come by. At the time there was only one such specialist, Dr. Suratgar, who chaired the English Department at Tehran University. He was a short, heavy-set, elderly gentleman with a thick British accent. During my second semester at the National University, John Woods, who had chaired the department, left suddenly and the dean asked me to take his place. As department chairs of the two major universities in the capital, Dr. Suratgar and I paired up to attend various meetings, including a trip to Isfahan, the beautiful capital of the Safavid dynasty, the following semester to help found the Association of Teachers of English.

At the time, the Abraham Lincoln Library at the Iran-America Society in northern Tehran was a popular space for Iranian intellectuals and artists, with a vibrant and stimulating atmosphere. The society held film screenings, many of which were based on novels and plays we were reading, among them Shakespeare's *Hamlet* and Herman Melville's *Moby Dick*, and regular panel discussions on topics that interested the students, such as "The Changing Role of Women in Iranian Society." I would often meet my students at the Lincoln Library to show them how to conduct research.

Richard Arndt, the American cultural attaché and his capable wife, Lois Roth, who headed the Iran-America Society, were well connected to the intellectual community in Tehran and soon joined Gholam's and my circle of friends. I was not surprised to get a call from Richard at my office that fall, but I was surprised when he said, "I have a gift for you!"

"Will you deliver it yourself?"

"No, she'll walk in."

And so the poet Tahereh Saffarzadeh came to see me. She was a short, stocky woman with pale skin, intelligent eyes, and a soft smile. She had recently returned to Iran from the United States, with a degree in creative writing from the prestigious Writers' Workshop at the University of Iowa. Previously she'd published poetry in Iran, and her work—romantic, verging on sentimental—had been very popular. But she returned from America with an entirely different approach to her writing. After our initial greetings, I asked her to read a few poems from her new book—the only one she ever published in English, *The Red Umbrella*. These were sensuous poems, rich in physical detail and innovative in style:

> we travel towards the enjoyment of salty waters
> in a boat with no compass, we travel from nowhere
> to somewhere from somewhere to nowhere
> cruising in the song of our bodies
> my breasts trust every word that your hands
> —hands with suppleness of the gentle heart—whisper[1]

We discussed poetry for two hours. I was impressed with her work—its open physicality and search for spiritual connection and meaning:

> The exquisite sound of *Azan*[2]
> like the pious hands of a man
> caresses my healthy roots
> no longer a lost, isolated island—
> I join a mass prayer
> my ablution is the dark smoke-filled air of the city
> My Mecca is the future
> My nail polish no barrier to prayer
> prayer for a miracle
> prayer for change.[3]

I felt no hesitation in asking her to join our team at the university to teach creative writing.

Tahereh and I became close friends. Aside from our love of the English language and literature, we had our home province of Kerman and love of the desert in common. In her life as well as her art, she seemed to be searching for something beyond the increasingly materialistic existence that surrounded us as the country moved toward modernity, urban living, and industrialization. Her poetry reflected an interesting mix of Sufi mysticism and feminism. She asked me to join her in her Friday evening *Khaneghah*—Sufi spiritual meetings—something I had always wanted to do, and came to our house many an evening for quiet gatherings of music, poetry, and shots of ice-cold vodka.

My friendship with Tahereh was easy, but navigating the classroom was more challenging. I had been warned by my American-educated friends about differences in classroom cultures between the United States and Iran. I had been told that in Iran I should keep a certain formality and avoid any familiarity with my students. Above all, I was told I should avoid kidding around or any kind of humor—advice that I ignored, much to the benefit of our class discussions. The difference in the atmosphere, I found, was not in the interaction between students and faculty—the most palpable difference was in the way the young men and women related to one another in the classroom. There was a tension between them—a combination of tentativeness and uncertainty. Women had been attending mixed classes at universities in Iran since 1938, when women first enrolled at University of Tehran. The idea that men and women should sit together in a classroom was not new, but cultural norms still made interaction, especially outside the classroom, awkward. There were no established rules for navigating this complex dynamic, but this was nothing compared to the more complicated question of how to continue the relationship outside the classroom. Should a young man and woman continue a conversation that had begun in the classroom, on a bus? Should they talk about other topics, including personal ones? Should they tell their family about these conversations, risking conflict, or not divulge them and be somehow dishonest?

There was something powerful about the exchanges inspired by looking at characters in English and American fiction—so real and well defined—who were leading lives and making choices that were very different from ours. Our discussions led us to examine the puzzling contradiction between the urge to immerse ourselves in the life of a bustling metropolis and experiment with modernity, while not wanting to lose cherished ties with family and tradition. My young women students were deeply touched by what they read and were eager to discuss the protagonists in the novel and their choices. They talked about Henry James's Daisy Miller and Edith Wharton's Lily Bart as if they were real people. After each class, clusters of young women would walk with me to my office, excited and eager to explore the merits of the choices considered by the characters, and to consider how they would have thought and acted in their place.

When I had first discussed these works as a teaching assistant with students at the University of Colorado, it was in an American classroom. For the first time I was looking at the same works from an Iranian perspective. Daisy Miller, who seemed quaint and old-fashioned to my American students, was daring and unconventional to my Iranian students. They considered her mother to be almost neurotic in her seeming indifference to her daughter's behavior and her own lack of authority. "How could the father allow his wife and daughter to travel all over Europe with no supervision or protection?" they asked. While my students occasionally admired Daisy for her spontaneity, they couldn't figure out why she would risk losing a potential good match by flirting with another man. For my American students, it was difficult to understand why being alone with an Italian man in the Coliseum late at night would be such a terrible breach of trust. "What's all the fuss about?" they would ask. The "fuss," so irrational to my students in Colorado, seemed quite natural to my Iranian students.

Comparing the two groups and their reactions, I realized that it was the passage of time—in other words, history, and not culture—that determined how each group of students saw the world and how they applied their worldview to the characters in the novel; although we live at the same time, we are not contemporary. What had shocked Americans in the late nineteenth century when James had written the story had the same effect on Iranians now. But the Americans of the 1960s had moved beyond the cultural context of their grandparents. Iranians were at the cusp of a transition, not yet free, but eager to embrace a world of different possibility.

TO EXPLORE the contradictions that life in a fast-changing society presented, I worked with the women students to organize an informal group that eventually became the University Women's Association. Our first activity was a lecture series discussing aspects of tradition and modernity in classical versus modern poetry, Western versus Persian music, and realistic versus abstract painting. We invited prominent artists and critics to lead our discussions. Hormoz Farhat, a composer and musician, explained in detail how elements of Western classical music and those of the completely different Persian musical structures can blend together to form one seamless expression of modern musical performance. Tahereh Saffarzadeh spoke about her most recent poem, "Safar-e Aval" ("The First Journey"), and explained that the content of the poems determined their form and that often, emotions and experiences will not be contained within the constraints of traditional classical structures. She told us how breaking with traditional verse in no way prevented her from drawing on the myths and themes embedded in Iranian culture and religious experience.

One of the most eagerly anticipated sessions considered the role of religion in women's lives. We asked a well-known moderate cleric, Mr. Mohajerani, to speak on this topic. His presentation was disappointingly sermon-like, and in the question-and-answer period he insisted on the traditional line with no flexibility.

"I consider myself a believing Muslim," one young woman said. "I pray regularly. I think prayer deals with the mind's focus on God and his dictates. I don't believe God has a particular preference for the dress or appearance of the believer. Why am I told that if I wear nail polish while praying, my prayers are not accepted?"

"If you are a believing Muslim," Mr. Mohajerani replied stiffly, "you will not wear nail polish while praying."

Undeterred, the young woman pressed on: "Do you mean that if I don't remove my nail polish five times a day, and the choice is between doing that and not praying, it would be better for me not to pray?"

"Your prayers are nullified if you wear nail polish," he said.

I was shocked. For one thing, where in the Quran had he found a reference to nail polish? If a supposedly moderate cleric offered this advice, what hope was there for reform through traditional religious channels?

As we continued to hold these conversations, I began to realize that the role of women—their sexuality, their status in the family and in the community—is the pillar that holds up the entire edifice of culture, religion, and tradition. Once this pillar is shaken, the entire structure begins to tremble. I also realized that real change must come from women themselves. They are the ones who will have to assert their right to refuse to choose between faith and freedom. Once they understand their power to choose, and to interpret their faith as they see fit, they will be in a position to define their relationship with their faith so as to derive the spiritual sustenance they look for in religion without taking away their liberty.

Chapter 4

With the Iranian Delegation at the United Nations

I N A LITTLE OVER a year the University Women's Association had grown to 400 members. Women joined from a variety of backgrounds. We visited the Women's Organization of Iran (WOI) centers in the slum areas of Tehran where several students volunteered to work, and we became increasingly aware of the living conditions of poor women and the challenges they faced; we also learned about their courage and their desire for change. We realized that we could change things if we worked hard, together. We had no theories about how change happens, but we were eager to experiment and discover. We began with what we knew—dialogue based on stories, just like our literature classes, but this time the stories were real—stories that women told us about their lives.

One day Simin Rejali, a colleague in the Department of Psychology who had recently accepted the position of secretary general of the WOI, asked me if I would align myself with the WOI. She told me the WOI was founded in 1966 by a 5,000-member assembly of Iranian women from diverse backgrounds and regions. Its mission was to educate women on cultural, social, and economic matters and to make them aware of their rights, duties, and responsibilities. I realized there was nothing about equality in the list she mentioned. "I took this position, hoping that I could get other women involved," she said. "We need new research, and information to push forward ideas about women's status. And we need new blood—young women who can take the organization away from its emphasis on charity and welfare."

I had little interest in any field other than literature and teaching, but I was excited about the discussions I was having with my young female students. My conversation with Simin led me to consider more seriously the idea of expanding our programs beyond the academic arena. "Our goal is to discuss the changing role of women," I told her. "We want to look at music, poetry, culture, religion—we want to know how to negotiate our need to connect to a new world while keeping rooted and connected to our values and our relationships."

"Wonderful idea," Simin smiled. "I like the 'we.' It's great that you feel you are one of them!"

A few days later I was giving Simin a ride back to the university from a lecture in town. She mentioned that Princess Ashraf, the shah's twin sister and honorary president of the WOI, who chaired the Iranian delegation at the General Assembly of the United Nations each fall, was interested in including women in the delegation in order to expose more women to international diplomatic work. At that time, there were no women in the diplomatic cadres of the Foreign Ministry. Simin had been asked to suggest two women, one proficient in French and the other in English, to join the delegation. She already had the French speaker. "You wouldn't be interested in going, would you?" she asked me.

Without thinking, I told her I would love to go.

"It takes at least six weeks," she said. "Can you stay away for that long?"

I told her I thought I could arrange for someone to take over my classes, and that I was fairly confident my husband could take care of Babak. Having a well-organized household with live-in help made it a far cry from just two years ago in Colorado, when the only way to get around was to carry Babak on my back from home to school, to grocery store—nearly the entire day.

A few days later Simin called to tell me I had been approved. She gave me a contact in the Foreign Ministry, and within a week I received a packet with my tickets, passport, per diem, and the address of the apartment hotel in New York where we would be staying.

THE FRENCH-SPEAKING delegate, Soheila Shahkar, and I shared a small apartment near the United Nations. We hadn't met before: I only knew that she taught at Tehran University and had studied law at the Sorbonne. She arrived the day before me and when she opened the door, I was pleasantly surprised to see a slender woman, younger than I had anticipated, with large, slightly slanted brown eyes, a profusion of long brown hair, and a smile that lit up her face. Coming from a mixed French-Iranian family, she was more comfortable speaking her mother's language, French, and was a little uneasy in the Iranian environment. We were both excited about the prospect of working at the United Nations. We had no idea what our duties as "advisors to the Iranian delegation" would be. There had been no instructions from the Foreign Ministry. In the first few days after our arrival, no one contacted us from the Iranian Mission.

Princess Ashraf had not yet arrived—and even when she did, we were not her first priority. She had wanted women to be included in the delegation, but she had many other things on her agenda. So for a couple of days we went sight-seeing in New York. We also checked in at the United Nations but were told we needed a delegate's pass to enter the building. We had heard that Princess Ashraf was staying at the Pierre Hotel, so we decided to call her.

A man with an authoritative voice and a thick British accent answered the phone. I introduced myself and said I wanted to talk to Her Highness.

"What is it about?"

"We would like to know what we are to do here?" I said.

He said, "Give me your number and I will call you."

I realized I didn't know our number.

In a slightly disdainful voice he said, "You don't have your number?"

"We just arrived." I said, "We don't know anyone, and we haven't had an occasion to call ourselves."

"In any case, the delegation ought to decide what you must do. Call the ambassador."

Before we had a chance to call, we were contacted and asked to pick up our passes and assignments from the mission offices. We supposed the princess's message had been received. I was assigned to the Special Political Committee, responsible for Palestinian refugees, and Soheila to the Third Committee, dealing with humanitarian matters. A senior diplomat was the main representative of each team, and an advisor or second delegate was invited to act as an alternate. Committee meetings took place in enormous rooms with high ceilings and thick carpets that muffled all sound. The chairs for the delegates were arranged in a huge circle, in alphabetical order by country, with two rows of chairs behind them for alternates. The name of each country appeared on the desk in front of that country's designated delegates.

Though these diplomats came from all sorts of backgrounds and each had his or her own style and temperament, when their turn came each spoke in a quiet voice devoid of all expression. The fact that most were heard on headphones, through simultaneous interpretation, helped to reinforce the solemn mood of the room. At first we were impressed by the formal tone of the speeches. But since the diplomatic discourse leaves little room for imaginative expression, soon they all began to sound alike, and it was easy for newcomers like us to become uninterested and distracted, even though we very much wanted to understand why and how these proceedings worked. Soheila and I amused ourselves by turning the knobs and listening to bits of the speeches in Chinese, Russian, or Arabic, and eventually, through a process of immersion, we began to get the drift of things. Listening to the speeches and then hearing them analyzed in our delegation's morning meeting, we began to detect the nuances that suggested changes in a country's position and to understand the logic governing the way Iran's responses were drafted.

We were given assignments related to the princess's role as head of delegation and to her own interests in women and human rights. One of my first assignments was to prepare answers for the princess to a set of biographical questions for a national radio program. I could deal with questions that were historical, social, or political. But in response to questions like, "What was your father like?" I had to use my imagination: "My father, Reza Shah, was a stern and sober man." And so on.

In answer to "What is your favorite food, and do you ever cook yourself?" I wrote, "Yes, I love to cook. My favorite recipe is *fesenjan*—duck in walnut and pomegranate sauce," which was, of course, my own favorite. It was sort of like writing dialogue for a film script.

"What is your motto?" "To thine own self be true, for then, thou canst not be false to any man." I wrote. I didn't share the general view that Polonius, the old courtier in Shakespeare's *Hamlet,* was a dense and stuffy character. I thought his advice on parting with his son contained some good practical wisdom. Here was an opportunity to bring high-level support for my minority view of the old fellow. I don't believe the princess ever used the material I prepared for this interview. But she did use some parts of the speeches I wrote.

Soheila and I had an image of the princess based on the mythology surrounding her—as the "power behind her brother" or one who lived the high life in casinos and nightclubs. What we saw was a frail, small woman, simply but exquisitely dressed, who came to work punctually each day at the delegation offices on Third Avenue. She met diligently with the members of the delegation and discussed the events of the day before, what might be expected in the coming day, and what Iran's position might be on upcoming issues. She did not hesitate to ask questions when she did not know the background on an issue and had no hesitation in challenging an opinion she did not agree with.

At the General Assembly the princess sat with the Iranian ambassador to the United Nations, Fereydoun Hoveyda, and listened to speech after speech, carefully taking notes. At noon she attended lunches hosted by one of the ambassadors. These were occasions where much of the diplomatic give-and-take took place. Having witnessed her daytime schedule, we assumed that the glittering social life we had heard so much about must be taking place in the evenings.

Then one day we received an invitation for dinner at the princess's town-house. Her home was elegant but not luxurious. The living room had beautiful river views. Much to our surprise, we found that her evenings were an extension of her daytime routine. We were a bit disappointed but also quite relieved. The atmosphere was formal: ambassadors, journalists, intellectuals, and artists sat around in dark suits talking politely about innocuous subjects. A noncontroversial conversation over dinner was followed by a few speeches and toasts to the health of the leaders of this or that country whose ambassador happened to be the guest of honor. It took a few dinners to discover the significance of the guest list and the fact that sometimes the first moves toward very important political developments, such as the rapprochement between Iran and the People's Republic of China, were made at these dinners.

Fereydoun Hoveyda, Iran's ambassador to the United Nations, was well known in European societies as a novelist, film critic, and intellectual. He was the source of the directors, painters, and writers we met over time at the princess's house. Fereydoun was the brother of the prime minister, Amir Abbas Hoveyda. I admired Fereydoun's progressive ideas and his interest in arts and literature, and I appreciated the access he provided to talented artists. But as my grasp of international relations and the potential of our UN connections grew, our goals often clashed. His role demanded more attention to diplomatic relations, mine to furthering the cause of women. He was conscious to temper the feminist side of our work that was invariably supported by the princess when he saw conflict with the views of ambassadors from the more conservative countries in the region.

At one of the delegation's morning briefings the princess announced that she would like Soheila and me to be given a chance to participate in the debate in our committee meetings. This was not customary: the senior delegate in each committee generally gave Iran's presentation. To assign the country's speeches to two inexperienced young women was quite aggravating to the men. The Foreign Ministry was a hierarchical, bureaucratic system, and diplomats competed fiercely for the visibility and prestige of making a presentation at a committee of the General Assembly. The fact that the text would be wired to the Foreign Ministry and reported to the shah made this even more important. The intervention by the princess added to the resentment the diplomats felt about the fact that a woman—and an outsider to the Foreign Ministry—chaired the delegation.

I was assigned the speech on Palestine, which I began to prepare with a great deal of excitement. Iran had good relations with Israel, though this was kept as low-key as possible, given our ties with other Muslim countries and our sensitivity to the treatment of Palestinians. I would have to be careful not to offend the Israelis while making a strong case for the Palestinians—no easy task. Ever the diligent student, I went to the UN library and took out piles of books and articles. I was busily taking notes when Ambassador Abbas Nayeri, who worked in the office next to mine, asked, "What are you working on?"

"I'm preparing a speech for the Special Political Committee," I said.

"Listen," he responded, "I have been in this field for many years. Let me give you one bit of advice: Reading books and articles will do nothing but confuse you. What you have to do is just take out the file of previous years' speeches and make minor changes. This has nothing to do with you. It's Iran's position. The slightest innovation will likely have diplomatic consequences."

Part of our training was to understand the possible implications of our words. Each word, each pause, each phrase, boring and colorless as it may seem, carried meanings and implications. We learned also that you had to be careful in approaching representatives of the countries Iran was hostile to or had to appear to be hostile to, such as Israel. Iran's position on Israel was a pretend hostility. So you avoided situations where you came across the Israeli ambassador.

Later I learned that conversations at dinner parties were relayed back to foreign offices and inferences drawn from them. So it was not possible to just walk up to someone you liked and give them a handshake or a hug, followed by a casual conversation about the events of the day, without consequence.

On the day of my speech, I was last on the list. Prince Sadr-ul-din Agha Khan was chairing the committee.[1] At that time, he headed the UN Relief and Works Agency for Refugees (UNRWA), which provides assistance and protection to Palestine refugees.

Sometimes the context of events creates an impact quite out of proportion to the event's actual significance. That is, accidents make a substantial difference in one's life. It just so happened that the princess was free that afternoon and decided she wanted to attend my speech as a show of support for the women she had brought to the United Nations. An entourage of ambassadors accompanied her. Before my speech, she asked if I was ready.

"I'm terrified," I said.

"You must take a Valium," she replied. Then she added, "But be careful, because if you take too small a dose, it's not going to help, and if you take too much, you're going to start yawning in the middle of your own speech. Not a good thing."

It was too late to experiment with the tranquilizer, but her concern had a calming effect. What I said followed closely what had been said the year before. I made only slight changes that made the language more palatable. I was glad of this when I heard that the mission had sent the speech to the shah after he had inquired about it in the regular briefing by the foreign minister.

After my speech the meeting ended and everyone got up to leave. Many stopped to congratulate me, and for a while there was a long line of diplomats waiting to shake my hand. Then Prince Sadr-ul-din Agha Khan came down to do the same. If the meeting had not ended with me, no one would have thought to come by, but as it happened, this whole event, which had little to do with the content or delivery of my speech, left quite an impression on the princess: I was invited to join the delegation again the following year.

The next year, shortly before we were due to leave Tehran to return to New York, I was called for a meeting with Abdolreza Ansari, the former minister of interior, who was at that time deputy to the princess. He told me that Simin Rejali's term at the WOI was coming to an end in a few months and that the princess was searching for her replacement. He said the princess wished to appoint someone young and well educated who could bring new ideas. My performance in New York and my work with the University Women's Association had caught her attention. Would I be interested in expanding that work through the WOI?

I told him that I was an academic and would be happy to conduct research, but that I knew nothing about how to manage a national organization. He said it was easier than it seemed and asked me to think about it.

My family and friends were all strongly opposed to the idea. My husband feared that the job would take me away from my life of teaching and writing. My sister, Farah, who had joined the Union of Marxists, an offshoot of the Confederation of Iranian Students in the United States, was working against the Iranian regime. She was adamant that the system was corrupt and that nothing of worth could be accomplished within it. Some of my colleagues were worried about my lack of familiarity with civic work. Some worried about the rumored intrigue and infighting within the WOI.

"They won't let you do anything," I was told again and again, leaving me to wonder who "they" were. But I assumed that "they" were the established government elite. I shrugged and decided that if that happened, I would quit. Five years later, when I joined the cabinet and attended my first meeting of the High Council of Welfare, chaired by Queen Farah and attended by half a dozen cabinet ministers, I was amazed to hear everyone there refer to the illusive "they" as a group distinct from them, bent on spoiling everything. It occurred to me that for many Iranians, regardless of their position or power, "they" were anyone other than "us." It could be the power elite; foreign powers such as the United States, Great Britain, Russia; internal conspirators such as the mullahs, or the leftists, or the intellectuals; or any combination of these. During and after the Revolution the culprit was the shah, who was considered the single force for good or evil, depending on whether you supported him or opposed him. This was how as a society we surrendered our agency as citizens and became in our own mind a tool of some force outside ourselves.

IN SEPTEMBER 1970, Soheila and I took up the same apartment in New York and the same committee positions as in the previous year. One day the doorman called and announced with skepticism, "Someone who claims she is your sister wishes to come up."

It was wonderful to see Farah, though her combat jacket and boots, and her hair that she wore in the style of an Afro, made her hard to recognize. I had last seen her when she was eighteen, before I left the United States for Iran four years ago, and the last thing I expected was for her to show up in New York during the General Assembly. She shared her usual goofy anecdotes about the various activities of her group—recently they had chained themselves to the base of the Statue of Liberty to protest some cause or other. This time, however, she seemed to have moved to a different level. Of all the heads of state who addressed the General Assembly, she only wanted to hear Enver Hoxha, who ruled Albania with an iron fist and who, although he came from a Muslim family, had banned all religions. Riding with me in the princess's Rolls Royce to run an errand for the mission, my sister tried to raise the consciousness of the elegantly uniformed chauffeur and mobilize him to protest.

Despite her intense political perspective, Farah had the same innocence and honesty I remembered in her as a child—the kind of unrelenting bluntness that always made me regret I had nudged her under the table more than once to warn her about a comment that might upset someone, only to have her expose my intervention when she turned to me and said, "What's the matter, did I say something I shouldn't have?" Although she was no longer interested in her favorite pastimes—film and music—the more time we spent together in New York, her joyous, funny self emerged, and her Marxist rhetoric slipped into the background. I promised to go to California to visit her and Mom before returning to Iran.

The following week I was told that the princess wanted me to join her for lunch. Her chauffeur drove us to a Chinese restaurant a few blocks from the offices of the Iranian Mission. The owner met us at the door and offered many courtesies as he showed us to a booth. When the waiter asked if we would like a drink, I ordered a vodka martini, hoping it would calm my nerves. The princess seemed amused by my choice. She did not smoke or drink.

She asked, "Do you like teaching?"

"I love it, Your Highness. I love English literature and I enjoy bringing something new, a new culture and language, to my students. It gives them a broader outlook on life—access to a more global culture."

"How do you manage with your child?"

"Being a university professor allows one to have more flexibility—more work that can be done from home. It helps that my husband has the same type of work as I do. He is not a nine-to-five employee."

"Do the students take someone who is not much older than themselves seriously?" she asked.

"It's interesting, I feel very close to them, since I am only a very few years older than they are. But that has worked as a kind of bond. As if we are on the same road, traveling to the same destination. I love it that once in a while one of them says, 'I want to be like you!'"

Then she asked me about the WOI position. When I told her about my reservations—that as an academic I knew nothing about managing a national organization, she observed that a man in a similar position would readily accept the offer.

"Women are not as adventurous. They don't like to take risks," she said. At the end of the lunch, flushed by my unaccustomed drink, intrigued by the possibilities of making a significant difference in the lives of women in Iran, and miffed by the suggestion that refusal would indicate that I was less of a risk-taker than a man—I accepted the position with the caveat that I would remain on the university faculty, teach part-time, and be on loan to the WOI. This would enable me to keep my place in academia and continue to conduct my research.

WHEN I went to Monterey, California, a few weeks later to visit Mother before returning to Tehran, Farah and several members of her Union of Marxists group came to Mother's house. One of them, Faramarz, was an engineering student. He had dark hair, bronze skin, and piercing green eyes. I could see how Farah had fallen in love with this intelligent, charismatic man who carried himself with considerable dignity.

They were a well-educated and pleasant group of young people. At that point, some of them still attended classes while working their way through university, waiting tables at restaurants or serving at gas stations. Soon, though none of us knew it at the time, they would become full-time revolutionaries, spending their time studying their favorite leftist writers like Frantz Fanon, Herbert Marcuse, and Jacques Derrida, composing tracts attacking the regime in Iran, and taking training and networking trips to work with various radical groups in the People's Republic of South Yemen, Iraq, Oman, and Palestine. Farah and her crew were very much against my soon-to-be-announced WOI position, an organization with Princess Ashraf as honorary president. But I was too late in the process of their ideological development to make a dent in their radicalized views. What may have had some impact two or three years before was useless now. With Farah, I tried anyway. "Iran has its problems, but it is changing and moving ahead," I said. "You know me. I wouldn't get into this type of work if I didn't believe in the possibility—actually, the inevitability—of reform."

"It is impossible to reform this regime," Farah told me. "Good, honest people like you give it legitimacy and delay change."

I stopped myself from reminding Farah that she had left Iran when she was ten and knew nothing about the life of the people or the ways of the government. Even though she and I found ourselves talking often about politics, our conversations were invariably interrupted for a ride to the beach or a long walk in the moonlight. In those moments, we were sisters again, not opponents. And then she would be gone, leaving behind all of the Union of Marxists' notes for their upcoming meetings. I teased her on the phone about her sloppiness in the face of the ruthless efficiency of the security system she had sworn to dismantle. I was glad she was still capable of being amused by a joke with political implications.

Farah and her group became increasingly dogmatic and inner-directed. They developed practices they imagined that Che Guevara lived by. Even taking a daily shower or putting on lipstick became signs of bourgeois complacency. Dancing, movies, and music were all taboo unless they held a correct message about the downtrodden masses. They believed the downfall of corrupt capitalist regimes was inevitable, but it had to be pushed along by fighters for the cause. No opportunity should be passed up to show one's commitment, even if it was as small an act as destroying grapes in a chain grocery store to score a point against Pinochet's Chile. Farah became the spokesperson for the Union of Marxists. She was often in the press with statements and opinions that Mother took care to tone down and explain to me as best she could. Mother was a natural peacemaker.

Mother was also an ideal immigrant. She loved her adopted country and took her civic duties very seriously. She studied all candidates, local and national. She always voted. She never displayed any interest in Marxism, but she loved all three of her children and gave support when needed, without judgment. Whenever any of us met a barrier, or a catastrophe, we came back to her, never doubting that she would welcome us. She told me how proud she was about the work I was taking on, and she said I would be helping to realize her dreams and the dreams of my grandmother. At the same time, she tried to ease my mind about Farah's activities.

BACK AT the university, Tahereh was unhappy about my decision to accept the position at the WOI. She thought of the whole field as a misadventure. "The problem is not women. The problem is the disintegration of values," she said, sounding like the young Marxists who thought women's issues were a distraction from the class struggle.

"What if this offers the possibility to work to make life better for millions of women?" I asked.

"You would be looking in the wrong place for the wrong reasons for solutions to problems that are all too real," she replied. "The better place for you is teaching literature—the least dangerous for the soul." But the path that led me to the WOI *was* teaching literature.

We agreed that we would not dwell on our differences on this issue. We would continue to share the part of our lives that had to do with her poetry and my personal life. But it was hard to keep things separate. On the day my appointment as the WOI secretary general was announced, I was at Tahereh's apartment going over an article on haiku. Sima Dabir-Ashtiani, a journalist from Tehran's major evening paper, *Ettelaat*, who would become an effective ally in the years that followed, had requested an interview. Since I didn't want to change my appointment, I asked Sima to meet me at Tahereh's apartment.

Sima watched us work for a while and asked a few questions. She seemed puzzled by the incongruous image before her: a Western-educated young woman writing about Japanese poetry in English on the eve of taking on leadership of the Women's Organization of Iran. At the end of the interview, she asked about my family. Tahereh scolded, "Please keep those wonderful people out of this." Tahereh loved Babak, whose attempts at writing poetry she very much appreciated. She also respected Gholam and didn't want either exposed to the very real potential of negative media attention that my controversial new position was likely to encourage.

The whole time I was at the WOI, Tahereh was part of my life. I felt that as long as she was with me, I was on the right path. But even this had its limits. All the major Iranian poets worked with us at the WOI when the occasion warranted, but not Tahereh. She worked with me personally, but though she needed additional financial support, and we needed her translation and editing skills, she never accepted to work with the organization.

As my WOI work began to take me to all corners of Iran and around the world, I found myself spending less time with Tahereh. When we were together, I noticed that she was moving steadily away from her Western cultural inclinations, her feminist positions, and her interfaith probings—and into an increasingly narrow view of Islam. She showed me her poem *Safar-e Zamzam* (*Journey to the Well*),[2] an original and powerful long poem that used the concept of religious martyrdom to challenge the political system. When I asked her where she intended to publish it, she said, "I don't think they will allow it to be published."

I said, "Let me show it to Dariush Homayoun." The editor of *Ayandegan*, Tehran's major morning paper, was a connoisseur of poetry, and his journal was respected among intellectuals.

She said, "I know he will never print this."

But Dariush loved the poem. When it was printed the following week, Tahereh was visibly upset. I was disappointed to see her show the familiar attitude of some intellectuals who judged the validity of their views by the extent to which they were opposed by the censors. I didn't know then that she had already begun the journey toward political Islam that would place her among the ruling elite when the revolutionary government came to power in 1979.

Chapter 5

The Women's Organization
of Iran

O N MY FIRST DAY as secretary general of the WOI in 1970, I was
installed in a rather sumptuous office with no particular plan for
the day until Mrs. Kamrani, a secretary who over the years would
never fail to address me in an affectionate, motherly, but extremely polite
tone, handed me a leather folder, embossed with the WOI logo, with my day's
agenda. There was to be a press conference in the adjoining meeting room in
the morning, and in the afternoon I was scheduled to visit the WOI's capital
office that housed the headquarters of the affiliated organizations, where I was
to meet with the fifty-seven leaders.

At the press conference I came face to face with a group of curious but
not unfriendly journalists. My hope was that being honest and speaking from
the heart would help me through this novel experience. They asked about my
plans for the organization, and I told them the truth, basically ad-libbing. "I
don't have any plans," I said. "This organization is about the women of Iran. I
intend to meet a whole lot of them and to ask them what it is they need their
organization to do for them."

"You'll be traveling a lot, then," said *Ettelaat's* Sima Dabir-Ashtiani, "Do you know where you will start?"

"I'll start with my hometown, Kerman, and the cities around the desert," I said.

A man who introduced himself as the representative from *Kayhan*, Tehran's other major afternoon paper, asked, "Who do you want to talk to?"

"I suppose I will have to see a cross section—factory workers, teachers, agricultural workers, housewives. I will also try to see the policy makers to get their take on our work."

By the end of the press conference I had a plan of sorts. Sima's article in the newspaper that day was headlined, "The New Secretary General of the Women's Organization Will Initiate National Dialogue on Women."

The afternoon meeting was more intense. I entered the large conference room of the WOI's capital branch, where some sixty women, mostly middle-aged, almost all in dark suits, were waiting, expectant and skeptical. Women who had worked for many years representing a professional or minority group, or a specific cause such as expanding education for girls, would most likely not be receptive to an unknown woman half their age theoretically in a position of leading them—and I couldn't blame them. If the roles had been switched, I would have been skeptical of myself. I listened to Heshmat Youssefi, who had been deputy governor of Khuzestan province and had served as the acting secretary general during the first year of the WOI, go through my brief CV. She then turned to the group and said, with a hint of sarcasm, "Ladies, allow me to present the Secretary General of the Women's Organization of Iran!" I wished for more gravitas—perhaps if I weighed ten pounds more or had worn my prescription glasses! But I thought, "I am who I am," and went on to say, "I feel there is not much I can say to you at this point, but there is a lot to learn from you. I would like to begin by getting to know more about your work, your challenges, and your achievements." As we moved around the room, with each leader talking about her organization's work, an air of animation and excitement developed. I was genuinely impressed by the wealth of experience and expertise in the room. There were lawyers, nurses, journalists, and many activists who had devoted their lives to supporting religious and ethnic minorities—the Baha'is, Jews, Christians, and Zoroastrians—as well as those working on a variety of other areas such as environmental protection.

By the end of my first day I had the contours of a mission: I wanted to get to know as much as possible about the diverse lives of Iranian women and to hear these women's concerns and aspirations. Over the next couple of weeks I met with women leaders in academia, government, civic organizations, and the arts. They were supportive but, as a rule, pessimistic about the prospects for success—there are too few women with any real knowledge or expertise, I was told, and many of those who do have expertise have no interest in women's issues, and men are by and large uninterested and uncooperative.

ONE OF the first formal visits I received at the WOI was from Farrokhroo Parsa, minister of education and the first woman appointed to the cabinet in Iran. I had known and admired Khanom Parsa—as we all called her with awe in our voices—since my grammar school days in Kerman, when she was the principal of one of the two best girls' high schools in Tehran. She was well known as a stern but caring headmistress. Shortly after returning to Iran three years earlier to teach at the National University, I had received an invitation to a lecture by Mrs. Parsa at the Council of Young Women and Girls. At the time, I had no idea what this council did, but I was curious to know more about Iran's only female cabinet minister. So I set out in my Volkswagen from the university at the foot of the Alborz Mountains and steered my way through downtown Tehran's congested streets. I didn't yet know the city—I had only spent one year there, twelve years earlier, after my parents' divorce. The roads were crowded with vendors selling everything from cigarettes to paper flowers to kites, and the hawkers thought nothing of passing in front of the cars that were slowing down for traffic lights and walking up to drivers' windows to present their wares. The drivers themselves were oblivious to road signs and rules and seemed to think that any maneuver was warranted and acceptable if only one honked loud and long. Needless to say, I found the lecture hall with some difficulty and parked with the help of a young "machine bepa," who steered me into the space and reassured me he would watch my car until I returned. Paying a few coins to the boy provided a kind of insurance as well as the services of a parking attendant. In a dramatic gesture he removed the striped towel from his shoulder and moved jauntily forward to clean my car's windows. I wished he would not mess up my windshield with his filthy rag, but I didn't have the heart to ask him to stop.

Inside, the large hall was packed, and I recognized no one. I sat in the back and listened carefully to Mrs. Parsa, a portly, dignified woman who received the master of ceremonies' accolades with calm patience. She spoke in an authoritative and measured voice about the importance of girls' education as the foundation for national development and modernization. The atmosphere in the hall was strangely formal and humorless; the crowd of largely young women sat stiffly. There were no giggles, no loud whispers, no shifting around in their seats. It seemed that Mrs. Parsa's stern reputation hadn't changed since

I was a child. I liked her, and what she said seemed reasonable, though it was hardly novel.

Mrs. Parsa's heart was in the right place. In the 1920s and 1930s, her mother, Fakhr Afagh Parsa, was a leading member of the women's movement in Iran. With her husband, Fakhr Afagh established *Women's World Magazine*, with the goal of "understanding the need for women's education" and "familiarizing them with their rights." Although the magazine had a moderate tone about women's education, after publishing articles on the need for girls' education and the need for revision of the family laws, Fakhr Afagh had been exiled in order to placate the clerics. When she returned, she joined the Jam'iyat-e Nesvan-e Vatankhah (Society of Patriotic Women), one of the most active women's rights societies of the time.

Fakhr Afagh brought up Farrokhroo as a feminist, although at the time the word was not in use anywhere, and she urged her daughter to pursue the double goal of education and public service. Farrokhroo became a medical doctor, then a teacher and headmistress of one of the best girls' high schools in the country. Her work made her well known on the national scene. When women gained the right to vote in 1963, she was among the first six women elected to parliament. In 1968, she was appointed as the first woman ever to serve in the cabinet, as minister of education.

At the time, Iran's literacy rate for women was very low, even though primary education was compulsory for both girls and boys.[1] Mrs. Parsa made it her goal to ensure that parents actually *allowed* girls to attend school, especially in the villages and rural areas that were harder to reach and where people tended to be more conservative. She was helped by the establishment of the health and education corps as the sixth point of the 1963 White Revolution, which brought young women in their military uniforms to villages and small towns to teach children.

In my WOI office, as I awaited Mrs. Parsa's arrival, I rehearsed in my mind the many things I wanted to ask her. After all, she was much more experienced than I was and so much more powerful. In fact, she was the WOI's logical connection to the government, both as a woman and as minister of education.

Mrs. Parsa arrived wearing a black suit with a gold pin on her lapel, holding a rather small black leather purse. As I crossed my legs and we began to talk, I noticed that she had not crossed hers—her legs were firmly squeezed together, heels touching and the toes of her sensible shoes pointing straight ahead. Her purse remained squarely on her lap. She seemed as stern as she had been at the podium, addressing a crowd of women. But as we began our conversation, she looked at me with kindness and spoke warmly. The stern demeanor must have been a product of years of steering thousands of unruly adolescent girls, and later of having to prove her authority as the first and only woman in a cabinet of twenty men.

After the initial formalities, once the mandatory cup of tea was brought in, I told her how much we counted on her as an ally and spoke about how hard it would be to change the prevailing culture of discrimination without changing children's early education learning materials.

"How can a little girl think she could be a minister if all the women she sees in the textbooks are cleaning house and tending children?" I showed her a picture in the third-grade schoolbook with a girl throwing a ball up into a tree where it was stuck and in the next image, a boy climbing up to fetch it down again. I continued, "Time and again in the texts, the girls cause problems and boys solve them. Dads go to work, moms stay home and cook. Dads are in suits and ties or in various professional uniforms. Moms are wearing aprons. We need to show women like you in these books. We need to change the images and the stories."

Then there was the question of the chador. "Our members in the small towns and villages across the country are teachers. They want to put aside the chador, but they face too much pressure from family and community. If there were to be a directive from the Ministry of Education that at schools, girls would be free of their head covering and teachers would be unveiled, it would give support to those who wished to put it aside."

She smiled at me and said, "I will do what I can, my dear, but you must remember I am minister of education, not minister of women." On leaving, she shook my hand and wished me luck.

Thinking back on what she had said, I realized that she had a point. Although at that time there was not a post of minister of women anywhere in the world, it seemed like a very good idea. It would be useful to have someone in the government whose business was to put together a good team to study, plan, strategize, and advocate for equal rights for women and to work with other ministers as a peer.

Soon after our meeting Mrs. Parsa followed through on what we had asked of her—the school textbooks were revised to reflect a more equitable image of women, and a new regulation was passed allowing female teachers and students to have the choice not to wear the chador.

ON THE sixth day of the month of Bahman, January 26, 1971, Iran held a national parade to celebrate the anniversary of the 1963 White Revolution. The legislation of that time had included granting voting rights to women despite strong opposition from the clerics, and it was important to me to celebrate this enormous milestone. So it was with excitement that I accepted an invitation to join the prime minister, the cabinet, parliamentarians, and the mayor, among others, on a reviewing stand in front of the Senate building. Despite the cold day, I was buoyed by the celebratory atmosphere of bands, banners, and the brilliant colors of the many marching groups. But after a while, the bitter wind cut through my coat. I was shifting from one foot to another and looking around for respite when Mehrangiz Manouchehrian, one of two women senators and a longtime defender of women's rights, approached me. She took me by the hand and guided me inside the main hall of the Senate "for a little break from the festivities."

She beckoned a waiter and ordered two Turkish coffees, as senators and cabinet members stopped by to greet her and exchange pleasantries. This was my first contact with the ruling elite at work. The Senate's imposing hall, with its high ceilings, plush light-gray carpets, and simple furnishings, provided an atmosphere of understated opulence. An air of cordiality and camaraderie made it possible to gloss over the differences and rivalries.

After we had finished our coffees, Senator Manouchehrian said, "Turn your cup over, I'll tell your fortune." I smiled, pleased with the diversion. This was far more appealing than standing outside on the platform, and I told myself I was cultivating a potential ally. She picked up the cup, turned it over, looked carefully at all sides, studied the patterns, and said, "I see snakes—you have enemies, but you will not be harmed by their poison. This is you standing at a height, holding a bucket—you are giving ordinary women something from the bucket—you will be as good to them as you are to your friends. The bird whose wings spread—here, above your head—is luck. It will stay with you because you will keep a balance between your goals and your means. Here, do you see the balance? You will be given many versions of each event, but you will ask a number of disinterested advisors before you take any action. See the crowd huddled together, here near the bottom? You will be praised and pushed toward arrogance and pride, but you will know to keep your sense of proportion and you will remember that it is the chair at the head of the table and not the occupant that they bow to. I see here people sitting around a table. Can you make them out? You will learn not to be afraid of power, but you will not be obsessed with seeking it. Here I see a tiara, a powerful person—a great help, but an even greater danger. You must be very careful and avoid the temptation to get too close. I see a wide-open road leading to the heights. You know your way. You will get where you are going."

She put the cup down, smoothed her skirt, and smiled. "That's all for today, my young friend. Call me if there is anything I can do to help."

I followed her outside into the cold air, feeling reassured by her expression of friendship so delicately camouflaged, yet a bit frightened by her view of what lay in store. One thing the senator had perhaps anticipated for me at the WOI was interference from the princess's male staff—one of whom had been assigned to represent her at the WOI's board meetings during the time of my three predecessors. As a result, it would take a long while and an uphill battle to arrange direct contact between me and the princess. What I would learn in the years to come is whatever problems I had communicating with the princess, and whatever fallout I experienced from associating with her, she was a woman of loyalty, strong political instincts, and bluntness. I could deal with her and at least get the most from her involvement. Any middleman would be a man, and he would be in the middle, not daring, not wanting, not wishing, not understanding, and not approving whatever radical measures were to be taken on behalf of women.

My learning curve at the WOI took other forms, including missteps. A year later, legislation before the Senate included an item that required a husband's permission to issue a passport to a married woman.[2] In a naive effort to influence legislation, I wrote an open letter, which was published on the front page of the newspapers, to the president of the Senate urging him to reconsider this legislation. I referred to Iran's role in the committee that had conceptualized the UN Declaration of Human Rights and the article that refers to freedom of an individual to leave her country and return freely. Various WOI members also took part in public discussions and news interviews, pressing for elimination of the husband's permission as a prerequisite for issuing a passport to a married woman. Using the media for advocacy was unusual in Iran at that time and caused quite a stir. This effort, like a number of others, came partly from a belief in what we were doing and partly from a lack of awareness of the nuances in the political forces that we were up against in society. Our public advocacy for women's rights brought a vociferous backlash from the conservative groups—most importantly from the clerics, who accused the women activists of promoting travel by mothers to the West so they could indulge in gambling, drinking, and corruption, leaving their hard-working husbands and innocent children alone and abandoned at home.

I had no idea at that point what could or could not be done within the system, and I underestimated the clerics' influence over what I had come to see as a modernizing government. When discussion of the "passport permission" legislation began in the Senate, Senator Manouchehrian spoke eloquently about freedom of movement as a basic human right. She reminded her audience that one of the five pillars of Islam was the Hajj—it was every Muslim's duty to make a pilgrimage to Mecca at least once in their lifetime, if they were able. She was about to make the point that since no reference is made to gender in the Quran in relation to the Hajj, no mention of special permission needed for women, and in fact no indication that anyone's permission should be necessary to go on the holy pilgrimage, it must therefore follow that women may travel freely and of their own volition and that the requirement for a husband's permission for a woman to obtain a passport was incompatible with religion. The president of the Senate, panicked by her reference to Islam and the possible reaction of the clerics, quickly and harshly interrupted her speech, "Keep Islam out of this discussion!" he almost shouted. Senator Manouchehrian walked out of the chambers in anger and handed in her resignation.

Homa Afzal, the senator's former student who was now the WOI's legal advisor, and I went to the senator's house and pleaded with her not to give up her powerful position, especially since the president of the Senate had visited her home and apologized in private. We told her how important her position was to the women of Iran. But she would not accept a private apology; she insisted on a public apology. We told her that it might not be possible at that moment for him to make a public apology, and said that while we understood her position, her resignation would be a substantial blow to women. To be strong and principled was one thing, but to leave the arena was quite another. Other options to heal the rift will come along, I said, and I urged her to stay and fight. But she was determined to leave.

In the long run, my open letter to the president of the Senate may have caused more harm than good.

DURING THE first six months of my tenure at the WOI, I traveled to some forty towns and villages around Iran. I kept our visiting group small—a member of the research team and a board member—so that we could keep the atmosphere informal and comfortable. We wanted to find out what changes would be most useful to the women themselves. What were their priorities? What were their greatest challenges and needs? In every town or village we went to schools, factories, farms, homes, prisons, city councils, teachers' associations—anywhere—to learn about the lives and challenges faced by women. We talked to different groups, asking, "If you had your wish list, what change would you think is the most important?" But just as instructive as these larger issues were the struggles and challenges faced by individual women we encountered.

In Bandar Abbas, a port city on the Persian Gulf, we looked under a young woman's burqa (the mask-like covering over a women's eyes) to see the blisters on her face caused by the rubbing of the rough texture of the material over the skin in the 104 F degree heat.

In Abadan I talked to a woman of twenty who had killed the sixty-year-old husband who had raped her repeatedly since she had been given to him in marriage at the age of nine.

In Yazd we passed a woman in a dusty, winding street who was crying as she walked. We stopped the car and asked her why she was crying. She said she was the legal advisor for the WOI branch in Yazd and her husband had just beaten her, forbidding her to set foot in the WOI center. She implored us not to intervene and to let her solve her problem within the family.

In Isfahan we asked a woman in a textile factory how much she was paid, and she said twenty-five tomans a day.[3] We kept asking how much they paid the men; she kept repeating she was paid twenty-five tomans. Finally, tired of our insistence, she said, "They also get twenty-five tomans here—but it's not enough for *any* of us."

In Kashan a teacher told us she wanted to teach a class in carpentry, but the young women said even though a carpenter is paid much more than a seamstress, they were afraid that no young man would marry a carpenter.

The most important lesson I learned in all the exchanges was that the basis of the problems was women's powerlessness and lack of control over their lives. I had experienced this myself: when I returned to Iran and went to open a savings account for my child with my own money, the bank manager said, "You can't do that. You can open an account, but your husband has to cosign, and *he* is the one who will be able to withdraw funds from the account, not *you*." Even though it was *my* money, for *my* child, it took a male to make the decisions.

We had begun our travels around Iran conscious of the legal challenges women faced and the oppressive conditions under the existing laws. We had all experienced or knew someone who had experienced the injustice of a legal system that dictated the subservience of women, and we had seen the violence that resulted from such subservience. We had assumed that free choice in marriage, equal rights to divorce, custody of children, and the right to hold a job or to travel would be the essential and primary demand of women. But time and again women who were oppressed by the laws would ask, "What would I do if I could freely divorce the husband who beats me and insults me? Go back to my father's house and serve *him*? What would I do with my children and how would I support them?" It became apparent that economic independence was the prerequisite for self-determination. Economic independence, however, required political change, and that in turn depended on access to power to change policies. But underlying it all was for women to have agency, and that would depend on changing *culture*.

By the end of our journeys we had a focus. We would work in areas where we had found women with maximum need for change. We would focus on building skills—from literacy to income-producing trainings. In practice, we learned that for a woman to be able to leave her household and attend one of our workshops, she needed a safe space for her children. So we offered child-care facilities alongside the classes.[4] Then it followed that once women learned skills and were able to secure a job, they would have to be able to control their fertility. So we added a family planning unit. And since often these changes brought about some level of discord and conflict, we provided counseling and legal advice for these newly emancipated women.

The WOI centers, often housed in small rented spaces in the slum areas of the cities and towns, grew like mushrooms. They melted into the fabric of the neighborhood and were within walking distance of the women's homes. Their programs, chosen by the women of the community, were flexible. The members added functions as needed in response to women's demands. Some offered rather sophisticated skills, like the repair of small electrical appliances. Some offered religious and language instruction and taught women to read the Quran. Some taught embroidery or how to make artificial flowers. Although our intention was to prepare women for jobs that paid well, no one insisted that they pursue specific vocations. The main purpose was to create a socially acceptable way to bring the women out of the home to work in groups, to realize their own potential, take charge of their lives, and learn the power of solidarity. Our first challenge was to make sure that a woman would simply be allowed to leave her home for a reason other than attending a family gathering, the public bath, or shopping for the family. That in itself was a radical change. To achieve it, the volunteers at each WOI branch did whatever they needed to bring women in. In one place they invited and courted the women in the family of a powerful local mullah, to provide legitimacy in the eyes of the women's male family members. In another they offered classes in the arts or sports or more unusual skills, such as carpentry or bookbinding.

By 1973, we had secured a grant from the Iranian government to build new centers, provided that the local community paid half of the cost. With the centers growing increasingly popular, our provincial activists were able to raise the matching funds from individuals and from the local governments. In those years there was no tradition of grants from international organizations, as there is today. Local philanthropy in Iran, as in most of the developing world, was limited to religious endowments or charities that catered to the needs of the poor. It was through the UN conferences of the mid-1970s to the mid-1990s that nongovernmental organizations (NGOs) began to flourish, women from across the globe began to learn from one another, and funding for women's rights programs began to become available.

By the end of 1975, the UN-designated International Women's Year, the WOI had successfully established 349 branches and 120 centers across Iran. Fifty-five independent organizations were now affiliated with us, including ones that represented journalists, nurses, lawyers, and minorities such as the Jewish community, the Armenians, and the Baha'is, among others. New groups and committees of women were popping up organically in communities across the country. Once they reached a minimum of thirty activists, the groups could ask to join the WOI, and we helped them carry out elections for a secretary and board of directors and create a local branch. The secretaries participated in the WOI's annual general assembly to elect the National Board of Directors and develop the plan of action for the year to come. WOI members were volunteers, and the secretaries were often teachers or homemakers interested in philanthropic community work. By 1977 over 1 million women participated in the activities of the WOI branches and centers.

The most important lesson we learned during this period of rapid growth was to avoid making theoretical assumptions and strategic decisions without hearing from the people who would be affected. Through our work with women across the country, we learned that their aspirations and needs were widely shared, but for each project to succeed, it had to be fine-tuned and adapted to fit the specific needs of the women in each constituency. Our experiments led us to create a system whereby each province had one or more staff members, assigned to them as liaisons, who traveled to the various branches on a regular basis. These women were on the road three weeks a month and returned for a week to the WOI's central secretariat to report what they had seen and heard, exchange experiences, and take any new ideas learned from other liaisons to their area. The liaisons were trained for two years in the WOI School of Social Work established in Naziabad, one of the largest of south Tehran's underprivileged neighborhoods. They lived in the school's dormitory and interned in one of the twelve women's centers in the area.

When I first took on the position of secretary general, the customary position of the WOI was that women were capable of performing all of the functions and duties assigned to them as wives and mothers while also holding responsible positions as workers and citizens. Speeches often contained such statements as "men and women are like two halves of an apple," completing each other. At the WOI's 1973 general assembly, while listening to such a presentation, I decided to take a chance and test the opinion that seemed obvious in view of the hundreds of working women I had met in our fact-finding trips around the country. I walked up to the lectern, my heart pounding, and said, "I think it is time for us to make clear that no one can bear the burdens of family and work by herself—that if women are to have an equal role in society and the workplace, they need support from the family and from society. And I personally prefer to be a whole worm rather than half an apple." I stopped and looked at the faces in the hall. It took a few seconds, then the applause showed me that we had reached a point when we can say that we *do* want it all, but we can't do it by ourselves. The WOI's constitution was unanimously amended to declare the duty of the organization as "defending the individual, family, and social rights of women to ensure their complete equality in society and before the law."[5]

IN 1973 we at the WOI received an invitation from Valentina Tereshkova, the president of the Women's Committee of the Soviet Union, to visit her country in the hope of establishing ties between the women of our two nations. We had learned so much from our own people that we felt it was time to look to other societies to see if there were strategies we could learn from them. We decided to accept the invitation.

The WOI board selected Homa Rouhi, a former WOI secretary general who was now deputy minister of mines and industries, and Heshmat Youssefi, coordinator of the WOI-affiliated organizations, to accompany me on this trip. The Iranian Foreign Ministry gave us an intensive briefing, most of which focused on being careful about what we discussed among ourselves. They were convinced our rooms and telephones throughout the trip would be tapped and told us we would be filmed twenty-four hours a day. We were intrigued by the thought of being filmed constantly and laughed as we pretended to pose for the cameras. I'm not sure how comprehensive the surveillance was, but I know for a fact that straying even a few steps from the route that took us directly from the entrance of our hotel to the elevator was made nearly impossible by minders who either did not or would not speak any language other than Russian.

Our official hostess, Valentina Tereshkova, was the most famous woman in the Soviet Union at the time. She was the only woman cosmonaut in the world, a member of the Supreme Soviet, the Soviet Union's most powerful and authoritative legislative body, and later the head of the Women's Committee that represented the Soviet Union at the UN conferences on women in Mexico City and Copenhagen.

Valentina was immaculately coiffed and wore a light beige Chanel-style suit when she came to receive us. She spoke briefly about her role in advancing the participation of women in science and in space exploration. Then, her blue eyes sparkling and voice more animated, she added, "I strongly believe that a woman should always remain a woman and nothing feminine should be alien to her. I feel that no work should enter into conflict with her ancient 'wonderful mission'—to love, to be loved—and with her craving for the bliss of motherhood. These two roles should complement one another."

"So much for communist egalitarianism," we thought to ourselves. But we did not talk or say this—or even whisper to each other—until we walked into the open air.

Throughout our travels in the Soviet Union, there was an obsessive focus on the "domestic economy." The topic came up again and again in relation not to women but to the country in general. Our main guide and translator was a slender blonde woman who communicated with us in English. At one point she was translating a statement by the health minister about reproductive health. The term didn't seem to come to her immediately, so she pointed to the lower part of her body and said, "The minister is referring to this *here* domestic economy!" No reference on the trip was made to abortion, which at the time was often used in the Soviet Union as a substitute for contraception, sometimes leading to many such procedures in a woman's lifetime.[6] Neither was there any discussion of the absence of women from political leadership or of their lower pay and prestige in fields such as medicine.

In Alma Ata, the capital of the Soviet Republic of Kazakhstan, we met with members of an agricultural commune; women in the agricultural sector seemed to be comparatively better off. Each night there was a large group dinner. I had been warned by a friend who had been the Iranian ambassador to the Soviet Union that the only way to deal with the unending toasts of vodka would be to take a big dab of butter on a small piece of bread before each meal to line our stomachs. As head of the delegation, I had to respond to the endless toasts. I was told that as the highlight of the dinner I would be presented with a sheep's head and was expected to cut an appropriate piece for each member of the host party. I was petrified until our translator confided that I had the option of passing this honor to the leading local dignitary.

In Leningrad, in addition to the usual scripted meetings, we visited the incredible Hermitage Museum and Winter Palace. Heshmat Youssefi, our more adventurous colleague, wondered out loud, "If whatever existed prior to the communist regime was so bad and whatever happened after it was so good, why is it that all of the nice things we are being shown belong to the bad period?"

We had expected repression and control, but having heard the consistent message from the Soviet Union and its satellites that equality between men and women was a given under Marxism, we were taken aback by what we saw—even the laundered version of reality. Though women were working in large numbers, childcare was supplied by the government, and substantial numbers of women were educated and trained in various professions, they rarely held high decision-making positions. It seemed to us that patriarchy was still very much alive in the Soviet Union.

AT PRINCESS Ashraf's dinners in New York I had seen the beginnings of friendly discussions between the Iranian and Chinese delegations to the United Nations. President Zulfikar Ali Bhutto of Pakistan, a good friend of the princess, had played an important role in facilitating the dialogue that led to her pathbreaking trip to China in 1972. On our return from the Soviet Union, we discussed China as another interesting model and decided to visit. It was 1973, during the Cultural Revolution when China was mostly closed to the outside world, so the WOI board was excited about the trip. We asked the Iranian Foreign Ministry to facilitate a trip for us and we were told that in the special case of China, we would need to clear a possible visit with the court.

I composed a letter to the minister of court, Assadolah Alam, who delivered the response by phone: "I presented your request to travel to China to His Majesty and His Majesty inquired, 'What for?'"

It seemed a rather comical give-and-take, but I said, "We would like to describe our strategies for bringing women to fully participate in the process of development and establish ties of cooperation with Chinese women."

He called back to say we had the green light.

Everyone at the WOI was eager to go to China, and in the end we literally flipped a coin to decide on the delegates. Our team included Dr. Iran Alam, a gynecologist and chair of the WOI board; Shamsi Hekmat, the specialist on early education; Haleh Esfandiari, the deputy for international relations; and Parviz Homayounpour, the deputy for education and program development, a former Marxist and the only male.

On arrival in Beijing I was alarmed to discover that our host was the man in charge of tourism. On the drive to the city, I told him, "We are pleased to be in China and eager to learn from our Chinese sisters about their success in achieving full participation with men. As Chairman Mao has said, 'Women hold up half the sky.'"

I couldn't decide from his perplexed expression whether the issue was a faulty translation or something deeper. "We hope you will enjoy both the natural beauty and the arts and architecture of China," he said noncommittally.

The next day, on our visit to the Iranian ambassador, we discovered that the difficulty we had faced had its origins in a misunderstanding with our own Foreign Ministry, which apparently could not comprehend that one of the first delegations from Iran to China would be a group of women who might want to carry out serious business in that country. The agenda they had worked out with the Chinese was basically a tour of interesting sites. No meetings with women—nor with men for that matter. Highly respected by the diplomatic community, the Iranian ambassador was an elder statesman and former foreign minister. He was adamant that this was the message he had received.

I told him that we were in China on business and if we could not do the work we came to do, we would leave on the next plane. "We need to meet ordinary women and women leaders in the fields of education, health, politics, and academia. We would like to pay a visit to a university and speak to students. We would like to see a factory, preferably a textile factory," I said.

"This is a very difficult post, unlike any other," he sighed. "They have only a handful of foreign embassies here. It's hard to communicate and hard to arrange any meetings."

"I would appreciate it if you would convey our request to the Chinese Foreign Ministry," I replied. I was confident that there was interest in opening up avenues of exchange to Iran and that once the Chinese were told about our mission, they would cooperate. This was indeed the case, for in our next meeting with the ambassador, we were presented with a new agenda that looked a lot more like the trip we had envisioned. It included travel to Shanghai to visit a textile factory, schools, youth centers, and a neighborhood committee, and travel to Hangzhou, where we would visit a tea plantation and a commune. On our return to Beijing, we would have an appointment to meet the minister of health at the Great Hall of the People. All our journeys were to be by train, and we were accompanied by two translators—one for our French-speaking members, Dr. Alam, Haleh, and Parviz, and an English-speaking translator for Homa, Shamsi, and me.

In Hangzhou, a beautiful small town by the serene Lake West, surrounded by green hills and tea plantations, we discussed with our women hosts the merits of living in communes. We visited a kindergarten where we listened to the children's songs and sang an Iranian children's song for them. The children were bundled up in heavy quilted pants and jackets. The rooms were very cold, so the children dressed the same indoors and outdoors; the pants had a slit that allowed the children to use the restroom without having to take off their clothing, by simply squatting on the holes in the ground that served as toilets. On the wall of the kindergarten classroom a huge mural depicted a fierce, but adorable, chubby-cheeked boy wielding a huge spear against an invisible enemy. We were told that the enemy in this, as in most other cases, was the wicked Lin Biao, about whose evil ways we had already heard in Beijing.

Whether we were speaking with groups of women or visiting a kindergarten, the campaign of "Criticize Lin Biao, criticize Confucius" was in full swing. A curse against Lin Biao would find its way into the conversation, reminding us of the complexities of the political culture in this amazing, enormous nation, about which we knew so little. This was largely due to China's isolation at that time and its lack of interaction with the rest of the world. The ignorance was mutual. It was hard to believe that in 1973 the citizens of the People's Republic of China still didn't know that a man had stepped on the surface of the moon.

Parviz, the WOI's resident former Marxist who had mellowed to being a socialist, was better informed than the rest of us. He explained that Lin Biao was one of the great generals during the Chinese Revolution. He later became party vice chairman and Mao's chosen successor. He was one of the founders of the Cultural Revolution and the famous "Gang of Four," as well as a close ally of Mao's wife, Jiang Qing. Lin Biao helped spread the cult of Mao by promoting Mao's famous *Little Red Book*, which for a time was required reading for all Chinese, especially in the armed forces' training programs. Billions of copies were printed; it was translated into twenty languages in the 1960s and sold in 117 countries, including Iran. Parviz owned a copy.

In 1971, Lin Biao's alleged plans for a coup against Mao had been "discovered," and he and his family had died in a mysterious plane crash as they tried to escape China. When we arrived, the Cultural Revolution had come to an unhappy end. Some of our hosts quoted from the *Little Red Book*, oblivious to the intricacies of the Iranian web of international alliances and relationships. We heard several toasts to the "Iranian masses and their battle against all US and European reactionary forces who represent real dangers, and in this respect are like real tigers. But the struggle will reveal that they are paper tigers."

One of the twenty-five or so themes into which the quotations in the *Little Red Book* were divided was about women. It stated, "Women represent a great productive force in China, and equality among the sexes is one of the goals of communism. The multiple burdens which women must shoulder are to be eased." What we came to see, though, is that women in many ways were still carrying far too much. We were struck by the similarity between the working conditions in the textile factories we visited in China and the ones back home: the same back-breaking standing posture, the same dusty and polluted air thick in the sunlight, the same exhaustion on the faces of the women workers engaged in their monotonous work. Once again we wondered why nothing was done about the air quality, and why there were not better physical arrangements for these working women who constituted nearly 100 percent of the labor in these factories. Why couldn't they sit on stools? Why weren't they provided with masks? There were as few answers here as in our own textile factories in Isfahan.

There weren't many answers to childcare, either. When we arrived in Shanghai, our very pleasant and gentle female guide and translator asked whether we would mind if she left us for an hour to visit her child, who lived there with her grandmother. Our guide hadn't seen her child for six months. She explained that there was no national plan to provide childcare for working women, and grandparents were the main resource available to women. Later in the trip, at the Great Hall of the People in Beijing, the minister of health gave a rather disappointing, canned speech about the achievements of the People's Republic in the area of health, with no specific focus on women's health. Although she listened patiently to our description of our challenges and achievements, she had no questions or comments. When we asked about women's presence in the higher policy-making positions in China, she repeated Mao's oft-quoted line that "women hold up half the sky." But when pressed, she told us there were no women in the Politburo, the highest decision-making body of the Communist Party. She pointed out that women were fully integrated into China's educational system and the workforce and said that arrangements for childcare facilitated their workplace participation. She also confirmed our guide's statement that grandparents or other older family members were a major part of that solution.

The most instructive part of our trip to China was the small neighborhood committee we visited in Shanghai and the elderly woman who headed it. There we learned that the general, current ideological message we had heard in the Great Hall from the minister, "Criticize Lin Biao, criticize Confucius," and again at every stop down to the neighborhood committee, was an example of how ideology and administration were centrally managed. Messages were developed carefully, came from the center by a structured path through various institutions and communities, and reached every part of the country. While the ideological framework was centrally determined, the administration of ordinary matters of daily life was left to local committees that managed the needs of families and neighborhoods. This combination was highly efficient and effective. It was a one-way version of the two-way process we had developed at the WOI. At the WOI, we listened to and learned from local women around the country, compiled and analyzed the message at various levels of policy making, and took the results back to local communities to be acted upon in ways that reflected their conditions and priorities. In the Chinese case, there seemed little if any local participation or consultation in the development of the ideological goals and vision. We learned from China the importance of keeping the message simple both in concept and expression so that it could be shared as widely as possible. Implementation would be local and adapted to the context and circumstances.

At the end of our trip, we said goodbye to our interpreters with hugs and tears. We had broken through the rigidly programed conversations so that they joked with us about some of their own prescribed statements. Our female translator kidded her male counterpart, saying, "Before the Cultural Revolution his name in Chinese meant 'the poplar tree that bends in the wind'—after the Cultural Revolution he changed his name to 'the unbending Banyan Tree.'"

The China we saw would soon change dramatically, but at that time the streets were almost without cars. Everywhere we went we saw endless lines of male and female bicycle riders in identical gray uniforms. No visible local commerce, no shops, no restaurants. The national TV broadcast only for a short period every day. The news was highly selective, with little information about the world outside China. There was a simplicity and sparseness to everything. One day in Shanghai we decided to take a walk by the water, where we chatted about the view and the wonderful food for an hour. As we turned to return to our hotel, we saw a mass of gray-clad men and women following us and talking excitedly among themselves. It felt strange to see ourselves—ordinary Iranian women—as extraordinary, as we must have appeared to the average Chinese who had never seen people like us or anyone from anywhere else for that matter. We had a hard time processing all of this, but once we were immersed in China, it was almost painful to be suddenly bombarded by the sights, colors, smells, and sounds of Hong Kong, which was like a giant mall. We were repelled by it. We didn't want to shop. We didn't want to go sightseeing. Instead, we talked about our affection for the people of China and our dislike for the cocoon in which they seemed to live.

By the time I wrote to Farah, who at the time idolized China, I had a clearer grasp of our experience. I told her about all I had seen and asked, "Does it take the selflessness, efficiency, and order of a beehive to feed and clothe human-ity and take care of their survival? The ballet *Red Detachment of Women* was beautiful, just as *Spartacus* had been in the Soviet Union. But is art only to be valued in relation to ideology? Is there no worth to beauty for its own sake?"

Chapter 6

West Meets East

I N 1973, WHILE I was in New York as a member of the Iranian delegation at the United Nations, I got to know Betty Friedan, the founder of the National Organization for Women (NOW). I remembered Betty from my student days in the United States as the author of *The Feminine Mystique*, which was credited with starting the US women's movement. She was a short, stocky, plain-looking woman, not much older than my mother, but she reminded me of my hard-working, no-nonsense grandmother, Tooba Naficy. Betty was a bit abrupt and impatient and not too keen to consider the customary cultural nuances in her communication. This was also true of her personal interactions with people of different backgrounds in her own country. But her public persona was not without humor, and I appreciated her innate humility and her honesty about limiting her focus on women of her own background. Her willingness to share her thoughts and experiences so that others might take what they wished from them also made her a successful communicator. We took a liking to each other immediately, and the similarities I saw with my grandmother made me trust Betty as a mentor. Different as they were, the two women seemed refreshingly dedicated to ideas beyond their own self-interest. For her part, Betty seemed quite curious to learn about my experiences and work with women in Iran.

Having visited India, the Soviet Union, and China, I thought it would be very helpful to learn more about the feminist movement in the United States. While we were in New York, Betty introduced me to feminist activists in the United States and brought me to meetings she thought representative of the discourse in the feminist community. Betty also talked to me about a Women's Bank she was helping to create. I couldn't quite fathom a bank just for women, but I was curious to learn the reasoning behind the project. Years later, the Moroccan writer Fatema Mernissi asked me, "Why do you think Western feminists insist on segregated spaces—schools, conferences, projects? Is it because they have never experienced segregation of a harem?"

The next step for us at the WOI was to better understand some of the different approaches to the status of women in the West. Once I was back in Iran, I drew up a reading list from what I had learned on my trip and passed it on to our WOI board and staff. Some of the pieces were more appealing than others. I particularly responded to the second chapter of Kate Millet's *Sexual Politics*, "Notes on a Theory of Sexual Politics." In her analysis of the predicament that we—women and men—face so long after there was any reason or justification for it, Kate discussed the causes and consequence of the division of roles and functions that society provides for men and women. She realized decades before others that the global condition of women takes shape in the family. But some of her other statements made cross-cultural communication a bit challenging. One such example was the experience of Dr. Alam, the gynecologist who chaired our board, and an eager student of the liberation texts. A friend who was one of her relatives cautioned me to be a little more discreet with my reading choices. He told me that on a weekend family get-together Dr. Alam, whose second language was French, had looked up from her reading and turned to him, asking, "What is this word 'fook' this lady keeps talking about?"

The Feminine Mystique was more familiar and more approachable. In it, Betty Friedan described her conversations with a substantial number of women with lives similar to her own, women who lived in rather affluent households with husbands, children, friends, cars, and sophisticated labor-saving appliances and who, by all accounts, were supposed to be happy but were not. Clearly there was a problem. At the WOI, we fiercely debated what that problem was and what could be done about it.

Our discussions of these texts gave me the idea to invite some of the leading figures in the Western feminist movement to Iran, so that we could hear firsthand their ideas and experiences, just as we had already heard from other women leaders in the Soviet Union and China. But talking to women in China and the Soviet Union—textile workers, teachers, political leaders—had reinforced our idea that the underlying structures that affected the status of women were essentially the same across the world. We also still felt that while women's aspirations were similar, the priorities and the strategies to reach these aspirations had to fit their specific circumstances. That is, each society had to find its own way to change the status of women, based on its own culture and way of life. But the very idea of the universality of women's condition convinced us that we needed to look at the roots of the problem of gender inequality and build some form of solidarity around our different experiences and challenges.

When I suggested to my WOI colleagues that we invite a few Western feminists to Iran to give lectures, visit our centers, and offer feedback on our work, reactions were mixed. Some loved the idea and thought it would be useful to engage in dialogue. Some were worried that the publicity around the visit might further typecast us as "Westoxicated" ("intoxicated by the West") a nebulous concept in vogue among Iranian intellectuals at the time. Others were concerned about what the speakers would say and the ramifications of their opinions for us. If the press or the radical clerics decided to use the visitors to attack us, they could quote them out of context, or, even worse, quote them *in* context. It would be no use for us to say that their opinions were their own. The natural question would be why we had invited them if we didn't respect what they had to say. This latter group had a point. The press seemed to follow an unwritten code when it came to the shah and the royal family, and in most instances, to specific government policies. But as far as women were concerned, we were fair game for criticism. We had friends, mostly women, affiliated with various newspapers and journals, who took a special interest in women's issues, but their influence was limited.

In the end, we decided to move ahead with the plan. I suggested we invite Betty Friedan, Kate Millet, and Helvi Sipilä, the first female UN assistant secretary general, the highest-ranking woman at the United Nations, and the person responsible for the first UN Conference on Women, scheduled for 1975 in Mexico City.

When I first mentioned the possibility of the visit, Betty had asked me many questions: "What does the shah think of this? Why would he want me to come?"

I told her that the shah had no idea that I was asking her, and I didn't know *what* he would think of it.

"Is there anyone who would want to listen?" she asked.

"I think so," I said. "There would not be masses of people, but there certainly would be hundreds. Language is the first limitation. But there are enough people interested. Besides, an important part of the visit for us is to have your feedback on our work."

"What do you think—a hat, a scarf?" she asked me. At that time Betty was excited that she had been invited for an audience with the Pope, and she wondered what she should wear to that event as well as on a trip to Iran. I found myself wishing that the amount of time women spent deciding what to wear to an occasion more often matched the time we spent on our worthier concerns.

When I sent her a formal invitation from the WOI, she accepted, with the caveat that she would have to have a personal meeting with the shah so she could do an article for the *Ladies' Home Journal*. I told her I would try my best to arrange one, but I couldn't promise.

I had met Helvi, an experienced diplomat and women's rights activist from Finland, in New York. A tall, dignified woman with impeccable manners and wide-ranging, firsthand knowledge of the status of women across the world, she accepted the invitation quickly and graciously.

Kate Millet, on the other hand, said she was working on a manuscript and would not be able to travel. In her place, we talked about inviting Simone de Beauvoir, whose *Second Sex* many of us had read and admired. But because language would present an added complication, I wrote to Germaine Greer, author of *The Female Eunuch*, who could represent the more radical wing of the feminist movement. She wrote back immediately, expressing surprise and excitement at the offer. She asked what topic would be of interest, then mentioned her work on reproductive rights and wondered if that would be an appropriate subject. I told her that would be fine.

I met Germaine, a statuesque woman with wavy red hair, for the first time when she arrived at Tehran's Mehrabad airport. As we sat in a corner to wait for her suitcases, she looked up at the large imposing portrait of the shah on the wall and said, "I can't talk with him staring down at me." I reassured her that we would be out of there soon, and there would be no photographs of the shah anywhere in our vicinity. Because we were both English literature teachers, we chatted about books, and I liked her from the outset.

Germaine was excited and a bit nervous about what was expected of her. Unlike Betty and Helvi, she had not been involved in organizational work, and as a speaker she was uncertain about her audience. A professor at several academic institutions in England and Australia, she was more sophisticated, more intellectual, and in her discourse, clearly a member of the elite. She seemed bent on being controversial and radical—wanting to shock, provoke, and out-do the others and sometimes herself. I had expected that someone as intelligent as she would see that it was not too difficult to shock a couple hundred middle-class Middle Eastern women, especially at that moment in history. To make these women understand and sympathize with someone of her background would be the real accomplishment. But I was drawn to her fragility and vulnerability.

As much as I enjoyed all three of our guests, it became apparent during their time in Iran that they did not have much admiration for each other. Their approaches to women's issues, their past histories, and their lifestyles were so different that often they seemed more alien to each other than to us. Helvi was an experienced diplomat, very correct in her behavior. With a long and distinguished career in law, she had been a leader in several women's organizations in Finland. Her work at the United Nations had also brought her into contact with a wide variety of cultures and life experiences. As a result, she had been exposed to many approaches to women's issues across the globe and had a good experiential basis for comparing the work the WOI was doing in Iran with that of others. By contrast, Betty had a quick and empathetic mind, and her frankness made her ask questions bluntly, to which she received more spontaneous and honest responses. Brilliant but emotionally volatile, Germaine was younger and centered her understanding of women's condition on her own personal experience. She delved into her own psyche to search for the insecurities, pain, and fear that she expressed in vehement and colorful terms that often touched the individual women who read her work or listened to her. Her work, however, did not include formulas for personal, let alone collective, action once this illumination had taken place.

During their first panel discussion I took care to explain to some 200 women and three dozen men in the audience that "the views expressed by the panelists are not necessarily the views of the WOI" and hoped for the best. Helvi opened the session with a discussion of the United Nations system and the participation of women within the UN Secretariat which, she pointed out, was dismally low. She read Article 23 of the Declaration of Human Rights, which states the right of each individual to work, choose a profession, and receive equal pay for equal work. She referred to the Declaration of the Elimination of Discrimination against Women, which focused on women's right to receive vocational training and equal access to benefits including vacation, and especially maternity leave and childcare facilities. She then asked everyone to take the declarations home and read them and ask themselves how their situation compares to the articles of the declarations. She concluded her lecture by mentioning a conference in Tokyo on population that she recently attended: "You can imagine how I felt to see that 141 men and only 4 women were gathered to discuss population issues. I hope all of us, men and women, can join together to make the International Year of Women the beginning of the end of discrimination, so that in 1985, at the end of the Decade for Women, the question of women will not exist in the way we knew it in the 1970s."[1]

Betty then talked about how the theme of the "feminine mystique" described the emptiness of life for the middle-class American suburbanite, and she went on to an in-depth discussion of the causes of that discontent. She also described the establishment and vision of NOW. The audience responded warmly to her down-to-earth presentation style and appreciated that her critique was based on a group she knew well and grounded in a question rather than a formulaic solution.

Finally, Germaine spoke about women's reproductive rights and the toll that early pregnancy, botched abortions, and lack of maternal care took on women, especially in developing nations. Finally, she wondered why while Islam does not object to birth control and the Quran does not consider the fetus alive until the fourth week of pregnancy, Islamic governments refuse to introduce legislation to make it possible to obtain abortions without penalty. I winced at her reference to Islam and the Quran, recalling the recent resignation of Senator Manouchehrian.

For the question-and-answer session that followed the panel discussion, we asked to have the questions from the audience in writing, partly to avoid the long speeches from the floor that are sometimes offered in place of a question. Also, we wanted to be certain that a variety of concerns were addressed. Most important, however, we wanted to avoid controversial references to Islam that could lead to politically contentious responses from the speakers. We needn't have worried—the questions were quite benign and the answers reasonable. We were relieved by the extensive and positive press coverage the next day. Except for a reference to Germaine's recent interview with *Playboy* magazine, no controversial statements and no nastiness appeared.

As usual, we walked a tightrope. We wanted our guests to feel free to say what they wished, and we wanted the widest possible audience for them. But we did not want to own their words or be identified with them since we did not share their views in a number of areas. We were petrified of being typecast as "tools of Western imperialism" by the Left, and "godless enemies of family values" by the Right. Also, we were concerned about SAVAK, the intelligence agency that throughout the years of my work with the WOI had considered our activities, for the most part, to be needless provocation of the opposition, especially the religious fundamentalists. They thought we antagonized the extremists without creating any real power group in support of the system.

Our visitors' awareness of our complex situation was varied, but they generally held the view, prevalent in the West, that Iran was a dictatorship. However, if such a state had allowed them to be invited, then everything must be okay. They also saw no difference between closed totalitarian systems such as the Soviet Union and China and a relatively open society such as Iran. For example, at first our visitors made no distinctions between the WOI, the intelligence agencies, the state, and the various forces within Iranian society. At one point while visiting a WOI center, Betty asked bluntly, "How do I know these centers are not set up to impress us? How do we know they will go on after we leave?"

It was a testament to our lack of understanding of how Iran was perceived in the West that it had never occurred to us that someone might think such a thing. I was shocked and angry. "Who do you think you are that we would spend all this money and all this effort to put on a show for you?" I asked. "And if we were able to construct centers, put people to work, and bring women to impersonate learners just to impress you, what would stop us from continuing the work?" I believe that my indignation convinced her, and candor strengthened the bond between us.

In addition to limited understanding of the political situation in Iran, our guests had little understanding of our cultural context and the limitations it placed on our work. While Helvi was impressed by the work she saw at the centers and spoke of the possibility of using it as a model elsewhere, Betty wondered why the women in the centers were not more feminist. She understood after I reminded her that she would have a hard time finding many feminists in disadvantaged areas back home in the United States—that the Western feminist movement was largely formed among the intellectual elites of affluent white women. Then, on a visit to one of the women's centers in the slum areas of south Tehran, Betty struck up a conversation with one of the women in a workshop and asked, "Why are you studying hairdressing? That's such a traditionally female skill." We couldn't expect Betty to know what courage it took for a semiliterate, poor woman from the Naziabad slums just to want to leave her house and come to a class. Nor could Betty imagine what it must have taken to gain agreement from the men in her household that she do so. She asked another woman, "What would you do if your husband said you can't come to the center?" But she was familiar enough with the politics of powerlessness to grasp the meaning of the woman's answer: "The whole trick is to ask in a way that he would not say no. If he said no, that would be the end of that."

The rest of the speaking engagements in Tehran were, on the whole, successful. People came, listened, and raised questions. Helvi was solid, serious, and inspired respect, even if she did not excite the audience. Betty empathized with her listeners. She succeeded because what she said about her own constituency—middle-class women in America—appealed to the educated middle-class Iranian women who were listening to her. They liked her humor and her anecdotes and her humility about the status of women in her own country. Germaine assumed things about the audience that were not always correct—she supposed that their needs and priorities matched those of her audiences in the West. But she was articulate, charming, and intelligent, and for the most part received a positive response.

When our guests met with Princess Ashraf, Betty asked about the veil and its impact on women's lives. Princess Ashraf explained that before January 8, 1936, no Iranian woman could leave her house without a full veil. She said that her father, Reza Shah, had been influenced by Atatürk, and on his return from a visit to Turkey he had decreed that the women of Iran should no longer veil. She described the day he took her mother, her sister, and herself with him to the school where he made his famous speech on unveiling and declared his intention to involve women in the development of the country. She recalled her father's contradictory feelings on the morning of the ceremony—his tears at the thought of exposing his unveiled wife and daughters to the gaze of strangers and his determination that it must be so if his goal of progress for the country were to be realized. The princess went on to explain that during her childhood, a woman's existence did not count at all. If a man had three daughters and two sons and was asked, "How many children do you have?" he would answer, "Two." She also explained that there was no mandate in the Quran for women to be veiled.

Betty and Helvi said that they had been impressed by the women they had met at our centers and at the meetings organized for them. "But they are part of a minority of Iranian women," the princess said. "The majority is still illiterate and lacks skills and lives a cloistered life. You should meet the women in the rural areas to get a fuller picture."

When I told the princess that our guests would be traveling to Shiraz next, she recommended that they visit the tribal school for "barefoot doctors," a system of training men and women from villages in basic health care that the princess saw during her trip to China and helped adapt for Iran. She also talked about the upcoming 1975 UN Conference on Women in Mexico City, which she thought would help create a global agenda shared by governments and supported by the women's movement. The princess was genuinely pleased to meet the Western feminists and seemed to look upon them as comrades in arms.

Years after Betty's death, I saw that she wrote in her notes that Princess Ashraf and my mother, who was on her summer visit to Iran from the United States and joined us for a portion of the three feminists' visit, had the timidity of women who had been veiled in their youth. If I had seen Betty's notes that summer, I would have told her that neither woman—both of whom were from her own generation—had ever been veiled; both were extraordinarily strong and courageous women who took chances and flung themselves at possibilities, knowing full well the costs. I can't imagine too many women in the 1950s in the United States who would have left a luxurious lifestyle to travel to a faraway country halfway around the world to work in a cannery to support themselves through university as my mother did. Nor in the 1940s were there many twentysomething women who could have sat with Joseph Stalin and negotiated bilateral relations as Princess Ashraf had done. Manners and styles of communication that make people behave "not like us" are not an indication of strength or weakness.

After we left Princess Ashraf, I took our visitors to see Queen Farah. Their anticipation of the meeting was as varied as their personalities. Betty had no idea how she was supposed to talk to royalty or what "the queen of Iran" would be like; as the UN assistant secretary general and a citizen of a monarchy, Helvi had had occasion to meet with royalty before; Germaine's beautifully executed curtsy demonstrated her Anglo-Celtic familiarity with royalty-related customs. Despite the varied personalities and experiences, our conversation, encouraged by the queen's informality and spontaneity, went smoothly. The queen was open about the problems of women in Iran and said time and again, "We face challenges, but we are trying."

Betty asked about the shah's interview with Oriana Fallaci, an Italian journalist, in which Oriana's flirtatious teasing had elicited from him—as it had from other, more savvy politicians such as Henry Kissinger—shocking comments, including, "Women have not been able to produce any leaders, not even a great chef."

"Did you ask him about this?" Betty inquired.

"Yes," the queen replied. "He said he was joking and had been quoted out of context." The meeting, scheduled for half an hour, lasted an hour and a half. Everyone seemed to enjoy the freewheeling conversation about the problems of handling the many complicated roles we were expected to perform as women and as professionals.

We left Sa'dabad Palace for the WOI offices, where journalists were awaiting our guests. During the subsequent press conference, all three visitors offered effusive comments, but Betty topped them all, saying, "Queen Farah is one of the greatest feminists I have seen." I was surprised. I knew Queen Farah as an intelligent, caring woman, but she didn't consider herself a feminist, nor did we consider her to be one. When Betty returned to the United States, her cover article for *Ladies' Home Journal* was titled, "The Feminist Empress of Iran." I then realized that Betty's definition of a feminist was broader and more accurate than the general understanding of the term at the time, when the word was used to denote radical, antimale, antifamily activism. Germaine was also very positive about the trip, although later, after Betty died in 2006, she wrote the least generous "eulogy" for a feminist colleague I have seen, mocking Betty and calling her pompous, egotistic, demanding, and selfish. She added false and insulting anecdotes about the trip, and, for good measure, called us at the WOI "the shah's courtiers."[2]

The next day Betty had her meeting with the shah, which Queen Farah had helped us arrange. Betty was nervous leading up to the meeting and told me she had a queasy stomach; she wanted me to go with her. But I had given the court my deputy's name, so she accompanied Betty. Betty came back quite impressed, and in the same article for the *Ladies' Home Journal* she wrote a generally positive report about the shah: he described his "Great Civilization" project as "a little like the 'New Frontier' and 'Great Society' of our Kennedy-Johnson eras." About the Fallaci interview, she quoted him as saying, "Let us complete this matter of equality in education and opportunity, and then we will see what women are capable of. It is up to them. We have not seen great accomplishments of women in the past—yes, as I said, not even great cooks—because of lack of opportunity."[3] Unfortunately, her repeated references to having been invited by the shah "to advise his women," which she knew to be untrue, were strange and disappointing. I understood Betty's mixed feelings—the glamour and prestige that would come from a feminist having received an invitation from "the Shah of Iran," the powerful symbol of patriarchy. However, to translate this admiration for the shah's power into making us "his women"—as Germaine later did as well—handed over our initiative to him, totally ignoring the courage it required for us to provide her with a public forum to say whatever she pleased in Iran. Our courage had nothing to do with the shah or the government and everything to do with our conviction that our work was both important and necessary, however much it might be opposed by the clerics and fundamentalist conservatives. Even my passing up the occasion to accompany our guest to a meeting with the shah hadn't seemed to ring a bell of sisterly solidarity.

On the flight to Shiraz I sat with Helvi and we discussed possibilities for the upcoming UN First World Conference on Women, scheduled for June 1975 in Mexico City. I inquired about the possibility of setting up a new regional research and training center on women for Asia and the Pacific region, similar to those the United Nations had for Latin America and Africa, to be located in Tehran. We also talked about the possibility of setting up some sort of central institute that would be a clearinghouse for the global women's movements. This later became the International Research and Training Institute for the Advancement of Women (INSTRAW).[4] I thought I might be able to find ways to interest the Iranian government in supporting these initiatives. We brainstormed about holding a conference in the mid-1980s to follow up on the decisions made during the Mexico City conference. I mentioned that the Iranian government, sensitive as it was to international public opinion, would be responsive to the suggestions, declarations, and documents of the United Nations, so we thought we would use international pressure to support our national goals and plans. At the same time, Iran's position as a nation rich in human and natural resources and a government committed to modernization, with ties to East and West as well as the developing world, would help us negotiate our way successfully through the UN General Assembly and realize some of our ideas and projects. Helvi and I both took copious notes. There was no chance to speak with the others, so I missed some of the tension that was developing between Betty and Germaine.

In Shiraz, we organized a meeting for Germaine with women students at Pahlavi University. On a bright, beautiful day the young women sat in a circle on the grass and listened to Germaine's comments. The university was bilingual, so the students were well prepared to participate in a discussion in English. Germaine began in a relaxed tone, talking about women's problems and needs. I felt happy to sit near her in the circle of young women and thought to myself, "This is it. This makes the whole thing worthwhile." I knew the importance of the work we were planning with Helvi. But I loved the idea of the conversation taking place on a balmy day in this romantic city—the grass, the sunshine, the whole atmosphere of the conversation between the English teacher and author and the young Iranian students. Germaine seemed to think that the university students she was talking with were very much like the ones in her own classrooms. So I'm sure she thought that what works at home, saying something provocative that would ring true, something they could relate to, would reach and stir these young women as well.

But what worked at home did not go over well here. The girls began whispering to each other and shifting in their places. One girl said, "How can you presuppose what we want or need? Why are you preaching to us about our life choices?" Germaine was taken aback. It wasn't that she was saying something terribly radical. It was the impression the young women got that they were considered somehow in need of Western direction and guidance. It was unusual for the students to challenge a speaker, especially a guest from far away. Germaine tried to set things right by explaining that she had no such intention, and the young women relaxed and the conversation resumed.

Since that day I have seen this kind of thing many times. Even though the core issues that women face are similar, in cross-cultural dialogue *who* speaks is as important as the words spoken. Underlying the communication experience there has to be a deeply felt respect for the views and concerns and life choices of others. If that is felt, then one can fall upon the sameness of our experience as women and our shared oppression. I was sorry to see the young women's reaction to Germaine. Having been immersed in cultures of both the speaker and the audience, I knew how much they had in common. Yet none of that could be taken for granted. I am not sure what Germaine and her audience got from this conversation, but I personally learned a lot.

Later that evening we had invited the governor of Fars province, the mayor of Shiraz, and various other notables to join us. The guests were having drinks in the garden and socializing with Betty. Helvi was in her room, drafting a proposal to the United Nations on the basis of our conversation on the plane. My assistant pulled me aside and said, "Germaine is not coming out of her room and is saying she will not participate in tomorrow morning's panel." She added, "The word has gotten around about that, and the governor and the mayor were joking about the hair-pulling among the feminists."

I went to Germaine's room where she was lying in bed, and as I sat next to her, I asked how she was doing. She said she didn't want to talk on any panels anymore, that Betty was always drawing the crowds to herself and did not give her a chance to speak, and that she was tired of being in the background.

"Please, Germaine," I said. "We have talked about you three as being leaders of the feminist movement in the West. They are already talking about hair-pulling among the feminists. Think of what this means to us."

She pulled the covers up to her chin. "I'm not the leader of anything," she said. "I'm just a woman who wrote a book."

I realized she was right. Our supposition was *our* problem. "See how you feel in the morning," I said. "But do come outside. It's a beautiful evening. Let's have dinner." She agreed to join us, and the next morning she participated in the panel.

IN HER book *The Second Stage*, published in 1981, Betty talks about the need to create a women's movement that is inclusive of men and supportive of the family. She states that these are necessary steps to achieve equality. Once that happens, the issues of our bodies, sexual and reproductive rights, and other concerns, will be taken care of. One of her arguments is that full equality requires new structures for women's physical environment. At the WOI we had carried out research that resulted in the publication of *Urban Design and Women's Lives*, which considered what changes in city planning would support a family with two working parents. Betty seemed to refer back to our conversations in Iran when she suggested apartments with common spaces and functions such as communal eateries and childcare centers. Our idea at the WOI to have childcare on the premises of the workplace was a successful interim measure. Some four decades later, some level of communal planning with grocery stores stocking prepared foods, apartments with joint-usage exercise rooms, and other amenities have come about for many middle-class families.

The last paragraph in Betty's *Ladies' Home Journal* article I think best reflects our unity of purpose during her visit: "I looked at myself draped in the chador, in the Women's Center in Iran, and realized that that piece of cloth is easier to throw aside than those invisible veils trapping our spirits in the West. My sisters in Iran laughed at me in their chador and I realized how far we all have come out of our veil."

Later, I saw in her article Betty's wistful comparison of similarities between NOW and the WOI: "Having organized a national organization for women [NOW] with similar objectives myself, against obstacles, in a nation that considered itself much more advanced, and with no money at all, except from women's own pockets to this day, NOW's program, which is not too different from the Women's Organization of Iran, is considered too revolutionary in the USA to get foundation funds, much less government funds. I am bemused with envy and question marks."[5]

It's interesting to me that in the 1970s, Betty and I were talking and thinking about two national women's organizations in two completely different parts of the world. But as radical feminism marginalized the more moderate approaches, Betty's ideas and NOW's projects in support of working families lost much of their momentum, just as the combined efforts of the Radical Left and extremist religious forces in their reaction to the WOI destroyed Iranian women's achievements and soon spread to other countries of the region.

The visit of the Western feminists to Iran was very helpful for us at the WOI. We translated their presentations into Persian and published a booklet

that reached all our members and many others across the country. My conversations with Helvi gave us a concrete plan that helped us gain the support of
the government and led to Princess Ashraf's chairing the Consultative Committee for the First UN World Conference on Women in Mexico City in 1975.
The draft we submitted became the basis for the World Plan of Action for the
improvement of the status of women. This made us important players at the
UN Mexico City conference, where the two centers Helvi and I had discussed
were created. The first, the Regional Center for Training and Research on
Women and Development of the UN Economic and Social Commission for
Asia and the Pacific (ESCAP), was inaugurated in Tehran in February 1977.
But then came the Revolution, and so much was lost. The second center Helvi
and I envisioned, INSTRAW, could not be established in Iran after the Islamic
Revolution and was instead set up in the Dominican Republic. It still remains
an important part of the United Nations' work on women. Then, the 1980
World Conference on Women that had been scheduled to be held in Iran was
hurriedly transferred to Copenhagen, where the Islamic Republic fought every
progressive measure suggested to improve the status of women.

Looking back, I still wonder at "what could have been" and what our continued leadership on women's issues could have meant for Muslim women in
the region and the world.

Chapter 7

1975

INTERNATIONAL WOMEN'S YEAR

B Y 1975, THE UN-designated International Women's Year, the eight-story building on Tehran's Takht-e Jamshid Avenue that housed the WOI headquarters was, for those of us who worked there, the most exciting workplace in all of Iran. The building buzzed with activity, enthusiasm, and energy. The first floor held our childcare center, which provided an experimental model for other WOI centers across the country. Here children played with toys made of whatever was available in the household or in the natural setting in various parts of Iran. They experimented with making music using readily available objects. They role-played with costumes of various professions and jobs. I stopped by the center from time to time to watch them. One day I saw a three-year-old boy who was asked to try on a nurse's uniform refuse to do so, saying that nursing was "a girl's job." True to customary gender roles that he had already internalized, he asked for the policeman's uniform that a little girl was wearing. On the third floor, the young women who were liaisons with the WOI's 400 branches throughout Iran spoke on the phone with activists in various cities trying to obtain or provide information or make connections.

On the fourth floor, Ms. Yeganegi and her group were experimenting with various products and processes that were to be used to improve the quality of vocational training classes, provide markets for handicrafts, or help establish co-ops to eliminate the middleman between the women and their customers. The colorful cocoons that Ms. Yeganegi's silkworms produced were larger and better than the norm. In a corner someone was experimenting with a machine used in leather bookbinding classes.

On the next floor, Maryam Chamlou, our new women's studies instructor, was holding her consciousness-raising group, where the WOI finance officer and one of the cleaning women shared their experiences of divorce. In another room, the research group was discussing the feasibility of translating several Western feminist texts into Persian so they could be included as sources for discussion in the women's studies program organized by the WOI at the National University the following fall. In the International Relations Section, women were poring over the UN draft World Plan of Action. Each section of the WOI thought its work was the most important for improving the status of women. There were heated arguments, and occasionally even tears, but the essential spirit was one of cooperation, mutual respect, and general enthusiasm. People came to work early and seemed never to leave. They trained their families to respect their work and fall in with the accelerated rhythm of their lives.

Even more exciting than the WOI workspace was the measurable progress the WOI had made throughout the country. Our classes were building more marketable skills and women were earning more after graduating. The childcare centers were helping children learn healthy habits that were transferred home to siblings and parents. Simple habits such as frequent handwashing and brushing their teeth kept them in better health. Families came to accept the centers as safe and helpful places, and women came together before and after classes to participate in facilitated discussions about their lives and challenges.

Now we felt we needed a strong research base to make sense of what we were accomplishing and how we might do more. We had several academics on our board who offered help. Nikchehreh Mohseni at Tehran University undertook a project to study the impact of images of women presented in the media and in elementary school textbooks. Vida Behnam helped us connect with other faculty members at Tehran University who conducted several studies, among them a groundbreaking analysis of the impact of the penal code's Article 179, which granted near impunity to a man who murders his wife if she is found in an adulterous situation (a woman was considered the property of the male members of the family and adultery was considered a crime against the men). This was the first research on "honor killing" in the region. Honor crimes had increased as women began going to school, working, and generally having more of a life outside the home. Newspapers wrote about a brother or husband killing a woman who was seen in what appeared to be "the company of an unknown man." In one particularly outrageous case, a man murdered his sister because after she got out of a cab, a man got out. Cab drivers routinely picked up several passengers on their route, and this had been one such case. Other research topics included the status of women factory workers and the changing aspirations of tribal women.

Each month of the International Women's Year, the WOI branch in one of the twelve provincial capitals scheduled a seminar on a theme of its choice. Each seminar would agree on a resolution that would spell out their priorities for action. Each branch also commissioned papers on its area of interest and involved men and women, scholars, and activists. To ensure local government involvement at the highest level, we asked Princess Ashraf to open each seminar and the provincial governor to present a report on the "state of women in the province" during the first session. The governors all accepted, with the exception of Abdolazim Valian, governor of Khorasan province, whose capital city, Mashhad, housed the Shrine of Imam Reza, the most important holy site in Iran. In addition to the post of governor, Mr. Valian held the title of Nayib ul-Tawlieh, or "Guardian of the Shrine," and he therefore expected special consideration. Giving a presentation on the "state of women in the province" was not to his liking, politically or otherwise.

When I called him, he stated flatly, "Women are not my business."

I said, "Governor, women are half of the population of your state. This is the International Women's Year. How can they not be part of your business? Every other governor is doing this."

"My situation is not like every other governor," he said. "I am Nayib ul-Tawlieh."

I didn't know what to say to him. I called and explained the situation to Princess Ashraf. She said, "Tell him from me that I understand. He needn't take the time out of his busy schedule to attend the seminar."

When I called and delivered the message to Mr. Valian, he paused for a minute and then said, "Mrs. Afkhami, what disservice have I ever done to you to deserve this?" I could feel the self-mocking smile on his face from the tone of his voice as he continued: "Of course I will be there and will deliver 'the state of the women of Khorasan,' which, by the way, is unmatched in any other province."

The seminars generated a sense of excitement around the country and gave us and our issues more visibility, but our greatest success was the passage of the 1975 Family Protection Law, which significantly increased and safeguard-ed women's rights. After the law's passage, the minimum age of marriage for women increased from fifteen to eighteen. After a father's death, the guardian-ship of children would be assigned to the mother instead of a male member of the father's family. The right of divorce, which had previously belonged solely to the husband, was made accessible to both men and women through the family courts. While earlier, a man could marry four wives and have many temporary marriages, after the law's passage, a man could marry a second wife with the expressed consent of his first wife, who could then obtain an uncon-tested divorce if she wished. With the exception of Tunisia, it was the most far-reaching family legislation in the Middle East / North Africa (MENA) region at that time.

When Congresswoman Mehrangiz Dowlatshahi called from the Majlis to tell me the bill had passed, I was speechless with laughter and tears. I looked around my office, wishing to honor the moment. I knelt down and kissed the ground. It didn't seem an adequate response. I called a woman friend who had complained she had no control over her child's life after the death of her husband. "Afsaneh jan, I have news for you . . ." It was her turn to be speechless with tears and laughter.

Even more than four decades later, the 1975 Family Protection Law remains one of the most progressive in the MENA region. Its annulment was Ayatollah Khomeini's first decree after his return to Iran. To women activists, the fact that at that point there was not yet a government or constitution demonstrated the centrality of the status of women to the fundamentalists' fury and how it was a major factor in the fundamentalists' opposition to the government.

WHILE MANY WOI programs focused on women's social and economic empowerment, I was always looking for ways to bring literature and the arts into our work. While I was in New York in 1974, before the three Western feminists visited Iran, Betty Friedan took me to a conference on women in the cinema. She introduced me to Molly Haskell, the feminist film critic who had written a groundbreaking critique of the image of women in film, *From Reverence to Rape*, and to Eleanor Perry, whose screenplay for *Diary of a Mad Housewife* further explored the themes of *The Feminine Mystique*. There was enormous energy and excitement in the room. Young women—speakers and audience alike—were flexing their intellectual muscles and finding inspiration in their own rhetoric of discovery. As I listened to the speakers at the conference, I thought about how welcome such a project would be in Iran, where film was a much-loved form of both art and entertainment.

When I returned to Iran, I asked Hajir Dariush, the founder and organizer of the Tehran Film Festival, for his guidance. His advice was basically that without a big budget and a savvy staff of film aficionados it would be impossible to organize any kind of a film festival. Perhaps that was why there had been no such festival in the Middle East. My colleagues at the WOI, however, were intrigued by the idea. So I decided it would be worth a try. We wrote to several women filmmakers and festival organizers in other parts of the world and received several swift, positive, and encouraging responses. Soon we had commitments from filmmakers from eighteen countries (including Belgium, Canada, China, Egypt, England, Finland, Ghana, Hungary, Iran, Italy, Japan, the Soviet Union, and the United States) and the United Nations. By the time the festival opened some months later, we were able to screen fifty-two works, some of them award-winning films and documentaries. Molly Haskell, Eleanor Perry, Joan Shigekawa (producer of WNET's *Woman Alive!*), Amalie Rothschild (independent filmmaker and producer, director, and writer of *Nana, Mom and Me*), and Joan Hotchkis (a popular actress and playwright) all accepted our invitation to participate as panelists and judges.

The festival was one of the most successful events we organized in 1975. Volunteers and colleagues helped us in various ways, including my friend Guity, who spoke several languages in her deep, resonant voice. She agreed to tape the conference announcements in English, French, and Persian. The huge cinema that hosted the festival and screened the films was a regal space, with red velvet chairs and a spacious balcony where the princess and invited guests, among them ambassadors and cabinet members, sat on the opening night. Every night the place was full, with an audience of several hundred jubilant, mostly younger, women and men. The Italian director Lina Wertmüller's film *Seven Beauties* was honored as the best film. Even though we had improvised our way through the process, learning as we went along, we encountered few problems.

Our Western guests were wonderful, talented, kind women. They toured several cities and visited our WOI centers and engaged with our members. I couldn't spend as much time with them as I wished, but I thoroughly enjoyed the time I did have with them. When they returned to Tehran, I decided to have an informal, relaxed gathering for them in Guity's beautiful garden, with its ancient oak trees and gurgling stream. I thought they would enjoy sharing the private side of our Iranian social life. We invited Dariush Mehrjui, one of our respected film directors, our close friend Dariush Shayegan, one of Iran's best-known intellectuals, and a handful of others. Years later this same garden would be the safe house for my sister, Farah, when she was in hiding from the Islamic Republic.

It was a mild afternoon of conversation. I mentioned that the Chinese we had recently visited didn't seem to have a sense of humor about their leaders, and I added, on reflection, "Not that we have much humor when we speak about the shah."

I found the article Molly wrote in the *Village Voice* on her return interesting but disappointing; sadly, some inaccuracies reminded me of those Betty Friedan had written about her visit to Iran. Molly later wrote me a sort of apology saying that she had written what the *Voice* expected. She was clearly impressed with our colleagues and wrote perhaps the most complimentary paragraph that I have ever read about myself, but almost a quarter of her article was devoted to justifying her going to Iran: "To accept the invitation is to be pummeled with charges of collaboration by the knee-jerk Left," she wrote. After she had visited women's welfare centers and birth-control clinics in Shiraz, Isfahan, and Yazd, socialized with dignitaries, and mingled with intellectuals and activists, she said she began to wonder, "Why am I here? Am I here as a feminist bringing the message to the benighted, as one brings Christianity to the cannibals? Or am I here to receive the light and pass it on to my readers back home who have been getting a definitely poor impression of civil liberties in Iran?" One wonders how she would have taken such a statement had the shoe been on the other foot—if an Iranian woman had referred to Western women activists as cannibals. But she said she was also "bowled over by the women we have met—perhaps because we are surrounded by superwomen—smart, capable, funny, well-educated, womanly and yet ambitious women who read *Ms.* and Sylvia Plath AND who know where the strings are pulled."[1]

She went on to reveal that things had quickly deteriorated among the leading women critics and directors who constituted the panel of judges. Differing interpretations of feminism, compounded by personality clashes, were at work. But it could not have been just that, she surmised: "It is possible that such frictions would have developed under any circumstances, but surrounding each of us and preventing their release was a wall of silence, the wall imposed by Iran. The fact that there were certain subjects they couldn't talk about (and therefore withheld), and that we couldn't ask them about (without being considered insensitive) created an automatic barrier between us. There were things we might not have talked about anyway, but the fact that we couldn't, that there were locked closets in our relationship before it even began, made trust impossible."[2]

The wall of silence was entirely of her own creation, but the most telling piece of Molly's article related to our outing at Guity's garden. Molly wrote about the afternoon, quoting Dariush Mehrjui, who had said matter-of-factly that the Iranian public did not care much for good films and that "censure hampered the work of the artist." In the meantime, Eleanor Perry and Joan Hotchkis chatted with Dariush Shayegan, whose conversation Molly overheard: "But lo and behold, this bearded intellectual is baring his soul to Eleanor and Joan Hotchkis. Well, perhaps he can't keep it pent up any longer. He's just been in America, he tells them, where he had long talks with Gore Vidal. 'But here,' he said making a terrible face, 'they're bleeding us intellectuals to death.'"[3]

Eleanor Perry was impressed. She even suggested that this might be evidence that the Iranians they met with were free. "Look at the way he spoke out," she later told Iran expert Marvin Zonis.

"But don't you see?" Zonis corrected her. "That's exactly what they want you to think. What do you think he was doing there?"

I didn't know Marvin then. This was before he wrote *Majestic Failure*, his psychoanalytic profile of the shah, and long before he spoke to me at length about how the Iranian Revolution was by no means inevitable but could only be explained through the psychological traits in the shah's personality. We have all learned so much since then about other societies—some considerably more advanced and sophisticated than Iran in the 1970s—where lies become fact simply because they are repeated often, statistics become suspect because someone says otherwise, and scientific facts become invalid simply because a small group of people decide they don't exist. Had we known about "fake news" and the art of political sabotage, we would have taken more seriously the effect of propaganda orchestrated by trained opposition groups from the far right and far left on the West's perception of the Iranian system. I would have loved to have laughed with Marvin at the idea that I had planted Dariush Shayegan at Guity's garden party in order to brainwash the visitors.

Later I had a letter from Eleanor expressing her regret about the reaction of some of the group. I wrote back and expressed a hope for better days of East/West dialogue, a wish that is perhaps even more difficult to achieve now.

To know these women was an exhilarating but also eye-opening experience for me. There were obviously great differences between New York and Tehran. There were also major differences between our approaches to the unequal status of women and our strategies for change. In Iran, we didn't start from theory. Our only presupposition was that the status of women in our country was unequal and that the condition of women, especially poor women, was brutal. We had sat with groups of women around the country, listened to their stories, and asked them about their hopes for their daughters, about what frustrated and saddened them, and about what would change their lives for the better. Our programs grew from the ground up and were adapted and altered depending on the neighborhood, the city, and the focus of the activists in a given locality. Our programs all had one thing in common—our determination to encourage and enable women to develop their capabilities.

But the WOI's international activities would not have the impact they had, nor would they have brought us the stellar results that we achieved, were it not for the multifaceted, diverse, yet focused local efforts that provided learning and sharing experiences at the global level.

BETWEEN 1975 and 1995, for the first time in its history, the United Nations held four conferences specifically focused on women: Mexico City (1975), Copenhagen (1980), Nairobi (1985), and Beijing (1995). Two other closely related conferences were also held during this period—the Conference on Environment and Development in Rio de Janeiro (1992) and the International Conference on Population and Development in Cairo (1994). Each of these brought together delegates from governments around the world to discuss the status of women and to agree on strategies to involve them in developing their societies.

At each of these conferences, parallel to the government meetings, tens of thousands of women activists gathered to identify their own priorities and strategies. The conferences were the defining events in educating government officials on the significance of women's involvement in every matter they dealt with in their jobs—from agriculture, to education, from trade to labor, from environment to city planning.

In the world before today's instant communications technologies, these conferences offered invaluable opportunities for women from all backgrounds and every region of the world to witness the full splendor and color of their physical and cultural similarities and differences. East and West, North and South discovered each other and began to recognize the possibilities for global action. An important outcome of the conferences was to raise consciousness about not only the oppression of women but also the impact of that oppression on every other aspect of development.

The process also made visible the varying priorities of different groups and societies. The colonial experience was reflected in the relations between the developed and the developing worlds. Those who had begun by wishing to liberate the less developed societies from "the shackles of their suffocating traditions" felt resistance in the newly independent women who were experimenting with just what it was they wanted to change without disrupting their families and losing some aspects that they cherished in their way of life.

As the universality of rights and the superiority of democratic political systems became widely accepted, resistance grew among those in the developing world who felt they were being pressured to replicate ways of living that might not suit them. They stressed economic, social, and cultural rights over the political rights prioritized by the developed countries. This began to reflect itself in the work of some academics and was vigorously supported by conservative governments and religious figures who defended the traditional role of women and praised the idea of "cultural relativism."

Identity politics brought passion and commitment but also splintered our energies, experiences, and resources into small segments. What's worse, it numbed our sense of outrage about cultural and traditional practices that bring pain and lifelong damage to women because they relate to the suffering of a specific group to which we do not belong or because we feel we must respect what sometimes seem like other people's choices and lifestyles. "Culture" became a protective shield for those who perpetrated practices such as female genital mutilation, polygamy, bride burning, forced veiling, child marriage, and the like.

Feeling that criticism of certain traditional practices was an attack on their dignity, some activists from the Global South fought back and shunned support from Western human rights advocates on the grounds that the Westerners did not understand the nature of their problems. In a human rights meeting I was shocked to hear criticism of writer Alice Walker's efforts to mobilize public awareness against female genital mutilation. It seemed that people were dividing atrocities into "ours" and "theirs," as if these were natural resources. Some human rights activists introduced the concept of intersectionality to find a way of showing recognition and respect for activism based on identity and at the same time encouraged working together across identity issues and differences.

Other scholars from the Global South, especially from Muslim-majority societies, sensed a neocolonialist attitude in their Western counterparts. The large international gatherings of women included very few women from the MENA region. Even women from these areas with proven scholarship and high academic credentials or activist experience in the West were seldom asked to discuss their ideas and observations about the status of women anywhere but in their own society or region. But any smart and articulate Western journalist or academic who traveled to a country in the Global South, often without the benefit of familiarity with the country's culture, history, or language, felt empowered to write and publish books on the status, needs, and work of women in the developing world. There was a joke among our Middle

Eastern colleagues, who referred to these writers as "If it's Tuesday, this must be Tunisia" researchers.

After the Revolution, when I facilitated meetings between women activists in Iran with whom I had kept in touch and American journalist friends who wished to interview knowledgeable people in the country, the Iranians often complained about the way they were treated by the Westerners. As one of my friends explained to me on the phone, "They come, they talk to us, we entertain them, share our knowledge, before we know it they are gone and we never hear from them again—they don't even send a copy of the work they publish. We feel 'seduced and abandoned!'"

The incomplete connection and interaction between the developed and the developing world and Western interest in addressing atrocities against women in some developing countries brought an avalanche of images of violence and abuse that portrayed the women of those countries as helpless and without agency. A comment to me from Alicia Partnoy of Argentina, who was imprisoned during the dictatorship in her country, comes to mind: "When I arrived in America, journalists asked me if I had been raped and were almost disappointed that I hadn't been. I felt a tinge of regret that I wasn't raped. It seemed as if a human sacrifice was necessary to gain the concentration of the media." This attitude is exacerbated by a culture of "misery fundraising," where people are encouraged to "Save a slave for ten dollars a month," and trafficking campaigns that feature a small, big-eyed little girl with a tear rolling down her face as incentive. The leader of one international NGO said, "Our work is turning into constantly carrying a tin cup and settling petty disputes." In short, there was and is considerable confusion in the activist community.

The disillusion with governments in the Global South and the dynamism in the women's activist community on the other led to a major change. Funders began to shift substantial funding to NGOs. The largely volunteer organizations that had attended the NGO forums during the UN conferences of the last quarter of the twentieth century were provided with resources for work that they, by their volunteer nature, were not prepared to undertake. As a result, substantial professional organizations and networks, largely in the West but focused on the developing world, came into being. Unlike the small, thematic volunteer entities focused on advocacy and movement building, these new NGOs focused on services such as health, welfare, and education. The new culture began to spread in the small organizations in the Global South countries, and a lot of good work was done. But often the indigenous passion, knowledge, and vision were no longer there.

Sustainable change comes from people themselves. They cannot be empowered when the image they see of themselves is one of helplessness. In the end, without their leadership and involvement there is little chance to change a situation permanently. Even well-educated, skilled women in the United States—a 200-year-old democracy with plenty of resources—fail to exert their will and demand their most elementary rights, such as paid maternity leave and decent, affordable childcare, unless they get involved in organizing themselves and demanding their rights.[4]

THROUGHOUT THE process leading to and following the 1975 UN Conference on Women, the Iranian delegation was arguably the most effective. It developed and followed up on the conference's three major objectives in relation to equality, peace, and development for the decade: (1) full gender equality and the elimination of gender discrimination; (2) the integration and full participation of women in development; and (3) an increased contribution by women toward strengthening world peace. The most important of the conference outcomes was the draft for the World Plan of Action, which was presented and approved in March 1975 at the conference's Consultative Committee in New York headed by Princess Ashraf.

The Consultative Committee meeting held at UN headquarters in New York on March 3–14, 1975, as a preparatory meeting for the first World Conference on Women, in which I represented Iran, included delegates from twenty-three countries from diverse geographic, cultural, and political blocs among the UN member states. We argued not only about what to do but also about what to say. For example, every time that a statement referred to the "unequal status of women around the world," the Soviet bloc insisted that there should be an exception or qualification for socialist countries. The fact was that the situation of women in the Soviet Republics was in some respects worse than in many European countries. And there were often arguments about the particular preferences of certain blocs. The developing world resented the prominence of "political rights" at the expense of economic, social, and cultural rights, which had equal or greater urgency for them.

As the representative of Iran, I proposed creating the ESCAP Regional Center for Training and Research on Women and Development, to provide authenticated research on the existing conditions in the region. The center would initially collect and disseminate data and information on existing programs and policies relating to women in UN member countries in order to advance action-oriented research and new strategies to enable women to play a more active role in development. This proposal received the committee's enthusiastic support.

Princess Ashraf, who was elected chair on the first day, had a challenging but important role in moderating the discussion. This sometimes made life difficult for me. If she decided that some point had to be made in response to a delegate's statement but that she as the chair could not be the one to make it, she would call on "the distinguished delegate of Iran," even if I had not raised my hand. I thus had to be on guard, since at any moment the chair might respond positively to my undeclared request to comment. Elizabeth Reid, advisor on women's issues to the prime minister of Australia and an articulate and highly intelligent feminist, was vice chair of the committee and a strong ally during this time. Her role in her own country demonstrated the importance of having a presence in government of a capable woman to represent the cause. In 1977, when the UN ESCAP Regional Center for Training and Research on Women and Development was established in Tehran, I suggested that Elizabeth be its first director.

The conference designated the period 1975 to 1985 as the Decade for Women, during which the national plans of action were to be approved, setting targets to achieve for women's full participation in development. Iran's delegation successfully lobbied for a middecade conference in 1980 to review progress and offered to host the conference in Tehran.

A decision was also made to establish INSTRAW in Tehran. Iran offered $2 million as well as in-kind support for INSTRAW's local facilities, support services, and staff. For us at the WOI, these developments were the realization of a dream. Early on, we had learned that developing connections with other countries and the United Nations creates an incredible energy and dynamism that works in a circular fashion. We gathered information and conducted research at the local level and shared it with our foreign ministry. Lobbying our own foreign ministry involved it in the issues and led ministry officials to reflect on their position at the international level. Once the United Nations approved an initiative or passed a resolution and announced it internationally, we would then lobby our own government, citing the international document. It was a circular movement, each stage of which led to another stage, leading to yet another, and back to the beginning; the whole helped us learn more about the way global decision-making worked and how our goals could be furthered by involvement with international organizations.

In 1975 there were very few NGOs that had consultative status with the United Nations. The Mexico City Conference was a conference of UN member-state governments, but it also provided space for NGOs to take part in parallel meetings. The philanthropic institutions and donors realized the significance of this participation, especially of the national and regional gatherings in preparation for the conference. The process became a learning opportunity for all and ended up strengthening civic organizations and increasing support for their activities. The growth in the number of NGOs brought media attention, giving voice to the activists. By the Fourth UN Conference in Beijing in 1995, the number of representatives of NGOs reached 35,000.

Iran's delegation to the UN General Assembly, chaired for ten years by Princess Ashraf, had an unusually strong interest in women's issues. Helvi Sipilä's relationship with me and the princess and her appreciation of the WOI was also helpful. Most important, Iran enjoyed a friendly relationship with the United States and a reasonably amicable relationship with the Soviet Union, as well as a leading role among the Group of Seventy-Seven,[5] an informal union of developing countries that had shared experiences with some form of colonialism as well as the power play of the two major blocks led by Marxist and capitalist world leaders. Iran was also a prosperous nation, able to make the initial contribution to the various projects it supported. The combination of the WOI's work at the local level, which was translated into research and planning that was shared with the international community through Iran's delegation at the United Nations and thus impacted decisions on the global level, and its policy of reversing the process back from global to local empowered the national organization and its grassroots constituency. By the end of the International Women's Year, Iran was in a unique position in the international women's movement—it was a true global leader in women's rights. As an active participant in this process, I was grieved when the backlash came and a series of events, small and large, converged to create a perfect storm that destroyed all we had worked so hard to achieve.

Chapter 8

Appointment to
Iran's Cabinet

WHEN I WOKE UP on December 30, 1975, I knew the day would be important, but I had no idea that my life was about to change. My initial excitement was for the WOI national meeting to be held that day: hundreds of delegates elected by members of 400 WOI branches in cities and towns across Iran, as well as representatives of the fifty-five professional and special interest women's associations affiliated with the WOI, were in Tehran to take part in heated debates about the WOI's platform for the coming year.

By the afternoon session, members of the board had been elected with much anticipation and uncertainty, and now the board and several key delegates had walked back from the meeting hall across the street to the WOI headquarters. We sat in my office going over the events and engaging in a lot of cheerful banter. Fakhri Amin, Iran's deputy minister of education and a member of the WOI board, recalled that every time she looked, Princess Ashraf had her hand up in the air, voting for someone or something. "Does her vote count?" she asked. Everyone laughed. "Seriously, is she a member?"

Homa Afzal, our lawyer, said, "The royal family cannot run for office or cast a vote for municipal or parliamentary elections," but the group had lost interest and moved on to outbursts by the president of the Nurses' Association, one of the autonomous organizations affiliated with the WOI. Atefeh Bijan was a pioneer in the field, so I had encouraged her to stand for election to the WOI board. She had lost and was not happy with me.

In the midst of the conversation, Mrs. Kamrani walked in to say that the prime minister was on the phone. I took the call in her room. Mr. Hoveyda was less exuberant and upbeat than was his custom. "This past year has shown us the importance of the campaign to bring women into the process of development," he said flatly. "I feel we need to do a lot more in this area. I would like to ask you to join the cabinet and hold the post of minister of state for women's affairs."

He went on for several minutes while I tried to take in the full meaning of his words. "This is what we have been talking about," I thought to myself. "It's real—not one of many options—no longer an abstract concept. It's about my life." Then I noticed the silence on the line. The pause may have gone on longer than he expected.

"I would be honored," I answered, trying to sound cheerful.

"Excellent," he said. "Think about an appropriate English translation of the title."

For a moment all of this seemed surreal. When I was first offered the post of secretary general of the WOI some five years earlier, it took me over a year of thinking and consultation to make up my mind. Many of my intellectual left-leaning friends complained ceaselessly but vaguely about the conditions in the country and especially its closed political space. None of them wanted to change things drastically, but it was the norm to look at the politics of the country with disdain. I shared their mildly negative view of the system, but I had never been an ideologue. Generally, I leaned toward the pragmatic. It seemed to me that the shah's statements and the government's position favored modernity and economic development and, despite the shortcomings in the workings of the government, the system seemed to be moving ahead. There were jobs for those who wanted them and opportunities for innovation for those who wished to set up a business or start an initiative. Political repression was talked about openly in spite of the millions of agents attributed to SAVAK, and freedom of religion and lifestyle rivaled any country in the region. Moreover, thousands of students who were studying abroad with government support were coming back in droves to take up the tasks of developing the country. It seemed to me that the current regime was by far preferable to any that had the remotest possibility of replacing it.

But five years earlier I had been invited to join a nongovernmental organization. The Women's Organization of Iran may have had Princess Ashraf as an honorary chair, but it was an independent organization that was free to set its own course and make its own decisions. This time, however, I would be joining the government, and joining any government was anathema to most feminists at the time. That said, my colleagues and I had often discussed various mechanisms through which women could impact the government on issues of priority to them. When Françoise Giroud, the prominent leftist French writer, founder of *L'Express*, and first woman in the world to hold a cabinet-level position for women's affairs, had visited Iran, we had discussed the pros and cons of her position. Elizabeth Reid and I had discussed her previous position in Australia and the possible impact of that type of government post. A thoughtful, well-informed woman, Elizabeth had suffered in her lonely position within the government, especially since at the time there was little support and no guidance from our feminist colleagues. She cautioned me and said that the best way for women to improve their status was to stay outside the apparatus of government.[1]

My colleagues in Iran focused on the degree of access to information and high-level policy making that various positions might offer. There was talk that we should lobby instead for a post of deputy prime minister or a high-level position at the Plan and Budget Organization. Throughout our discussions, some continued to favor distancing ourselves from the government. But the WOI's High Council for Cooperation,[2] in which several cabinet ministers participated, had helped us realize the importance of access to information and interaction with decision-makers—not acting merely as outside pressure groups, but from within. The prime minister's phone call nevertheless came as a surprise. Mr. Hoveyda assumed that I would take the post, and I surprised myself by accepting without hesitation.

I put the receiver down and sat for a minute thinking about the implications of my own unequivocal response. Until now, the issue had been abstract. I had spent no time thinking about the possibility of this event in relation to myself and how it would affect my life personally. But this was not the time to think about that. My colleagues were waiting in the next room. Just as I was about to leave, the phone rang and it was again the prime minister, who this time asked me to meet him in his office in the morning so that we could travel together to the airport where he would present me to the shah after the departure ceremonies for the president of Syria. He then urged me to keep the appointment a secret from everyone.

When I reentered my office, the WOI board members' smiling faces turned to me expectantly. Everyone wanted to know what the prime minister wanted.

I said, "He was asking about the result of the elections of the WOI board." I thought they would surely not accept this and press me for the real cause, and I would have to make light of the call and kid around with them. But strangely enough they seemed to think the WOI election a very natural concern of the prime minister. I didn't understand the urgency and secrecy around the appointment and felt uncomfortable withholding information from my colleagues on a topic of such importance to them all. Am I already distancing myself from my allies? I wondered. Have I already become "one of the boys" and started playing by their rules?

At home I gave my husband the news. He was not surprised; rather, he seemed thoughtful and quiet. He had probably considered the possibility more seriously than I had. I wondered that we had not discussed it at all. I knew he did not like the idea: his concern was for me since he, more than anyone, knew how temperamentally ill-equipped I was for public life. He was perhaps one of the few men in Iran at that time who could tolerate his wife's being in such a high-profile public position. He was also perhaps unique in not resenting my making the decision without consulting him. He understood that this appointment was the logical conclusion of all the breakneck local and national activity and a whole year of highly visible national and international events related to the first UN World Conference on Women. For Babak, who was eleven, there would be little difference between my being secretary general of the WOI or a member of cabinet. I was already overworked and had a lot of public visibility. But the struggle to carve out enough time to be with him was excruciating. I was lucky that my husband's work did not require much time away from home.

The next morning I said nothing to my driver, Zamani, except to ask him to take me to the prime minister's office. He began complaining, as was his custom on our morning drives. This time he lamented the price of bananas: "My kids each eat a banana a day, one toman each; it costs me five tomans a day. That's 150 tomans a month, for bananas! That's a big chunk of my salary. Life is not so easy, ma'am." I sympathized with him: he had five children and his salary was barely adequate for such a large family. But his family planning and budgeting could easily be improved. Why have a sixth child on the way and why insist on feeding each one a banana every day? Why not give them the wonderful melons from Mashhad instead of imported bananas? But I was immediately ashamed for my quick judging of Zamani's budgeting and family-planning skills and decided not to meddle with the system that he and I had devised after much trial and error. He tolerated my reading of the morning papers in the back seat and did not expect me to make serious or lengthy reactions to his comments. But he reserved the right to make those comments as he pleased, almost without interruption.

There was a bit of theatricality in choosing to announce the new position of minister of state for women's affairs on December 31, 1975—the last day of the International Women's Year—but Prime Minister Hoveyda relished ceremony and was drawn to playing for effect. He reflected this in his own appearance: he was always impeccably dressed with his paisley-printed ties, shirts that picked up the predominant color of his tie, and a matching pocket handkerchief. The color scheme was highlighted by the miniature orchid from his wife's farm that always graced his buttonhole.

The prime minister's office was located in the building where the cabinet met and where the ministers without portfolio and their assistants were located. As I walked to Hoveyda's office, I was pleasantly surprised by the simple elegance of the surroundings. The guards and waiters walked quietly and spoke in subdued tones. Doors were opened as if automatically by dark-suited, white-gloved young men. The office was furnished with off-white, clean-cut, simple furniture that had a European air. The understated simplicity of the décor was accentuated by large, abstract oil paintings by Iran's esteemed poet and painter Sohrab Sepehri. Hoveyda's secretary, Afsaneh, an urbane young woman who resembled a Modigliani model with her long neck, narrow face, large dark eyes, and alabaster skin, was in perfect harmony with the décor.

Hoveyda walked up to me, kissed me on both cheeks, and asked me to sit down and have a cup of coffee before leaving for the airport. I would be presented to the shah just after the departure ceremonies of Syria's president at 10:30. He leaned back in his chair and waited until the attendant who had brought the coffee left, closing the door behind him. He told me then how much he admired my work. The growth of the WOI had been exceptional, and our work was most important to the future of the country. He asked again how we should word my title, worrying over the French and English translations. Then he said in his offhand way, "You will not be communicating with Princess Ashraf in this aspect of your work. Government concerns are government concerns. I hope this will not be awkward; I know you will be able to manage it. I also know that you will manage to balance your contact with the queen. She should be briefed periodically on women's issues. These issues are of great interest to her. In fact, it would be good to pay a courtesy call on the queen as soon as possible."

I sensed he was worried about Princess Ashraf's reputed rivalry with the queen. I could not fathom his fear that the princess might seek to interfere in government affairs through me. He attended the princess's twice-weekly dinners for her brother, the shah, where her close circle of friends and a few political leaders were a fixture. I was not part of this entourage. In fact, with the exception of accompanying her on travels inside and outside the country for meetings related to women's issues, I only saw the princess two or three times a year for a brief hour-long courtesy call and an occasional lunch. On these occasions I would give her a report on the goings-on in the WOI and the international women's movement. She seemed interested but never too curious. Often our talk drifted to my family or recent travels.

Hoveyda's view of Iranian politics, I came to learn, was based firmly on personal power alliances. He was careful to make it worth people's while to be a friend and unprofitable to be an enemy. As we came to be friends over the next two years, he counseled me to help as many people as I could with their plans and projects. "Don't keep track of what they have done to or for you and whether they have been friend or enemy. Treat everyone as a real or potential friend, except in the very rare case when someone's enmity begins to interfere with your goals."

That morning, as we walked out of the building, I closed my eyes for a second to adjust to the bright sunlight and the icy air. Hoveyda's small Iran-assembled Peykan was parked at the foot of the steps to the main entrance of the prime ministry. I sat next to him in front, holding his walking stick. He drove, talking of generalities, while his guard's radio droned on endlessly in the background. Other husky guards followed in a Mercedes-Benz that was theoretically the prime minister's vehicle. We drove to the army post a few blocks away. As we passed the guards at attention at the gate, Hoveyda waved casually, and we stopped next to the helicopter. The pilot saluted; Hoveyda shook his hand and asked how his wife was recovering from her operation.

As we flew over Tehran, Hoveyda pointed out the beauty of the cityscape—the touches of bronze and turquoise in the tiles that graced the buildings here and there. A few moments later he pointed to a number of huge ditches where squatters had constructed clusters of shacks with piles of bricks, pieces of wood, large sheets of plastic, and flattened cans. Above the roar of the helicopter he shouted, "Remind me to tell you about this later." This was the first reference to the additional post he would offer me as his deputy for the South Tehran Urban Development Project.

When we landed at the airport, a man who was waiting with a briefcase handed him a folder and walked with him, whispering. I slowed my pace to allow them privacy, and in a moment the man left. The prime minister waited for me to catch up and as he looked at the chief of the queen's bureau, the court protocol officer, and others standing just inside the glass doors of the royal pavilion, he said, "If anyone asks what you are doing here, just say you are presenting a report to His Majesty." And with that he rushed to meet the shah's helicopter, which was landing a few hundred meters away. I looked at the waiting plane, the honor guard, and the queen's slender form as she descended the helicopter steps in the distance.

I was not particularly excited or nervous. Instead, it felt as if I was on the sidewalk watching a parade. The strains of the national anthem were coming to the final phrase when I suddenly realized that in the excitement and urgency of the Syrian president's departure, the protocol officers had neglected to brief me about what I was supposed to do. I looked around and was relieved to see the smiling face of my husband's young cousin, Mehdi Zolfaghari, the newest addition to the court's Department of Protocol. I hastily kissed his cheek and asked him what to do. "It's my first assignment, too," he said, and grinned. "We will muddle through together."

By now Hafez al-Assad had boarded his plane, and the shah and the queen were walking back to their helicopter. Was I to walk up to them, or was I to wait while they walked over to me? Court protocol was made for days before helicopters and airport ceremonies, I thought. I began walking toward them, but thought immediately that this seemed too casual—as if we were running into each other accidentally. I looked over at Mehdi and saw he was simply following me—no help to be expected from him. So I stood while the royal couple, accompanied by Hoveyda, walked up to me. A lone photographer who lagged behind as the rest of the press corps were leaving the airfield sensed that something was going on and took a picture that appeared on the front page of the afternoon paper, much to the prime minister's chagrin. By arranging that particular time and place for the presentation and by not issuing a press release, he had made every attempt to downplay the importance of the appointment. At the time I had no idea of any of this, but I soon learned that he was concerned that there would be a backlash to all of this attention on women and the unique visibility of the newly created cabinet position.

"Your Majesty," Hoveyda said, "May I present Mahnaz Afkhami, the new minister for women's affairs?" The shah said something about the importance of women's contribution to the development of the country, then he asked where my office would be. Hoveyda said something to the effect that I could keep my office at the WOI. The shah said, "She is not going to be a minister of women only but a member of the Iranian cabinet. It seems appropriate for her to be with the other ministers without portfolio at the prime ministry."

Here again I was a bit puzzled. I wondered why the shah and the prime minister were concerned about the location of my office. But obviously there was a lot of symbolic significance to where the Ministry for Women's Affairs would be housed, as well as an indication of whether it would be ghettoized from the outset. The shah may have been thinking of the joint responsibility of the cabinet. The prime minister, though in principle supportive of women's participation, was worried about the historical and repeated clashes between the religious forces and those who struggled for women's rights. The most important of these was the first Khomeini uprising in 1963 when the shah announced the White Revolution. Hoveyda would have liked a gradual process, keeping the position as low-key and out of the loop as possible, but the shah thought of it differently. The queen smiled pleasantly but said nothing. When they turned to leave, she said, "Good luck."

After the royal pair's departure, Hoveyda noticed my driver, Zamani, who had come to pick me up, and asked me to send my car away and return with him in his helicopter. When we got to his office, he placed his unlit pipe in his mouth, stretched his legs and propped them up on his desk, and told me once again that I should inform the queen periodically about my work. He also asked why I hadn't curtsied. I told him I didn't know how, so I had bowed briefly to both. "Symbolism means a lot at court," he said.

"I will make a note of that," I said and smiled.

In the past, on the few occasions when I had talked to him, he had adopted a light, bantering tone, but this time he was almost solemn. I tried to compose an expression of high seriousness. Then he told me that I must never "confer with the shah alone." That comment ruined my new, somber expression. The idea of going to the shah had never entered my mind. "Conferring with the shah alone" conjured up an unlikely scene—the shah and I in close consultation over a cup of tea—that I found quite funny. I smiled once again, and once again I was surprised by his solemnity. He didn't seem to think this a farfetched or comical possibility.

The prime minister called in Mr. Hadi Hedayati, minister without portfolio for administrative affairs (one of several cabinet ministers who had a previous history of membership in the Soviet-backed Tudeh Party), introduced me, and asked him to show me the cabinet room and offices. The cabinet room was an impressive place, with a long table and some twenty armchairs upholstered in soft, green leather, a small microphone in front of each. On one wall was a huge, detailed map of Iran. On another, framed pictures of all previous prime ministers hung in chronological order.

I looked for and immediately found the portrait of my husband's grand-father, the first prime minister of Iran after the Constitutional Revolution of 1907. Gholam Reza's nanny never tired of telling us that Vazir Afkham was the "minister of all ministers." I found out from my mother-in-law that as important as his post was, he held it only for a few weeks. But here on the wall there was no indication of the length of his tenure. I pointed him out to Hedayati with considerable pride. I was reaching out to my patriarchal roots for validation of my present place in the hierarchy.

THAT SAME day, in the afternoon, we had scheduled the WOI's final seminar of the International Women's Year, to be opened by the prime minister. I was still shaken by the fast-moving events and anxious about the Tehran seminar. Although the newspapers hadn't yet covered the story, my colleagues had somehow heard about the appointment.

When I entered the hall accompanied by the prime minister, the crowd, having learned of my appointment, jumped to their feet, yelling, clapping, whistling, and stamping in an unruly display of joy at what they considered their own triumph. The prime minister, obviously impressed, was much more upbeat and relaxed than he had been in the morning.

The meeting of the country's governors, a first in history called by an NGO and focused on women, was scheduled for January 1, 1976, the day after my appointment. The governors, who were invited to discuss the approval of the National Plan of Action, were jovial and supportive. Most of their suggestions on economic viability and political implications had already been negotiated at state-level meetings. Our plan had been toned down from its first draft approved by the WOI board and become less ambitious. But as I explained to some of the more radical members of our council, it was better to have full support from the governors than to have a plan closer to our lofty aspirations that did not enjoy their support.

The princess joked after the meeting, "Do you realize that women are the only ones except for the prime minister who can bring all the governors together at one time?"

"It's your support," I replied.

"That helps," she said, "but it's the recent history of the WOI's work. Without that it could not have happened even a year ago." She was right. Three years ago when I started my listening tour across the country, I needed a letter of introduction from her deputy, Mr. Ansari, just to get an appointment with the governor of each province.

The most important product of our National Plan of Action was the unique implementation mechanism that Hoveyda helped create. It was based on an idea that decades later became an accepted part of feminist activism: "*All* issues are women's issues." The implementation of the plan was made the responsibility of twelve government ministries. The ministers met annually at a meeting headed by the prime minister and reviewed and evaluated the progress made toward full participation of women in all aspects of the ministries' work and to discuss resources and programs for the coming year. Every month the senior deputy ministers from the twelve ministries met with the minister for women's affairs to review and evaluate implementation. No such mechanism existed at the time anywhere, nor has one been put in place since. The closest approximation is the President's Interagency Council on Women during President Bill Clinton's time in office. But this initiative lacked the resources or the clout of a cabinet position and remained at best an advisory entity.

The plan was finalized in May 1978. Seven months later, in February 1979, Ayatollah Khomeini returned to Iran. There was no time to see the impact of the plan or to share its outlines with the international community.

MY APPOINTMENT as minister for women's affairs was announced on a Wednesday, and I was scheduled to present a report on the status of women to the political bureau of the Rastakhiz (Resurgence) Party that Saturday,[3] the beginning of the work week in Iran. In the party's conference room Prime Minister Hoveyda took the center seat, flanked by the minister of culture, who was married to the shah's older sister, Princess Shams, and the minister of labor, a former communist and graduate of Karl Marx University in Leipzig. My friends and allies in the group—the head of the Plan and Budget Organization, the minister of the interior, and the minister of health and welfare, all of whom were also members of the WOI's High Council for Cooperation—were attending a meeting chaired by the queen and would be delayed.

I sat across from Hoveyda. He began the meeting with no congratulatory reference to my new position. I thought vaguely that the absence of any comment about my appointment was rather unusual, but I didn't dwell on this and began to present my report with confidence. The picture I offered of women's lives in Iran was rather dismal. I concluded my talk saying,

> The stated position of the government of Iran is to reach equality between men and women in all areas. The real situation of women in the country is, as you have seen, quite far from that goal. For centuries women have been delegated to the private sphere in this country, as in almost all other countries. Their subservient position has been reinforced by societal arrangements across all fields of endeavor and has been strengthened by the subtle support of literature, myth, and the arts. To change this, there will have to be a commitment to change

that will cover the entire range of human relationships. We will have to examine all aspects of our development planning, from skills building, job distribution, family support systems, and school curricula to city planning and legislative reform. Achieving the goal of equality will take a revolutionary stance on the part of the government.

My previous professional experience had been limited to academia and the women's movement. I had little knowledge of the political sphere and little experience of diplomacy—my presentation was rough and raw. My aristocratic grandmother, Shah Jan, would have been appalled at my lack of nuance and by its revolutionary stance. My radical grandmother, Tooba, would have been proud.

Hoveyda decided to clip my wings and reassure the various interests represented in the political bureau by stating, in so many words, that what I was saying on the first working day after my appointment was not sanctioned by the government. He interrupted me with a set speech about the advanced state of women in Iran, the dangers of disrupting the family unit, and the blessings brought upon the population when women were freed by His Majesty through the White Revolution.

The deputy court minister, who like several other ministers was a former member of the Soviet-backed Tudeh Party, upped Hoveyda's discourse by arguing that women's homebound position and their status as a complement to the role of men was a cornerstone of order and felicity in the family and in society. In what appeared to be an honest, spontaneous outburst, he sternly said that he doubted "the sanity of the position that openly proclaims the intention to cause an upheaval in the roles of men and women."

This led another elder statesman at the table to proclaim that "a man's authority over his family resembles a monarch's benevolent concern for and leadership over his people. The dangerous attempt to unseat the father as chief of the family would lead to a more devastating upheaval in the nation and would threaten the role of the monarch as head of state."

The analogy was quite well-taken, I thought. At the WOI we were well aware that the democratization of the family unit would eventually create pressure to democratize the entire social fabric, although we did not dwell on this in our open discussions. Many years later, working in the international women's movement with women in Muslim-majority countries, we referred to this as "incomplete theorizing," a strategy that would allow us not to delve into the full consequences of what we were proposing until a time when the possibility of wider public support would materialize, making it possible to take our arguments to their logical conclusions.

Hoveyda summed up the meeting by emphasizing the excellent conditions women enjoyed in Iran and added pointedly, looking at me, "It seems our colleagues do not share your opinions."

I could see my hand shaking on the file in front of me. I flattened my palm on my papers and pressed down hard, but still could not control the trembling. Hoveyda triggered a rush of anger in me that resulted not so much from the public affront as from the injustice of the attacks. I had thought that my appointment represented a commitment to change the status of women, at least by the prime minister. I pushed my chair back and started to rise. My friend Ahmad Ghoreishi, who had been teaching at the University of Colorado when I was a graduate student there and was now chancellor of the National University of Iran, was sitting next to me. He held fast to my arm under the table and forced me to sit still. "Please don't," he kept repeating, as tears welled up in my eyes.

Fortunately, the meeting adjourned following Hoveyda's remarks. The minister of economy, a friend from the right wing of the cabinet, walked up to me and held me by the elbow. "My friend," he said, "The most important thing we learn as cabinet officers is never to cry in a meeting! All will turn out all right, you will see." His patronizing smile stopped my tears.

The minister of health and welfare, who had arrived late, said, "Please have a cup of coffee with me before you go back to your office." Then he whispered, "Don't say anything about this to anyone," as we walked out of the meeting room. In his office, he ordered a Turkish coffee and tried to calm me by telling me stories about the media attacks on him supported by the medical establishment. He said, "Right next door is a team whose main task is to address all the press stories and petitions sent to the shah with complaints about me."

On the drive back to the office I reflected on my presentation and realized that I would have to discipline myself and learn the difference between activism and effective action inside the government. I also realized I was not adequately aware of the nuances in the battles between the country's social forces, of which Hoveyda was acutely aware. Later I would learn that Hoveyda had his way of showing displeasure or sympathy through a somewhat theatrical and not so subtle set of gestures. He would shake his head, whisper to his neighbor, or write a note, scrunch up the paper, and throw it across the table—behavior for which he would have been reprimanded had he been in a classroom rather than a cabinet meeting. He also had a way of casting a veil of mystery around an issue by implying there was more behind his words and actions than appeared to the naked eye—that he knew things he was not able to discuss openly. Generally, Hoveyda was quite successful at making it appear that decisions concerning a given subject had already been made, that the discussion was really a charade with a purpose other than what was stated, and participants had better try to find out what the decision was and fall in line, short of appearing to be "not in the loop," or worse yet, actively "subversive." The implication was that the shah had given specific directions on the minutest aspects of each conversation and that any intervention would bring reward or punishment, as deserved.

I learned later how the game was played at court. The shah's interaction with the cabinet was primarily through the High Economic Council, headed by the prime minister and composed of cabinet ministers whose responsibilities related to economic issues, the managing director of the Plan and Budget Organization, and the head of the Central Bank. Other ministers participated whenever their ministry was involved. I attended the council meeting a few times as the prime minister's deputy on the South Tehran Urban Development Project. During those meetings I got a glimpse of how the system worked: on Sunday afternoon we would attend a meeting chaired by the prime minister, where the reports of various consultants and experts were closely studied and a preview discussion took place. The group formed their conclusions, and the next morning, in the formal council meeting chaired by the shah, the various ministers presented their respective pieces of the project. The shah asked a few questions and confirmed what appeared to be the rational conclusion based on the studies and reports.

Each week I scoured the minutes of the High Economic Council, which were regularly circulated to the entire cabinet. They reflected the same pattern I had witnessed in the meetings on the south Tehran project. Facts and statistics would lead one to a reasonable conclusion that was almost always agreed upon beforehand by those concerned and that subsequently received the shah's approval. What was, in effect, the government position gained added credence from the royal stamp of approval. Sometimes in practice a variation would be required because of changes on the ground. The scenario would be repeated and the shah would reach the new expected conclusion. It was an interesting way of doing business. The shah was presented with scenarios that had really only one clear-cut, reasonable conclusion, and the public was then told that the shah had decreed this or that.

Ministers had tremendous power within their own portfolio, largely unchecked by civic organizations or the press. No one person, not even the shah, could possibly know the details of the activities of the various ministries in a far-flung, modernizing, and increasingly complex socioeconomic system. Work was carried out rather efficiently and smoothly, the development process sped forward, and Iran achieved an exceptional rate of economic growth. Hoveyda, the chief architect of this system, made sure that we members of the cabinet were well equipped educationally for our jobs and that we had the resources necessary to do what we loved, unencumbered by public scrutiny or criticism. The shah believed that he was devoting time and energy above and beyond the call of duty to governance and that without his benevolent and disinterested fatherly guidance things would not get done with such speed and efficiency.

In reality his role was largely to push—relentlessly, it would seem at times—a vision of modernity and progress for the country. He had no way of knowing the particulars of how things were planned or implemented. The problem was that without public accountability, the various forces and opinions within our diverse population did not have a channel for release. Nor did this process create a sense of ownership for his vision of society. One of the more debilitating aspects of this process was that the governing elite also bought into the prevalent view and thought of themselves as functionaries rather than the leaders they actually were. Nevertheless, decades later under the Islamic Republic, in the face of a government that suppressed any sign or expression of modernity, the energetic pursuit of it by the country's youth showed that the impact of that era's modernizing efforts was deeper than was realized at the time.

Hoveyda could hardly suggest that the shah was against the advancement of women, since creating the post of minister for women's affairs was a radical and visible testimony of his support. But the prime minister could make it appear that there was more to the situation than the fact of the appointment would imply. I later came to learn the logic of Hoveyda's position. He was acutely aware of the influence of the reactionary forces in society and especially mindful of the power of the clergy. He knew of the backlash that was building against the radical changes initiated in the status of women, and he was afraid of the potential consequences of too strong a movement toward rapid change in the space where the private and the public intersected, where relations between the family, community, and society were negotiated. This was the area where deep-rooted beliefs were skillfully manipulated by the conservative clergy. He also worried about the reactions of other sources of power in the country, one of whom, Queen Farah, was a symbolic role model for women.

My conversation with Hoveyda left me quite depressed and worried. None of my discussions with colleagues had taken into account the web of relationships and interactions that I seemed to have stumbled into, and I was sure I was far from up to this aspect of the task. The prime minister seemed suspicious of my motives, and I sensed that he had been pushed, quite unwillingly, into appointing me. It seemed he thought I was closer to Princess Ashraf than I really was and that she had more power than she actually did, and he worried that I would be her agent in the cabinet.

Much to her credit, the princess never interfered in the WOI's policies, personnel decisions, or projects. I reported to her out of courtesy for her position as the honorary WOI president and also to be able to quote her as agreeing to the policies adopted by the council. The perception of her power was such that the impression of her support made things a lot easier for us. In later years, though, I came to regret the game we at the WOI played. We had adopted a policy of saying she had "decreed" that we do such and such. This was to co-opt her clout, real or imagined, and was intended as insurance against those who were suspicious of and hostile toward our programs. But it gave a false impression of how things really worked within the organization and alienated some of our natural constituency.

In fact, the WOI ran on a collaborative, participatory basis. The provincial branches decided on their own programs and strategies. They participated in determining the overall direction of the organization through their representatives at the annual general assembly and by electing the members of the board, which met every week for several hours to discuss programs and to monitor and oversee the organization's work. In later years, when I founded NGOs and served on NGO boards, I never saw any such an organization where the board met weekly and was so closely involved in reviewing and evaluating proposals or setting the agenda for its activities. Nor did I see a board where such strong emphasis was given to diversity in the members' religious, ethnic, and overall backgrounds. Yet despite the exceptional involvement of the membership at all levels of decision-making, and despite the fact that the board members oversaw our plans and programs every week, we regularly took the shortcut of prefacing important announcements and projects with a reference to royal decree—a practice that I regret to this day.

By the 1970s the princess, who had devoted considerable time to women's issues, had become absorbed in international affairs and relished her role as her brother's special emissary. She enjoyed her role as top diplomat and spent a considerable amount of time on her responsibilities and as the leader of the Iranian delegation at the United Nations. Her brother, it became clearer to me in later years, preferred for her to be preoccupied with matters outside of domestic affairs in order to avoid controversy. A powerful, outspoken woman would elicit strong reactions, especially among the more conservative elements in the society.

Interaction between the local, national, and global had become integral to our work, and she became interested in the WOI's international activities as they coincided with the preparations for the UN International Women's Year in 1975. The circumstances following my appointment brought home to me the degree of effectiveness of our own public statements—even the prime minister was taken in, thinking the princess much more involved with the WOI than she was. I was certain at this point that unless I had a clear-cut mandate for my new duties, I might end up the focus of power-elite games that had nothing to do with the function and purpose of the position I had just accepted.

Back in the office, I called the WOI's informal executive committee—my deputy, Ezzat Aghevli; the WOI's deputy for education and program development, Parviz Homayounpour; and the WOI's legal advisor, Homa Afzal—to my office and described what had happened in the meeting. Ezzat agreed that the style of my presentation had probably been too zealous but immediately saw that the problem was much more complicated. The reactionary tide was rising. The attitude of women in our centers was changing. Even younger women who had never favored wearing a veil before were beginning to come to classes veiled not in casual printed-cotton chadors, but in heavy black ones that were clearly designed to make a statement of cultural identity and solidarity with a more democratic, decentralized system that the intellectual community of the time was promoting. These were only the surface indicators of the strength of the conservative opposition. The prime minister was an astute politician: he wanted to preempt an inevitable backlash by avoiding the more controversial and radical pronouncements attributed to the government. When I spoke now, I was speaking for the government and would have to learn to moderate my tone.

Homa and Parviz were less worried about the backlash and more concerned about the need to shore up support among our own troops. We decided that we needed strong support from women at the top as well as at the grassroots. We had the built-in grassroots constituency of our membership and of the women who regularly attended the centers; the numbers were in the hundreds of thousands. But we had not yet developed a clear-cut plan for advocacy. As for the top, the simplest place to start was with the queen. I called her office and was granted an appointment for two days later. The queen's quick response to my request and the news that she would receive me within two days was reassuring.

I HAD never been to Niavaran Palace before. At the entrance a guard took my name and checked it against a list. I walked down the wide avenue, lined with tall cypress trees, toward the simple, elegant structure that was the royal family's winter home. It was not really a palace so much as a spacious house with a wide entrance hall, a large dining room that was also used for meetings, and a sizeable sitting room with tasteful selections of modern paintings, sculpture, and exquisite Persian carpets. Behind the reception area was a screening room, where the family watched films, and upstairs were the royal family's bedrooms. A guide in formal attire led me to an upstairs room, which served as a waiting room for the queen's visitors. It was a simple room with windows that opened to the avenue below, adorned with lovely antiques and an enormous, beautifully framed mirror over the mantelpiece. I had arrived the usual fifteen minutes early and the queen was running late, as I learned to expect in future meetings. I fidgeted, looked in the mirror, checked my lipstick, and examined the lampshade and the miniature tree made of jade on the side table. Finally, the door opened and another man in formal attire entered and held the door open for me. I followed him to the small room next door, the queen's office, where I found the queen standing directly in front of the door. I was taken by surprise: Princess Ashraf, the only royal I had ever visited, usually entered the room after one had been seated for a few minutes.

Queen Farah had a wonderful smile that gave her almond-shaped eyes a joyful twinkle. I took her hand and, mindful of the prime minister's recommendation, executed my first real curtsy. I had practiced a few times at home but it felt clumsy now that I had a very knowledgeable audience. A photographer who had entered immediately after I did took a picture and then was shown out.

The queen asked me to sit down. "How are things going?" she asked, simply.

I forgot all of the speeches I had practiced on the way to the palace and burst into a long, unrehearsed statement pointing out the importance of the position I had been appointed to for women and for the country as a whole. I described the prime minister's attitude and my understanding that it was based in part on his perception of *her* displeasure with my new post. I told her I knew nothing of the process that had led to my appointment—I only knew that the post was a very sensitive and controversial one and that it would only be useful if she were supportive. Her support was needed because of her position, because of the network of organizations she headed, whose work was interconnected with ours, and also because without some show of support on her part, the prime minister and naturally the rest of the government would not be cooperative.

I ended my speech by saying, "I am not interested in a government position, Your Majesty. I have accepted this post because I believe it can play an important role in improving the status of women. If you have hesitations or cannot support me, then it would be best for me to leave the post at an appropriate moment."

Looking down at her slender, impeccably manicured hands, she told me that she supported the position and would talk to the prime minister. But she knew that if she were to comment on his attitude, he would not admit that he had been negative. He would joke about it and say he had had no intention of upsetting women, or some such thing. She said once again that she thought I ought to continue my work and do my best. I showed her a few recent WOI publications and told her about a number of new projects that the organization had planned for the near future. When I left her, I had a bounce in my step and a great deal of hope for the future.

Chapter 9

Prime Minister's Dilemma

A FEMINIST IN THE CABINET

NOTHING I HAD DONE in my thirty-four years of life had prepared me for the position of minister for women's affairs. Shortly after my appointment, while on an official trip to England I was presented to Princess Margaret at a dinner at the Iranian Embassy. When I was introduced to her as the "Minister for Women's Affairs," she said with a mischievous smile and a hint of genuine wonder, "My dear, how *do* you manage women's affairs?" Well, this was exactly what I would need to do—not to *manage* women's affairs but to help define exactly what it meant. A year before, Françoise Giroud, the well-known French left-wing intellectual, had been appointed to such a post—the first in the world. Shortly after, when Françoise visited Iran, she and I accompanied Princess Ashraf on a trip to the Bakhtiari tribal area. We had many conversations, but her government role was too new at that point to have set a meaningful precedent.

I was a young woman with a thin résumé—not to mention an outsider—appointed to a job with no specific mandate. To make things even more challenging, women and politics had a tumultuous history in Iran. In the mid-nineteenth century, Tahereh Qurrat al-Ayn, a poet, progressive religious thinker, and leading figure in the new Bābi faith, cast aside her veil as she spoke to a gathering of her male followers, causing one of them to slit his own throat rather than endure the agony of his conflicting emotions. Tahereh was later hanged for heresy—that is, for daring to think, to voice her beliefs, and to lead. Memories of the 1963 religious uprising led by Ayatollah Khomeini in response to the six-point White Revolution reform project proposed by the shah were still vivid for most people, especially for policy makers. Of the six points—land reform, nationalization of forests, sale of state-owned enterprises to the public, workers' profit sharing, voting and political rights for women, and formation of the Education and Health Corps—two were exceptionally repugnant to Khomeini's concept of social organization: land reform and the extension of the franchise to women. The land reform measures were intended to abolish the feudal system by giving farmers ownership of the land they farmed. This was anathema to Khomeini and much of the religious establishment because the system of charitable donations to clergy mandated by *zakat*, one of the five pillars of Islam, enabled the ayatollahs to acquire huge plots of land and was the foundation of the clergy's wealth and power. But Khomeini found point 5, giving women the right to vote, even more dangerous and repugnant. While land reform weakened the clerical establishment's economic base, point 5— which made it possible for women to enter the public space—undermined Khomeini's view of societal organization, one founded on women's role as complementary to men in the family and society and on men's role as guardians of women.

Khomeini's opposition was virulent and wholehearted. He declared that giving women the right to vote was tantamount to an "expansion of prostitution" and issued a fatwa (edict) calling all the believers to the streets to express their opposition; the demonstrations began with seminary students in the religious city of Qom and led to clashes with the police. Mehdi Bazargan, a National Front leader who later became the revolutionary government's first prime minister, several other ayatollahs, and a mix of Islamist leftists such as the Mujahedin antimonarchist groups issued statements of support for Khomeini's stance. However, the shah won that round when the referendum on the White Revolution showed overwhelming support by a large majority of the people, and Khomeini was subsequently exiled to Iraq. But the nation had seen a preview of what was to come, and many of the leading political actors of the next decade became wary of the clerics' power and influence.

On the WOI's side, though, the future seemed anything but bleak. Women's condition had significantly improved in the decade since Khomeini's uprising, and my WOI colleagues almost unanimously felt vindicated when I became minister for women's affairs. They suggested a set of new initiatives to be made public as soon as possible. They thought we should take advantage of the interest of the national and international media to keep up the momentum that had been created by Iran's role in the UN Mexico City conference and by my appointment. They were also emboldened by the fact that we had several government ministers on our side who were also members of the WOI's High Council for Cooperation. These men held the government social and economic portfolios most important to us, and over the years they had become thoroughly familiar with our ideas and work.

My colleagues at the WOI and I discussed often and at length the most effective ways to use my new post. We could not hope for the cabinet as a whole to share our vision of the role of women in society, and we didn't attempt the impossible task of making the cabinet a "consciousness-raising" workshop. What we needed was access to the information and resources that would enable us to reach our goals. We began by seeking out projects of mutual interest. If, for example, the minister of labor faced a labor shortage at a time of strong economic growth, we didn't argue the right of women to equal opportunity. We argued instead that women made better skilled workers and presented fewer problems than imported labor, and we promised to present qualified women if our centers were supplied with trainers and equipment. A case in point was Iran's transition from ordinary traditional farming, where women were an integral part of the workforce, to more technologically advanced, machine-based agriculture, from which women were excluded. We worked with the minister of agriculture to include agricultural equipment training for women. When the minister of health expressed concern that women were unwilling to go to his department's male-run clinics or were not allowed by their family to do so, we asked for nurses and equipment to offer counseling and services at the WOI's women-run centers. In this way, we were helping the ministers solve their problems by finding mutually attractive solutions, and we needed their support and resources to bring skills and income to women. This was the first stage, but we knew that the process itself would inevitably bring awareness to men.

There was little history or precedent for my government position. In consultation with the prime minister, on the one hand, and the WOI leadership, on the other, we decided that I should keep my position as WOI secretary general as a way to maintain the connection with the WOI team on whom we relied for ideas, strategies, and information from the field. Ezzat, my senior deputy at the WOI, took on the day-to-day management of the organization.

The WOI's High Council was discontinued, soon to be replaced by a much stronger and larger team of ministers, headed by the prime minister, who met annually to review with WOI representatives the progress made in improving the status of women in each ministry. Our strategy involved looking, speaking, and behaving in noncontroversial, conventional ways, which helped us sell our radical ideas. I was reminded of this four decades later at one of our Women's Learning Partnership (WLP) partners meetings in the United States, when a conventional-looking straight woman told us how the Human Rights Campaign helped to secure marriage rights for gays and lesbians. She explained how articulating that community's demand simply as "marriage equality" instead of using the previous terminology of "same-sex marriage" had helped normalize and neutralize the issue. We learned empirically that it was better to use familiar and accepted language and avoid potentially inflammatory slogans.

AS I gained seniority, which a number of changes in the cabinet brought sooner than I could have imagined, I came to hold more authority. My work with the WOI had brought me into contact with people at the grassroots and made me aware of how they interacted with each other and with various institutions—and aware of grassroots demands, challenges, obstacles, and achievements. Now, with my position as minister and my regular travels with the cabinet and the queen that involved visits to a variety of national projects, I had access to the other side of the political spectrum.

The men I worked with often had to find a formula to take advantage of my unusual grassroots access, and the experience and resources it provided, without feeling threatened. In fact, my being a woman may have made this less threatening. It was a unique situation because I had been rendered gender-neutral by my position as a peer. Also, since I was not quite one of them, the usual power hierarchy or competition did not enter into our interactions. Nonetheless, there were all kinds of unexpected, and often ridiculous, inconveniences for a woman cabinet member. The cabinet was so indisputably a male domain that there was only one restroom near the meeting room, and that, of course, was a men's room. Every once in a while, I had to make the restroom unisex, much to every one's inconvenience. Decades later, in a meeting of women ministers of culture in Iceland, several of us exchanged similar restroom stories as part of our bonding.

On the cabinet's official tours to the provinces, we often traveled by army helicopter. Since we had to take part in regular meetings on arrival, I had to dress appropriately not for the journey, but for the arrival, and had to improvise ways of getting in and out of a helicopter in high heels and a skirt without too much fuss and in a reasonably dignified manner. Years later, when it became acceptable for professional women to wear pantsuits, this aspect of life became simpler. There were also smaller indignities—recurring signs of the novelty of the situation. During the first few weeks, the policeman at the entrance of the prime ministry formally saluted all cabinet officers as a matter of routine, but in his confusion about what to do on encountering a woman minister, he turned and twisted his arm every which way, in a gesture somewhere between a wave and an attempt to brush aside a bee. A messenger who brought a file to a room where I was chairing a meeting looked around in confusion—I was sitting at the head of the table, but I was not a man—and found the likeliest white-haired male and delivered the material to him. I chose to regard these incidents with humor. Anger is not very healthy or useful if it becomes a constant emotion, as it would have been had I lost my sense of humor.

Another issue was protocol. Most men had a wife to take to receptions or official functions. I had a husband, and that presented a problem. Not only did I have a husband, but I had one who was the secretary general of an important organization—Iran's National Committee for the World Literacy Program.[1] Usually at official functions husbands and wives were placed in the same box in terms of protocol. With the two of us, it was hard for the hosts to decide how to deal with the situation. Although in protocol my rank was higher than Gholam's, he decided that during formal occasions and ceremonies he would take the place assigned to his own position. I didn't question his choice. I assumed that as women took on more senior positions, each couple would make its own decision.

Things became more comfortable as time passed, and my cabinet colleagues eventually behaved toward me with less elaborate respect and more camaraderie. I realized how much things had changed when, on a trip to Azerbaijan with several of my cabinet colleagues, we stopped at a model farm that used the newest mechanized farming methods. After lunch outdoors, we were standing around talking when one of my colleagues whispered to another that his fly was unzipped. The colleague turned away from the local village men and faced me and our other two colleagues to correct the situation. "Huh," I said to myself, "finally I'm established as a peer, and that definitely trumps gender!"

THE CREATION of the minister for women's affairs post was clearly a victory for feminist activists. But partly through my first clash with Prime Minister Hoveyda and partly through my initial contacts with the world of politics and government, I had come to realize that as strange as that world was to me, my presence was at least as destabilizing to it. I decided to sit back and allow the event to sink into the public's consciousness, calm the nerves of the men who might be supportive, and try to get a feel for the existing political alliances within the cabinet. This decision was prudent, since all the men in the cabinet, by the time they had worked their way up to the top job, had a better sense of the politics of their domain than I did. Not only was I new to public service, the job with which I had been tasked was new to government and, by its very nature, controversial. I would have to learn a lot very quickly.

A couple of months after my appointment, I prepared a memo to the prime minister suggesting that preparatory material and drafts of all matters on the cabinet's agenda that might in some way relate to women be referred to my office for review of their potential impact on women. As a matter of course, the draft forms of these materials circulated among all cabinet ministers. But I was interested in the earlier, preliminary stages of preparation, before the final drafts of the bills were prepared and the language had been determined. Since this would be an internal cabinet decision with no public exposure, there was no particular resistance to the idea, though I soon learned that I would have to work hard to convince my colleagues of the wide range of issues that could be considered to be related to women. Decades later, the slogan "All issues are women's issues" validated my position.

The weekly meeting of the cabinet subcommittee for social and cultural affairs, chaired by the minister of plan and budget, offered an invaluable occasion for coordinating, pressuring, and educating the most powerful personalities in these fields on issues of special interest to women. We met at lunch each Tuesday and continued our meeting through most of the afternoon. We discussed bills, projects, and budgetary considerations at length, and most agreements reached here would pass through the cabinet without much opposition.

Integrating women's concerns in the process was challenging on many levels. For some members, my comments and interventions were their first exposure to a woman's perspective on issues related to their portfolio. For others it was the first time these subjects were presented not by a lobbyist or member of a pressure group but by one of their peers. This meant that a fine line separated my identity as a committed member of a pressure group and a responsible government minister.

Clearly, acquainting members of the Iranian cabinet with women's conditions and needs was an essential aspect of my job. And these highly educated men, many of whom held PhDs from the best Western universities and were familiar with a broad range of societies and cultures, were not averse to new ideas. But women's issues tended to touch on foundational concepts of culture, tradition, and human relations, and I knew I had to tread carefully and hope at least at first for only incremental change. As the WOI's council chair, Dr. Iran Alam, often reminded us, "We don't want to run so fast ahead of our constituency so that when you look back there is no one following."

Two years before, we had amended the WOI constitution to state that its ultimate goal was to achieve freedom and equality for women. These were big words, but how would we reach that lofty goal? We knew the breadth and depth of the multifaceted challenges we would face, but we had also learned how to build on past achievements and how to work to get other groups to support us. We had been told again and again by the women we had met and consulted with across the country that economic independence was the foundation of liberty: women need jobs before they can hope for any kind of independence. In the meanwhile, women were responsible for the care of children, and without dependable and safe childcare, employment in general and access to better pay and status in particular would be unattainable for them. This became my focus on the Social and Cultural Affairs Committee. I worked with my colleagues at the WOI on a "dream package" that, if approved, would give working mothers up to seven months paid pregnancy leave and then after the child's birth, part-time employment with job security and full-time benefits until children reached three years of age. It also provided childcare on the premises of their workplace.

I knew this package would not be accepted easily, not only because women's work was still seen as a luxury and not a right or necessity, but also because it would cause a disruption in employment procedures and budgeting within various departments. I thought if I presented segments of the plan in successive meetings of the committee, it might be less of a challenge. When I presented the part-time work with full-time benefits concept, the social welfare minister asked for statistics for the potential number of women this provision would cover and exactly how much it would cost the government, or, more specifically, his department's budget. I would have liked to have given him specific figures, but we only had general estimates. The plan and budget minister whispered to me, "Give him the numbers you have and let *him* go find the exact figures." This welcome advice pretty much solved my problem of the moment.

The Social and Cultural Affairs Committee finally agreed to all of these provisions and defended them when I presented them to the full cabinet. The minister of agriculture, a very pleasant but quite old-fashioned man, immediately began to list a host of problems, including the difficulty arranging for personnel to fill the remaining half of the work week, and insisted that the plan would cause "unbearable hardship" for his department. Faced with the support from a number of our committee members for the bill, he finally threw up his hands in resignation and said, "All right, I'll go along. But I'm warning you, if we don't watch out, the minister for women's affairs is going to have us send all women government employees home and just write them a check at the end of each month!"

The package was approved in 1976. To put its significance for women in context, more than forty-five years later in the United States, an advanced industrialized nation with a long history of women's activism, women still do not have paid maternity leave mandated by law, and safe and affordable child-care is limited to the affluent families who can shoulder its enormous costs. This remarkable package was approved in Iran largely due to the strength of the women's networks and to its strong and simple advocacy message: Women have not only the *right* to work but most often they *have* to work. Children are the shared responsibility of both parents and the greatest resource of any society. Their welfare and education must be a priority for the nation. It helped that in 1975, soon after the rise in the country's oil income, Iran had declared that free public education and daily meals from kindergarten through the eighth grade were to be a state responsibility.

A FEW months after our initial rather unhappy encounter, Prime Minister Hoveyda began to see me as a fresh face, someone who could break out of the government bureaucracy and hierarchy and have a kind of optimism and faith that he himself and some others might no longer feel. Perhaps based on this, he gave me two assignments that I found interesting and engrossing.

One of these assignments was the South Tehran Urban Development Project, a huge, complicated reconstruction and development effort for the entire large slum area in the south of the city. He had pointed to this on the day of my appointment as we flew over the area. Hundreds and thousands of women and men were living in *gowds* (literally "deep places")—shanty towns that were often flooded by water flowing down from the slopes of the Alborz Mountains, making them perpetually muddy and damp. Since these gowds were mostly outside the boundaries of the city, services were almost nonexistent, and drug abuse and other urban slum problems were rampant. Migration from the rural areas had brought many women to the city with their men, most of whom were unemployed or marginally employed. Because of this, the women were expected to care for the children as well as earn a living. The worst problems of the country's urban centers manifested themselves in south Tehran, and this particular project focused on finding solutions.

The prime minister headed the project and appointed me as his deputy charged with its management. The work was overwhelming. Each aspect of the project required coordinating with one or more ministries and dealing with their slow and cumbersome bureaucracies. To deal with their questions I placed large statistical maps of the area on the walls of my office. Almost daily, people—mostly women with children—came to see me to ask for help getting water, electricity, a job, or a childcare center for themselves or their neighborhood. At the time, I justified spending so much time on this project because much of the work concerned poor women and involved the type of programs the WOI had carried out in its centers in similar areas of the city. Looking back, though, I ought not to have allowed myself to become so deeply involved in a project that trapped me in a position of either being tied up in coordinating a labyrinth of government ministries or having to create a complex new entity with its own resources, both of which took me away from totally focusing on women.

The prime minister also asked me to set up an organization for exceptional and gifted children. Here, too, I was Hoveyda's deputy, and in this capacity I oversaw the creation of the new organization. In the end I was responsible for everything from finding a physical space for the campus to teacher training, designing teaching material, and administering tests, to selecting qualified children from across the country. It was fascinating work, but it also took away from my focus on women. Years later, international aid organizations, disappointed with the corruption and inefficiency of the governmental apparatus in some developing countries, began to turn enthusiastically to NGOs to take on similar development and service projects, to the detriment both of the projects and the largely volunteer-run organizations. The effort, more often than not, changed the very nature of the NGOs and weakened government agency and responsibility. In my case, a haphazard combination of NGO and government resources was at stake. My friend Shojaeddin Sheykhuleslami, the minister of social welfare, strongly warned me against taking on this new responsibility and diluting my focus.

"You are responsible for women's affairs. It's what you will be remembered for," he told me. "It's what the country expects of you. Don't let yourself get distracted in the name of 'good deeds.'"

I appreciated his counsel, which reflected my own concerns.

THE CABINET met every Monday morning. One of the highly respected senior members of the cabinet, Safi Asfia, minister of state for economic affairs, was very sympathetic to the women's cause and took on the role of my mentor and supporter. Prime Minister Hoveyda was also supportive, except where he foresaw mounting opposition from conservatives or clerical groups. By far the most astute politician in the cabinet, Hoveyda tried to fill the void that the lack of a working political infrastructure created by balancing the interests of various groups and constituencies. He kept an open and ongoing dialogue with representatives of religious, commercial, ethnic, and other interest groups. Nearly every day he had lunch with journalists, bazaar leaders, members of minority groups, or factions in parliament. My office was in the same compound as his, so he often asked me to these lunches, providing me with a fast track to self-education on the political forces in society.

My favorite among the cabinet members, however, was Minister of Defense Reza Azimi, a venerable four-star general who shared my love of poetry. Every Monday morning during the cabinet meeting, he would tell my fortune through the poetry of Hafez, one of Iran's most beloved poets. Following a popular Iranian custom of divination, he would write down the very first ghazal by Hafez that came to mind as my *faal*, or fortune, for the week. I loved reading the poetry written in his beautiful calligraphy. This was even more delightful given who he was, where we were, and the contrast with the prosaic discussions going around the table at the time.

My most challenging interaction was with the minister of justice, Sadegh Ahmadi, partly because of the legal system's inherent conservatism, but mainly because the status of women was a subject where civic and religious law most often intersected. This was the primary area of conflict between the government and the ulama (Islamic scholars). The conflicts were basically ideological and sprang from opposing views on modernity and development. The laws related to women were concentrated in the family status legal codes, which historically the clerics had devised and controlled. These laws were now increasingly brought under civil law, which for the clerical establishment represented a significant loss of power and financial resources. My interest was to change the laws to bring about more equitable rights for women. The justice ministry's interest was to make sure that no legislation that might be seen to be in direct conflict with Shari'a, a Quranic-derived interpretation considered the foundation of Islamic law including family law, would ever reach the Majlis, Iran's parliament. This did pose a challenge, but Ministry of Justice representatives were surprised by the expertise and skill of the WOI's legal team, headed by Homa Afzal, an able and persuasive negotiator who was careful to address the sensitivities of the more enlightened members of the clerical establishment. By offering language and arguments that would not appear to be in conflict with the religious texts, Homa and her team made it possible for the ministry, more often than not, to side with women in the vital process of reinterpreting religious texts and rethinking customary practice.

A typical discussion with Minister of Justice Ahmadi took place at a meeting of the WOI's High Council for Cooperation before I joined the cabinet. In one instance, the WOI had prepared a comprehensive document in support of its proposed revision to the Family Protection Law. One item concerned rescinding a husband's right to stop his wife from holding a job that he considered to be damaging to his "honor." The minister of justice couldn't understand what was wrong with that law. I argued that *all* lawful work is honorable and that a woman should have the right to choose her profession.

The minister asked, "Well, what if my wife decided to be a singer?"

Princess Ashraf, who chaired the meeting, turned to Abdol-Majid Majidi, the minister of plan and budget, and asked, "Do you have a problem with your wife's work?" Majidi's wife, Monir Vakili, was an opera singer and a respected artist.[2]

"I am proud of her work," Majidi said.

There was laughter among the group, and the minister of justice seemed embarrassed. But he stuck to his position in later meetings.

Finally, though, we were able to convince him and his colleagues to include the same right for the wife. I was proud of this on two counts. First, for a woman to have the potential power to refuse permission to her husband was a significant feat. Second, this was the first time in Iranian law that a woman was seen to have "honor" in her own right. This was more a matter of symbolism than actual change in the rights of women in the family, but in a culture where the symbolism around honor carried a great deal of weight, I considered it a victory.

Chapter 10

A Preface to the Revolution

P RESIDENT JIMMY CARTER'S DECISION to spend New Year's Eve 1977 in Tehran was unexpected. That November, the shah and the queen's visit to the United States had been marred by the leftist Confederation of Iranian Students' demonstrations in front of the White House, and the tear gas that the police sprayed to keep the protestors at bay also swirled around the two heads of state and brought tears to their eyes as the president welcomed the shah and the queen to the United States. Carter's follow-up trip so soon afterward was therefore anticipated in Iran with great interest. Designated as one of the official hosts, I was asked to accompany the president and First Lady to events and escort Mrs. Carter on her visits to museums and educational institutions.

The New Year's Eve state dinner in President Carter's honor was a stunning occasion.

Every object in the room seemed to be bathed in the sparkling light of the crystal chandeliers. The flowers, the gowns, and the décor were exquisite, but most striking was the jubilant atmosphere of the New Year's celebration that seemed to reflect the anticipation in the room of a special year to come. In his remarks at the dinner, the shah reviewed the long and fruitful relationship between Iran and the United States. He began with an allusion to the Reverend Mr. Smith, the first American to travel to Iran in 1832, who wrote that living among good people like Iranians and serving them was more pleasant for him than anything else, and that he considered the best days of his life those spent in this country. The American College in Tehran, established 100 years earlier, was an outstanding center for the education and training of Iranian youth. Our people, the shah said, carry such good memories of its beloved principal, Dr. Samuel Jordan, that one of the highways of Tehran is named after him. He mentioned Ralph Waldo Emerson's admiration for the poetry of Hafez, and Arthur Upham Pope's encyclopedic research on and contribution to the study of Iranian art. The shah then reviewed the political support the United States had provided to secure Iran's sovereignty during and after World War II and the Truman Doctrine and economic aid that had helped Iran's modernization. He ended by praising President Carter's human rights policies, saying that they elevated the US role as a global leader. In his toast to the shah, President Carter said, "The transformation that has taken place in this nation is indeed remarkable. . . . Iran, because of the great leadership of the Shah, is an island of stability in one of the more troubled areas of the world. This is a great tribute to you, Your Majesty, and to your leadership and to the respect and the admiration and love which your people give to you. . . . there is no leader with whom I have a deeper sense of personal gratitude and personal friendship."[1]

The dinner was followed by an intimate celebration in the private quarters of the Niavaran Palace in which a few dozen guests, among them President and Mrs. Carter, Secretary of State Cyrus Vance, and National Security Advisor Zbigniew Brzezinski, were joined by Amir Abbas Hoveyda, who was now minister of court, new Iranian prime minister Jamshid Amouzegar, Iranian ambassador to the United States Ardeshir Zahedi, the Iranian royal family, and King Hussein of Jordan. The spirit was carefree as we danced and cheered, and at midnight we brought in the New Year with kissing and hugging all around.

Just twelve months and two weeks later, on January 16, 1979, the shah and Queen Farah would leave Iran following a year of turbulent upheaval. Carter was later mocked for misreading the Iranian political situation. But at that moment he was not wrong—Iran was indeed one of the most promising developing nations and in many ways exceptional in the Middle East.

IN JANUARY 1978, the Iranian government still saw Khomeini as irrelevant. The cleric's 1963 attack was largely forgotten and considered an aberration that had been corrected by the White Revolution. No doubt Khomeini had some religious and political followers among the clerics and religious students in the shrine cities of Iraq and Iran, and his name was mentioned now and then by some religious opposition groups, which interested the intelligence community. But the idea of the *velayat-e faqih* (the guardianship of the Islamic jurist) was unheard of, except among some clerics, and the concept seemed bizarre to the few nonclerics who might have heard of it. As far as the government was concerned, the opposition consisted of two types: the intellectual liberal Left, and the union of what was known as "the red and the black." The first was not a serious threat, at least not to the liberal wing of the government, which in fact shared some of the Left's ideas, such as a more participatory political system. The second was based on *taqiyeh*, an Islamic juridical term whose meaning relates to when a Muslim is allowed, under Shari'a law, to lie.[2] In this case, the government saw the opposition's use of taqiyeh as a dissimulation to mislead the public about the underlying Marxist-Leninist ideology. The only danger therefore emanated from this group, which, as far as the Iranian government was concerned, was a passing phenomenon taking advantage of the open political space.

None of this even remotely suggested the possibility of a revolution, either to the Iranian government, the international community, or intelligence organizations.

LOOKING BACK, I see how what seemed like unlinked events at the time fit together and created a downward spiral into chaos. A few months earlier, during the fall of 1977 when I was in the United States for the UN General Assembly and other meetings, I had a call from my deputy, Ezzat. "There have been demonstrations by male students at Tehran University demanding gender segregation in the cafeteria," she said.

"That's crazy," I said. "Do we have any idea who is behind this? I can't believe that students would make such a preposterous demand."

"There are rumors that SAVAK may have orchestrated the demonstrations to make the opposition appear right wing and archaic," Ezzat continued, her voice sounding sad and exhausted. "Should we issue a statement or arrange for a reaction, event, or demonstration?"

I paused for a few seconds. "Let's hold off until we find out more about the situation. We certainly don't want to align ourselves with anything orchestrated by SAVAK or the unsavory elements in the opposition."

We never did find out enough information to react well to the demonstration, and the event faded into the background as the WOI continued to develop a progressive road map for intergovernmental collaboration—the National Plan of Action—which pointed to Iran's commitment to women's rights. A direct result of and link to the World Plan of Action that was announced to UN member nations in the fall of 1975, Iran's 1978 National Plan of Action remains today the most comprehensive example of collective government action for full integration of women in development.[3]

Coming up with the plan took three years: we at the WOI discussed and adjusted the draft National Plan at brainstorming sessions with our members in 400 cities, towns, and villages. We then took the draft to village, town, city, and state councils, nearly 80 percent of whose members were men, most of whom were not familiar with the demands of women activists. In each of the councils, a woman activist introduced the National Plan and facilitated the discussions. The feedback consistently suggested making the plan more conservative. We had expected this, but some WOI members were disappointed. Our chair, Dr. Alam, once again reminded us that "the most beautiful plan, if it does not get the support of those who need to make it happen, will end up framed and displayed for our visual enjoyment!"

The final draft of the National Plan was brought to a gathering of 10,000 members and supporters of the WOI on February 27, 1978, the fifteenth anniversary of Iranian women's winning the right to vote. Participants at the WOI Congress included men and women from the groups that had participated in the review process, members of WOI branches and affiliate organizations, minority groups, and university students, among others.

But ten days before this meeting, a massive demonstration in Tabriz shook the Amouzegar government. On February 18, 1978, although still small in number, Khomeini's followers helped organize a violent demonstration in Tabriz during which banks, cinemas, and other institutions were attacked, looted, and burned, and several demonstrators were wounded or killed. Over the next few months the Islamists used the time-honored fortieth day of mourning for the dead to mobilize people in other cities, taking over the mosques and causing new casualties. Riots broke out at a ceremony on the fortieth day of mourning for theology students who had come out in support of Khomeini in Qom, where, according to the opposition, sixty people had been killed by security forces.

In light of these events, the shah, who was to address the WOI Congress about the National Plan, had been advised that in view of the opposition's sensitivity to feminist positions, it would be preferable if I did not speak at the Congress. We prepared a speech for him but had no indication of what changes he might make to it.

On the day of the Congress, representatives of students, labor, profession-al women, homemakers, and farmers addressed the meeting in support of the National Plan, after which the shah came to the podium. To everyone's surprise, he spoke in stronger terms and with more commitment to women's participation than in the draft we had sent him. He referred to the fifteenth anniversary of the law that "had brought half of the population who had been put in the same category as criminals, minors, and the insane into active par-ticipation in determining the nation's destiny" and went on to condemn the recent demonstrations by the Islamist university students who were in favor of segregating male and female students in universities. "How can we, who work with the international community to battle apartheid in other countries, prac-tice apartheid against half of our own population?" he asked. He then pledged that Iran would continue on the path toward full equality, quoting a famous saying, "The moon will shine and the dog will bark," a politically inappropriate choice, with the government as the moon and the opposition as the dog, that would come to haunt him for quite a while.

That afternoon, as I accompanied the shah and Queen Farah to their heli-copter, he turned to me with a smile and said, "It seems we said all that you would've said and perhaps more."

"Thank you for your support, Your Majesty," I said. Strangely enough, he seemed a bit like a young boy who had done something he had promised himself he would not—but had enjoyed doing immensely. The developments in the following months and years proved to me that the shah was quite aware that the main cause of the Khomeini uprising was the fast-changing position of women in the family and its connection to the changes necessitated by moder-nity. Khomeini, for his part, well understood that changing the structure of the most foundational unit of society—the family—would shake the entire edifice.

Iran's National Plan of Action, finally approved by the cabinet in May 1978, offered the first instance of a government committing twelve cabinet ministries and other high-level institutions—health, education, plan and budget, agricul-ture, labor, higher education, radio-television, justice, culture, adult education, economics, and mines and industries—led by the prime minister, to annually review the progress of women and to find new funding to improve their material and social circumstances. In the interval, the senior deputy ministers would meet monthly with me to coordinate and evaluate projects. Little did any of us know we would never have the opportunity to put the plan into action.

IN MARCH 1978, not long after the shah's National Plan speech, I attended a Norooz (Persian New Year) ceremony at court where various groups, including the cabinet, met with him. As we stood in line and the shah passed by, smiling and nodding his customary greetings, he stopped in front of me and asked, "Where are these brave, independent, and freedom-loving women of Iran whom you tell us about regularly? Why is there no reaction to the demonstrators demanding segregation of men and women?"

I was taken aback by this unusual gesture, but before I had a chance to respond, he smiled and said, "Perhaps now that their fearless leader is back in the country, they will get their act together."

When he left, my colleagues gathered around me and asked, "What was that about?"

I smiled and said jokingly, "I am afraid I cannot divulge. National security, you know!" They laughed and we moved on.

Not long after, I received another strange communication from the shah. As I was leaving Prime Minister Amouzegar's office following a meeting on the South Tehran Development Plan, he said, "Could you wait? I have a message from His Majesty for you." He walked to his desk and picked up a folder. From it he read, "Tell Afkhami the Women's Organization is not worth a farthing!" He stopped and looked at me and added, "I told him you would be hurt, and he said he wanted you to be hurt."

When I walked out to join Safi Asfia, minister of state for economic affairs as well as my friend and mentor, I must have still looked amused at the conversation. Once I told him about the shah's message, he looked at me with a solemn expression and said, "My dear, I wouldn't take this lightly."

I suddenly realized that the shah was concerned that the radical fundamentalists were gaining ground. His unease was well founded: in August the nation would witness a series of demonstrations and arsons across the country, culminating on August 19, when the Islamists set twenty-eight cinemas on fire. The fire in the Cinema Rex in Abadan resulted in the deaths of 377 men, women, and children who had been watching a popular Iranian film.

The morning after the Cinema Rex tragedy, I asked Safi Asfia, "Why are we silent about this? Why don't we call this savagery by its name?"

"They are already attributing this to the government," he replied. "The more we say, the more it plays in the hands of the revolutionaries."

Shocked by the helplessness and inaction of my colleagues, I met with Prime Minister Amouzegar and explained to him the reports we were getting from our women activists around the country—the feelings of dread and anxiety from every corner of the country—and reports of the upheavals. I mentioned the suggestion our group offered—that he bring together a committee of cabinet officers as well as leaders of various civic organizations to discuss a strategy for confronting the revolutionaries. He said, "Why don't you speak with Asfia and go ahead with the plan."

"But we need your authority as well as intelligence reports. We have no clue what is happening and who is behind it all," I responded.

I couldn't believe it when he answered, "It's all in the newspapers."

Following this conversation, I decided to take my plea to the former prime minister, now minister of court, Amir Abbas Hoveyda. He received me pleasantly as always. When I described to him the reports we were getting, he said, "Why don't you speak to the prime minister?"

I described my conversation with Amouzegar and said, "At this point I believe we need a more holistic and radical reaction—something in the nature of the White Revolution with a whole new team to present to the people. At the very least we need His Majesty to make a strong statement and offer a plan."

After another hour of discussion, he picked up the phone and called the shah at his summer retreat. I listened to him render a more measured and less panicked version of what I had told him.

He put the receiver down and turned to me. "His Majesty agreed to have a television interview."

I asked, "Do you want us to get a group together and prepare an outline of a plan and some talking points for him?"

"No," he said. "He will make his own statement."

That worried me, but I decided to look at the positive side—the shah's acceptance of the critical nature of the situation.

On August 19, I attended a major event at the queen mother's residence. The interview with the shah was scheduled to air later that evening. My husband and I joined Hoveyda, the shah's half-brother Prince Gholam Reza, and a few others in the queen mother's television room to view it. After the interview, Hoveyda turned to us anxiously. It seemed as if he were hoping our reaction would be more positive than his own. Gholam and I were appalled. The shah had been completely unconvincing, had expressed no new ideas, given no justification or explanation for the fiasco that Rastakhiz had turned into,[4] and offered no specific path out of the nation's dilemma.

When we walked out into the garden, I turned to Hoveyda and said, "Please say something to the shah. Why are you silent? We have everything to lose and nothing to gain by silence."

Just then, the shah, accompanied by a few cabinet members walked toward us. As we stopped to let him pass, he asked Hoveyda, "Did you see the interview?" and before Hoveyda had a chance to answer, he turned to me and asked, "As a disinterested person, what did you think?"

All eyes turned to me. I glanced around and looked at him and said, "Me? Disinterested, Your Majesty? How could I be disinterested?" By then, someone else began talking, and he moved on.

Hoveyda turned to me with a sardonic smile and said, "Well, why didn't you say something? We have everything to lose and nothing to gain by silence."

Frustrated, I realized he was right, but I was also bothered by the rather unfair circumstance that made it challenging to offer a thoughtful and correct response, given the setting and the bevy of observers.

THE AMOUZEGAR cabinet resigned on August 27 following the Cinema Rex disaster. Chosen because of his connection to the more conservative clerical elements, Senate president Jafar Sharif-Emami was appointed prime minister, and the position of minister for women's affairs was eliminated as another gesture of appeasement to the right-wing revolutionaries. We all knew that the cause of women would be sacrificed in order to stop the revolutionary movement. I moved from my government office back to my office at the WOI. For a few days I felt numb. I read the papers with their contradictory messages and unverified news items with little emotion, except a diffuse feeling of dread at what seemed to lie ahead. Then I started thinking and wondering and planning again.

One of the first organizations to feel the brunt of the revolutionaries' rage, the WOI was a focal point of the attacks of the core revolutionaries, who feared and hated the accelerating change in women's condition and especially their changing role in the family. Our passage of the Family Protection Law had drastically reduced the power of the clerics throughout the country by taking the family out of their jurisdiction and bringing it under the umbrella of the secular judicial system. This, more than any other measure initiated by the WOI, angered the clerical establishment, since it not only negated their traditional beliefs about the role of women in the family and society but also threatened their livelihood and social clout.

That August my deputy, Ezzat, walked into my WOI office, looking agitated and angry. "The staff has decided to go on strike," she said.

"Really?" I smiled, rather pleased. My first thought was, "How wonderful to see women taking risks, speaking up, making demands." But seeing the expression on Ezzat's face, I wiped off the smile and walked with her to the large meeting room. There was little anger in our colleagues' faces. I said, "Friends, I would be the last person to discourage you from protest. However, I would like to bring it to your attention that if your protest succeeds and we close the offices, both the government and the opposition would be pleased. Unfortunately, we are not all that popular with either the government in power or with those seeking to replace them. It is useless for us to strike because we have no one to strike against but ourselves. In fact, we are at the center of the national argument. The government thinks of us as a nuisance in their effort to appease the religious opposition, and the opposition, even when it uses some of our own rhetoric as a camouflage, barely covers its intention of reversing all that we have achieved. And we, of course, have our grievances against both parties."

The staff went back to work. But they as well as some of the leaders were unaware at that point how hypocritical the opposition was in its statements about women and how many women were duped into thinking that the opposition's double talk about supporting freedom and democracy might mean a better agenda for women.[5]

One day I came back from a meeting to my office at the WOI and a sight that was, like many others during this period, both sad and incongruous. The toddlers sucking on their pacifiers were gathered outside the first-floor childcare center in the building waiting for their parents to pick them up. My colleagues told me there had been a telephoned bomb threat, along with a growing rumor that SAVAK was planning to destroy the building to give the revolutionaries negative publicity. For the first time in my life I picked up the phone and called the head of SAVAK. I asked him about the bomb threat.

He said, "Well, I know nothing of any such plan, but come to think of it perhaps it wouldn't be such a bad idea, of course on a day when the Secretary General is away from the building and . . ."

I realized the children's plight outside on the street had driven me to make myself the subject of mirth by the one person with whom I was not ready to share a joke.

The fact is we had contributed to the unrest by helping to raise the consciousness of Iranian women, who had been urged to know their own power and to mobilize themselves to assert their will. The director of the WOI's Kerman branch explained the masses of chador-clad women demonstrating in her city: "We kept saying 'mobilize the women.' We have, and now they *are* mobilized, and they're shouting, 'Down with the shah!'"

GRADUALLY THE atmosphere of unrest began to reflect itself in the schools and universities. Gholam and I had decided to enroll Babak for the fall 1978 term at his father's public high school, Alborz, which was led by the iconic headmaster Mr. Mojtahedi, legendary for his tough stance and high standards. Most of our friends' children attended French, British, or American schools; we thought that a purely traditional Iranian school would better prepare Babak for future leadership in Iran and spare him the personal conflict felt by those of our generation who had attended foreign-language schools—feeling at times superior and at times inferior to those brought up in a purely Persian context. Unfortunately, by the end of Babak's middle school period, the atmosphere among his classmates had become chaotic and divisive. His closest friend had been sent to Switzerland to attend the Institut Le Rosey, the boarding school the shah had attended. I wrote to Parviz Radji, our ambassador in Great Britain, to see if he could manage to get Babak into one of the better boarding schools there. He called to say there was too little time. "What's the rush?" he added. "Why don't you apply for next year? Why is everybody hysterical?" We decided to send Babak to my mother to attend high school in Carmel, California, where he was born.

In August 1978, the night before Babak left, he asked me, "When you went to high school in America, what did you say—how did you behave, so that the Americans would like you—what did you talk about?"

"Be yourself and I am sure the Americans will like you," I said. I knew from experience that the young Californians would be receptive and kind. Looking back, I was optimistic that being with Mother would provide him a kinder and softer transition than I had experienced. But my main concern was that in the United States he would be safe from any retaliation that might come from my work.

ON OCTOBER 5, 1978, as a favor to the shah, Saddam Hussein exiled Khomeini from Iraq to Kuwait. Rejected by Kuwait, Khomeini then was sent to France, where he was admitted after the shah told President Valéry Giscard d'Estaing he had no objection.

At the time, this seemed to me a good idea. In Iraq, Khomeini had been in constant communication with Iranian clerics and others who frequented the holy shrines there. In France, I thought, Iranian and other leftist students as well as the foreign media would discover his true worldview and recoil. I was wrong. Perhaps Khomeini's exotic behavior, image, and surroundings appealed to the progressives who wished for and imagined in him an Iranian Gandhi, as the leader of the hundreds of thousands of protestors on the streets of Tehran, even though they were by now shouting Islamist slogans interspersed with "Death to America and Israel!" I don't know whether their support for Khomeini was an act of willful denial, collective self-delusion, or both. But earlier, practicing taqiyeh, Khomeini's statements and slogans expressing belief in democracy, freedom of expression, and liberty had left a deep impression in Western countries, especially in the United States. The "unity of message" delivered by students like my sister, Farah, and her comrades in various splinter groups in the Confederation of Iranian Students was amazing—especially in the face of the fractious relationships among the groups and their animosity for each other.

WITH BABAK safely in California, I left Iran on October 8, 1978, tasked by the government to lead the negotiations with the legal team at the United Nations to draft an agreement between the government of Iran and the United Nations to set up the International Research and Training Institute for the Advancement of Women (INSTRAW)—the institution that Helvi Sipilä and I had envisioned and helped gain support for at the 1975 UN Mexico City conference. We had developed plans for the building and secured a site in Tehran. Our negotiations with the United Nations were mostly focused on INSTRAW's autonomy as a research and training institute. We hoped the board of trustees would be chosen on the basis of the members' scholarship and knowledge rather than politics, and that the institute would be as unencumbered by UN bureaucracy as possible.

During the early part of my New York trip, I stayed at the Waldorf Astoria Hotel on Park Avenue. Ardeshir Zahedi, the shah's son-in-law and Iran's ambassador to the United States, lodged exactly one floor above me and Hooshang Ansari, the minister of finance and economy, one floor below. One morning at a breakfast meeting in Ardeshir's suite, I sat sipping coffee as they each moved to the bedroom to speak with the shah and came back with news of his attitude and ideas. In those early days, every high-ranking member of the Iranian delegation wished to be part of my INSTRAW negotiations. But as we moved through the slow and cumbersome discussions, the news from Iran became increasingly dismal, and fewer and fewer high-ranking members joined in the talks.

By this time it had become obvious that Sharif-Emami had proved to be the wrong choice as prime minister. His strategy was to appease the clerics and other opposition members by arresting the regime's current officials, denigrating his own past, and promising to do what the clerics and opposition demanded. He, as many others, had misread Khomeini—the ayatollah was a "true believer": the more he was offered, the more convinced he became of the rectitude of his purpose and the inevitability of his victory. In fairness, it should also be said that Sharif-Emami did not have many choices available to him. The shah had refused to allow the military to take serious action, which would necessarily have led to bloodshed, given the opposition's adopted strategy designed to assure that such an outcome would be unavoidable.

In the first few days of November 1978, mobs ran virtually unchecked through Tehran, setting fire to the British embassy and dozens of other buildings in the capital. On November 5, Sharif-Emami resigned. That evening the shah appointed the military's joint chief of staff, General Gholamreza Azhari, a mild-mannered and clearly reluctant candidate, as prime minister. The idea of a military government kept the country calm for a while. Azhari bragged that he was in control and no one would dare to oppose him. Soon, however, the bravado stopped. The military regime proved unwilling to act, while the prime minister recited from the Quran and retreated as the opposition advanced.

In mid-November, after my daily meetings at the United Nations ended successfully with a draft agreement for the establishment in Tehran of INSTRAW, I ordered champagne. When we left the UN offices, my friend Mehdi, the only senior diplomat left on Iran's side, frowned. "You know I can understand that we would continue this work even while both of us know there is no chance that the government that sent us on this mission will be there when the agreement is signed. But what I can't fathom is your celebratory mood and the champagne."

"Well, I believe we have no choice but to go on as if . . ." I said.

At that point, I did not know that the UN Secretariat had suggested I lead INSTRAW in the interim.[6] When Jafar Nadim, Iran's deputy foreign minister, had presented the secretariat's suggestion to the Iranian cabinet, he had said that it was an excellent idea for Iran, but he then noted the downside: if I were to travel back to Iran, I would be using UN credentials and could not be arrested if the government's efforts to appease the revolutionaries required it.

EARLY IN the morning of November 27, 1978, came the phone call from Gholam that began my life in exile.

I could not go home, I did not know when or if I would see my husband again, and within months it would become clear that my safety even in the United States could not be guaranteed.

I decided I would go back to California, to my mother, grandmother, and Babak.

Chapter 11

Exile

THE FIRST MORNING IN my mother's house in Monterey at the height of the Revolution, I poured a cup of coffee and sat by the window. The rose bush looked weighed down with bright red flowers, and the grass, as always, was uneven and unruly. Everything seemed eerily similar to many other mornings I had spent there, except that Grandmother's arrival two years ago had brought a touch of the past with her. Now breakfast was more elaborate—a cheese tray with a variety of herbs, quince jam, whole apple compote with cardamom, homemade yogurt, and lavash bread—a colorful reminder of my childhood meals. Grandmother was more relaxed and content now that she was finally with her only daughter, in possession of a US passport, and supported by her Baha'i faith community.

As I began to imagine the day ahead, I suddenly realized this was the first working day in my adult life when I had no agenda and there was nowhere I had to be. No one needed me, not even Babak, who seemed fine in his new school in Carmel and in his own room in Mom's home. I began to realize that this was the beginning of life in exile.

My grandmother offered me toast, and my mother sipped her coffee while reading the paper. I looked at the three of us around the table and wondered what had caused us to make our choices. What would have happened if my grandmother had not decided that she needed the spiritual passion she had found in the Baha'i faith? What if my mother had been content to put up with the life my father offered—luxury, security, dependence? What if I had stayed at the university in Iran, teaching Virginia Woolf and offering advice to my students? Here we were, three women who like sparrows had hurled ourselves into a glass wall at every chance, with little hope of breaking out and reaching the sky. Somehow, though, we had ended up together.

Mother looked up from the paper. "Do you want to go to Carmel for a walk and a picnic on the beach?" she asked.

Grandmother began shifting in her chair, getting ready to stand. She knew there would be questions about her walking on the beach with her cane and the challenge of sitting on the sand. It also took her more time to get ready. She didn't want to provide any excuse to be left behind.

"It's still too early, Khanom Jan," I said, laughing, and they joined me, none of us knowing quite why we were laughing, except perhaps in appreciation of who we were and what we had done—my grandmother living for decades with diabetes, giving herself shots of insulin, never knowing whether at any moment, sitting on a bus or dozing off to sleep, her blood sugar might drop, putting her into a coma so that she would literally pass away. Each of my siblings and I had experienced such occasions when, quite by accident, one of us had awakened in the middle of the night and noticed her drooping in her chair over her sewing. Then we would feed her a glass of thick sugar water and watch her come back to life. Proximity to death had made her friends with it. She was not afraid. At eighty-three, Grandmother was still the most adventurous of all of us, ready to take part in whatever experience might promise something new, meaningful, or fun. Her smile crinkled the corners of her eyes and mouth and made me smile at my own predicament. "Come," she seemed to say to life. "Bring it on!"

Who was I not to follow?

Grandmother died on January 27, 1979, three days before Khomeini returned to Iran. Her last years were spent with her family in a country where she could live safely with her faith community. We buried her in the Monterey cemetery under a huge oak tree that from time to time one of us visits. I like to think of her presence there as a symbol that grounds five generations of our family in America.

I SPENT the next two months in a flurry of activity, as I monitored events in Iran—the growing number of demonstrations and strikes, the increasing violence—in a state of shock and disbelief. Cinemas and banks went up in flames across the country. The WOI centers received regular threats, but no center was actually attacked or burned. My colleague, Ezzat, led the organization bravely and efficiently. Unable to help, share the burden, or bring any solace to her and our other colleagues, I realized my connection to the organization was an added burden. I decided to write a letter of resignation. As I wrote "To the Central Council of the WOI," I pictured the faces of the women on the council, each one a leader of consequence either in the religious and ethnic minorities they represented or in the government or academia, and each a potential target of the revolutionaries. I began, "We have worked together and achieved much during the past decade. We have confronted many obstacles and succeeded in building a feminist infrastructure which will not be destroyed." I recalled the hours we had spent each week together, the tens of thousands of women we had reached throughout the country, and the lessons we had learned from them and from others in our travels around the world. I knew that no reactionary movement and no level of violence would be able to destroy what we had built. I ended with a pledge to continue my work for the women of Iran for the rest of my life. I read the letter to Ezzat over the phone, both of us fighting to hold back tears, both of us thinking not of the decade fast fading into the past but of the dark years ahead. I was reluctant to say goodbye, knowing that cutting the connection meant—literally—severing ties with my job, my cause, my country, and my home.

I put the receiver down, repeating to myself, "That's that. So much for that."

I PICKED up the phone. It was Farah. I heard only my sister's voice—I didn't think of politics. It was early February 1979, not long after Grandmother's death and just a week after Khomeini's return to Iran. Farah was in Germany waiting for the airplane the new government was sending to bring the revolutionary students back to Iran. It didn't occur to me at the time how odd it was that our positions had switched in such a short while. Nor did I imagine what the next turn in our fortunes would bring. I only thought of the last time I had seen Farah in America in her combat boots and sweatshirt, and I was sure the outfit would not work even in revolutionary Iran. "Do go to our house. You will need clothes. You will find everything in the closet. Sedigheh [our housekeeper] is there. She will help you."

"Yes," she said. "Okay."

"Take care of yourself," I said, and handed the receiver to Mother.

LATER THAT day Farah's husband, Faramarz, called. I greeted him as my brother-in-law; he was, after all, ready to travel to Iran after a decade. "When is your flight? Is the airport open?"

He paused for a moment. "You should return. You should answer for your deeds in the people's court."

I was dumbfounded. "Hold on," I said and handed the phone to Mother. Although Faramarz was the only one in the world who might call this number and talk to me like that, and although 90 percent of the calls those days were for me, I did not answer the phone again in my mother's house.

EARLY ONE morning after the Revolution, Senator Jacob Javits called. I had first met Jack and his wife, Marion, in 1975 at Princess Ashraf's house in Tehran. I hadn't seen much of Marion and Jack during that first trip to Iran, but Marion seemed to have decided from the outset that she wanted us to be friends. On her next trip, she wondered if she couldn't stay at my home. Her accommodations at the Tehran Hilton had an excellent view of the Alborz Mountains, but she said she preferred to stay with friends when she traveled overseas.

During the next few years, we met regularly in New York and Tehran and become close family friends. But hearing Jack's voice without an initial intervention by an assistant or intermediary on a working day, I knew the news would be important, and at that moment in history it could not be anything but bad.

He said, "Mahnaz, I wanted to call before you woke up and saw the paper. There will be news and terrible photos of the execution of Prime Minister Hoveyda and several other colleagues of yours. It is terrible. I am sorry. I just wanted to let you know that we have indications that this will be stopped. There will be no more."

I hung up and rushed to the front door to get the paper. I was afraid yet desperate to see the photos, and they were as shocking as Jack had said—there were my colleagues' naked, bullet-ridden torsos. Hoveyda and others had been executed by firing squads in the yard of Tehran's Qasr Prison shortly after their secret trials by an Islamic revolutionary court had ended with death sentences. Even worse than seeing the photos, Jack's prediction turned out to be illusory. The Islamic government was unlike anything the United States had dealt with, and the savagery would continue for quite a while.

It was during this time that Marion, Jack, and their children became my American family in exile. They included me and my family in every major event of their lives, and when not with my mother in California, I stayed with Marion in New York as I tried to rebuild some kind of life in the United States: I met with colleagues at the United Nations, political leaders introduced by Marion and Jack, and media personalities. I also found myself trying to prepare for the establishment of a new institution for Iranian studies.

Marion's conversations, filled with scenes of celebrities—senators, movie stars, and tycoons—came together smoothly in a colorful tapestry. She was a true choreographer of dialogue at her dinner table, bringing out the best in each guest and making everyone feel special. She always brought me into these conversations with affectionate good taste, but not without some creativity. For some months she described me as a poet, until I insisted that she save me from being asked to recite something. I explained that even though I had taught poetry, I had never written a single poem.

Even though Marion was nearer my mother's age, we could giggle together in girlish companionship on long walks through the streets of Manhattan. She loved the city and made every walk to a mundane destination an occasion in itself. At every step it seemed we ran into people she knew. She would exchange good-spirited kisses and hellos, trade quick bits of news, bring me into the conversation in some charming way, and on leaving would tell me stories of their past connections, their dramas, their enormously successful deals, films, political achievements, and their beautiful villas, yachts, wives, and lovers.

Manhattan was brimming with these stories, and Marion knew them all and witnessed many up close. This scene was different from what I had known in Iran, but in some way the same. At home, I would have walked into an event and there would have been connections, information, family ties, or joint interests with those around me. But it would have been less glamorous and more subdued. Moving through life in Iran was less like experiencing a festival, and more like flowing along with the waters of a river. Staying in Marion's home, watching her manage her life and relate to her friends, being part of her scene, was a diversion from the life I knew I had lost but whose loss I could not yet believe was permanent.

DURING THE first months after the revolutionaries came to power, chaos reigned in the exile community. The shah—frail, ill with cancer, and perplexed—was forced to move from country to country. Leaders of Western nations, always focused on Iran's oil and looking to a future with the Islamic government, shunned the man they had once courted so vigorously and praised so profusely. Some former high-level government leaders distanced themselves from their own past and criticized the shah in even harsher terms than the opposition. Several members of the elite who had been personal friends with Princess Ashraf were horrified to hear of her son's murder on a

Paris street, shot in the back by an Islamic Republic agent as he was entering his home. I had to encourage more than one friend to get in touch with her, reminding them of how hard it is to be isolated in a time of sorrow by those who once befriended you.

I had already decided I would not abandon her. Nothing had changed in her character or her history, and I could not alter my behavior toward her simply because her fortunes had changed. For me, this was part of an attempt to put together an identity for myself that involved ownership of my past and of the work that I loved and took pride in. The princess had been a significant part of that past. An aspect of putting myself back together was looking into my own eyes in the mirror each morning to check and see how much I had changed in my struggle for survival and to decide whether I could live with the change.

Nader Naderpour, Iran's beloved poet, once told me, "After the Revolution, our society feels like a banquet table where the cloth has been pulled away. All the objects are helter-skelter. Nothing is in its previous position or place. Politicians are now poets. Businessmen are politicians. No one is who he or she was. Our confusion and stress are in great part due to the chaos." Yet in the early days of the Revolution, Princess Ashraf's home in New York reminded me of the old order. I was fully aware that that world was rapidly vanishing, but there were still signs of the country I had known and loved, and from that I drew comfort and some illusion of stability. At her home, she was still the princess who gave her seat at the head of the table at a dinner to the young man who was the crown prince. To her, I represented the government. Her table was one place where people still sat according to protocol: everyone had their specific role and assigned place. But since tradition was now topsy-turvy, the room, the people—the entire scene—had an air of unreality. Yet there was comfort in it, like the blanket my little boy hung on to years after it had lost its original shape and use.

During the decade that I had worked with the princess, I had both over- and underestimated her. I had not known her during the early days of her brother's rule when she was more involved in political affairs, and I would learn much of her history from the memoir she later wrote. I only recently saw on YouTube a few clips of her at age twenty-five holding her own in a meeting with Stalin, the Soviet Union's brutal dictator, and the ceremony in which she received the Soviet Union's medal of honor. Over years of working with her, I found she was smarter and more courageous than I had given her credit for. She was also funny and self-deprecating, though quick to react to any attempt to cross the line of appropriate behavior. At times she was careless about other people's feelings and more materialistic than I would have liked. Other times, she would not sit still to read a document that I had worked on over days or weeks. She would say, "Tell me about it," yet not listen very attentively when I tried to explain. At one point when I told her that we really needed to work to bring about change in the employment conditions of women, she asked, "Haven't our women become equal?" But when I presented her with the grand plan that I had drawn up with Helvi Sipilä for Iran's collaboration with the United Nations, she immediately accepted the challenge, grasping the importance of making Iran a focal point for UN activities on women's empowerment. She saw that Iran's ability to offer financial support for these efforts, its special position among the nonaligned nations, and its friendly relations with both the Soviet Union and the United States made it an important player in the international community. Once she had a green light from the shah, she followed through, lobbying everyone concerned and mobilizing financial support from the government. She worked long and hard hours at the United Nations, meeting daily with the Iranian delegation and listening to their explanations about every issue that was being discussed at the General Assembly and Iran's position on each point. She prepared herself carefully for her presentations and sat through endless speeches during working hours and sometimes through excruciating shoptalk at the dinners she hosted or attended.

At the height of the Revolution the royal court announced that members of the royal family would resign from their charitable activities. I asked her if she would give up the title of honorary president of the WOI. She answered, "I will resign nothing that I have believed in or worked for. Let them fire me."

IN EARLY September 1979, a friend with good contacts in the revolutionary government called to tell me to urge Gholam to leave Iran. Almost a year after my husband had called me in New York to give me the queen's message to stay in America, I was in the unenviable position of calling him and relaying our friend's message that there would not be a chance for him to receive a passport and leave through the airport.

I knew how painful that would be for him, even though he had been living in hiding in Iran for several months already. He was and is such a totally "proper" person. Anything irregular, anything against the law, even though he did not believe in the legitimacy of the source of the law, was anathema to him. But even worse, this meant that once he left with a false passport, he would not be able to return. He found the very idea of crossing the border illegally—as defined by authorities on both sides of the border—distressing in itself.

A few days later, he called to tell me he had contacted the first postrevolutionary prime minister, Mehdi Bazargan, a former colleague at the National

University who was one of the remaining leaders of the broader revolutionary opposition movement, to ask his advice. Bazargan had responded that he was unable to help, and he advised Gholam to remain in hiding, which implied that Bazargan's own position was uncertain.

I put the phone down, wondering what to do. For the first time in exile I felt helpless and paralyzed. There was no option for regular travel, and Gholam could not stay in hiding indefinitely. I called the princess. She asked about Gholam, and when I started telling her about our dilemma, I burst out crying and hung up. It is a sign of our unusual circumstance that the only time I have hung up on anyone in my life it was on the princess.

A few weeks later I heard from Gholam that he had been contacted and told that arrangements were made for a clandestine border crossing. Even though she never mentioned it to me, we knew the princess had arranged this.

Finally, on October 20, 1979, Mother, Babak, and I met Gholam at the airport in Monterey. For nearly a year, I had hoped and prayed every day that he would be able to leave Iran safely, and that he would not be hurt on his own account as well as on mine. But the joy and relief of his arrival was tempered by the realization that my strongest connection with home was now severed. To make things even more uncomfortable, we were all almost shy and tentative with each other. He was wearing his old brown leather jacket and looked the same; not that much time had passed. But the drastic change in our world had changed how we saw each other. It seemed to me as if we were time travelers crossing paths, learning anew everything about each other.

Gholam told us of his border crossing—how he and his guide had to wait until midnight to bypass the Iranian border guardhouse undetected and run up the hill that separated Iran and Turkey; how once over the hill he had felt terribly sad and crestfallen when the guide said, "You are now in Turkey and safe." When I opened his suitcase to help him unpack, I discovered underneath other clothing his black tuxedo. He has never fully explained what made him pack it in the suitcase he knew he would have to carry as he walked—sometimes ran—in the dark, across the Turkish border. Perhaps it represented an image of the life he imagined he might live, or perhaps it was simply a gesture of defiance. We later learned that he narrowly escaped arrest when guards broke into his brother's apartment at dawn shortly after they had left to drive to the border to meet with the smugglers. His was a story we had heard many versions of from friends and colleagues escaping the horrors of the Islamist Revolution, and one that we'd go on to hear many more times. The most horrendous among them for me would become my sister's trek from Tehran to America a few years later.

It took us a few months to contact friends, including George Lenczowski, Gholam's professor and mentor at the University of California at Berkeley. He arranged for a visiting scholar position for Gholam at Stanford. For a year we lived in Palo Alto, where Gholam wrote his book on the Revolution, aptly titled *The Iranian Revolution: Thanatos on a National Scale*. As a political scientist, he could explain the shortcomings of the political system and the mistakes made by the leading members of the political elite, but he couldn't decipher what could logically drive not only the religious fundamentalists but also nationalists, democrats, and a wide range of intellectuals on the left and right to unite in massive demonstrations in support of something as absurdly outdated as velayat-e faqih. It must have been, he thought, a kind of Thanatos—death wish or mass suicide.

For a short while we led a reasonably normal life: Babak joined us to attend Menlo College, where he did well, and we lived in an apartment in the small town of Menlo Park. I had a chance to think through what I might want to do and what kind of job might be available to me. In my head I relived the day I walked down Market Street in San Francisco as a teenager, entering any establishment that seemed likely to hire a young woman with no special skills. The difference was that now I had the privilege of having unusual and valuable experiences, but I also bore the weight of the false reputation that was fast spreading about the government I was associated with and the institutions that I had worked to build. On the one hand, I was being considered for a high-level job at the United Nations, which, no doubt, the government of the Islamic Republic would object to vociferously. On the other, my letter inquiring about a possible temporary fellowship at Princeton was sent back to me, a sentence scrawled across the type-written text, "There is no position for you at Princeton!" I also thought of going into entirely different fields—selling real estate, opening a video-rental shop, teaching women's studies. Nothing was impossible, but everything was improbable. I knew already that to find the right path for my future, I would have first to put together the pieces of myself carefully and gently to avoid lasting damage.

I would have to build on the passions and learning of my past. But I also had to come to terms with my present, the condition of exile. I was now a woman for whom a change in government had become life-threatening, both inside and outside. In order to understand my own condition, I had to look at the lives of others. Was it accurate to say that women like me were in a state of exile in their own country before events made it impossible for them to remain? Were they ostracized, kept at a distance, ghettoized? Were they glamorized, made unreal, made bigger than life or different from the reality of their existence? Were they cheapened, defamed? Were their personalities and identities attacked? Were they first crushed and then thrown out or made to flee? Did they have to carry out a double battle of building their own identity while building a new life to suit that identity? How was it—the process of rebuilding an identity, figuring out who you are, despite the fears and doubts and uncertainties regarding self, values, and worth? Did they have to become more fiercely adamant about their beliefs, more assertive about their capacities and potential? Did they become meeker and more subservient and flexible so as not to break? What was the internal dialogue? How did they find the answer to "Who am I?" How did they relate it to "Where am I?" And then, "Will I ever go back again?"

The exigencies of each situation, the slow understanding of something gone, finished, over—something that can never be again: reality, like a bowl, has given shape to the liquid which is the self. If that is impossible to recapture—the innocence, the energy, the hope, the optimism, the laughter, the becoming, the bravery of those who have not been hurt yet, the courage of the child whose fingers have not been burned yet in reaching for the flame—all that is replaced by a vague muttering of "That's not it at all, that's not what I meant at all," and then "Would it have been worth it after all?"

ABOVE
Mahnaz Afkhami's
grandmother, Tooba
Naficy, in California.

LEFT
Mahnaz Afkhami's father,
Majid Ebrahimi.

Mahnaz Afkhami's mother, Ferdows
Naficy.

Mahnaz and Gholam on their
wedding day, 1959.

TOP	BOTTOM
Helvi Sipilä, Ferdows Naficy, and Betty Friedan, Persepolis, 1974.	Mahnaz Afkhami at the Preparatory Committee for the First UN Women's Conference in Mexico, 1975.

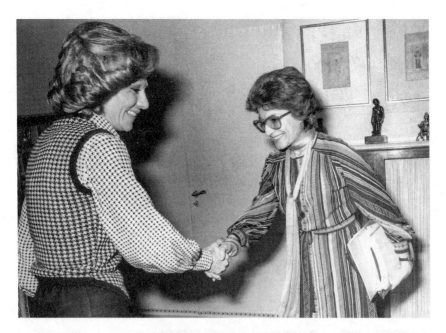

Mahnaz Afkhami meets with the queen
after her appointment to the cabinet,
January 1976.

Mahnaz with Princess Ashraf and the
governor of Khorasan at the grave of
Khayyam.

TOP

Mahnaz Afkhami, minister for women's
affairs (*fourth from left*), and Mohammad
Reza Shah at Norooz ceremony.

BOTTOM

Mahnaz Afkhami and Rosalynn Carter in
Tehran, 1977.

152

Iran Cabinet members with Prime Minister Amouzegar, 1978;
Mahnaz Afkhami in the second row.

Iran's "First Women" (*left to right*): Mahnaz Afkhami (first minister for women),
Nayereh Entehaj-Sami (first congresswoman), and Mehrangiz Dowlatshahi
(first female ambassador from Iran).

Board of Directors of the Foundation for Iranian Studies:
Mahnaz Afkhami and Princess Ashraf (*seated*), (*left to right, standing*)
Gholam Afkhami, Ahmad Ghoreishi, Amin Alimard, Akbar Etemad, and Abdol Samii.

Farah and Mahnaz with their mother, Ferdows, and Farah's daughter Neda with her pink panther on the day of Farah's and Neda's arrival in Washington, D.C.

TOP	BOTTOM
Sima Wali, Dorothy Thomas, Mahnaz Afkhami, and Hilkka Pietilä, UN Conference on Human Rights 1993 in Vienna.	Mahnaz and Hillary Clinton, meeting, autumn 1999.

TOP	BOTTOM
(*left to right*) WLP advisory members Hafsat Abiola, Asma Khader, Noeleen Heyzer, Leticia Shahani, and Mahnaz Afkhami at the State of the World Forum, 1999.	Leaders of the original WLP partners (*left to right*): Rabéa Naciri (Morocco), Asma Khader (Jordan), Mahnaz Afkhami, Amina Lemrini (Morocco), and Ayesha Imam (Nigeria), at the meeting to launch *Leading to Choices*, 2001.

TOP	BOTTOM
(*left to right*) Mahnaz Afkhami, Melanne Verveer, Madeleine Albright, Queen Rania, Marian Wright Edelman, and Mary Robinson, Global Women's Action Network for Children, 2004.	(*left to right*) Jacqueline Pitanguy, Mary Robinson, Mahnaz Afkhami, and Musimbi Kanyoro, at the WLP Transnational Partners Convening on Climate Justice, 2019.

TOP
Mahnaz with her sister, Farah.

BOTTOM
Mahnaz with the poet Nader Naderpour.

TOP	BOTTOM
Mahnaz with Marian Wright Edelman and Frances Kissling.	Mahnaz Afkhami's son, Babak, and granddaughter, Saphora, age two.

PART II

Chapter 12

Choosing Alliances
and Moving Forward

O N NOVEMBER 4, 1979, a group of radical students climbed over
the walls of the US Embassy in Tehran and took the diplomatic
personnel hostage. Their action was quickly validated by Ayatollah
Khomeini, who, sensing weakness in the American president, Jimmy Carter,
used the occasion to strengthen his own position and that of his allies inside the
country. He also grasped the opportunity to gain power and authority in the
Middle East and North Africa (MENA) region and elsewhere in the Muslim
world, especially among those who saw in his challenge to America a "David
and Goliath" humiliation of the powerful.

An Islamist revolutionary woman who called herself "Mary" became
spokesperson for the hostage takers. The woman, Massumeh Ebtekar, had
spent her childhood in Philadelphia and was chosen for her fluency in English.
During this period, I watched her regularly televised interviews with their
hateful messages about America's misdeeds. It was exceptionally difficult for
me to hear her anti-American rhetoric, but even more so because many in
the Iranian diaspora assumed "Mary" to be my sister, Farah—they were both

young, American-educated, media-savvy revolutionaries. However, Farah was a progressive leftist who even then did not attack America. Ms. Ebtekar's vehemence during this period led to a stellar career, and finally, to vice presidency of the Islamic Republic.

During this period, the regime had nearly limitless media attention and a global audience, as well as acolytes who devoted considerable energy to depicting themselves as representatives of the Iranian people and assigning guilt to the United States for a variety of misdeeds, chief among them the downfall of Prime Minister Mohammad Mossadegh, who had been instrumental in nationalizing Iran's oil a quarter of a century before. Never mind that Khomeini and his followers had no love for Mossadegh, a secular prime minister who belonged to the Qajar aristocracy and who had been associated with the power elite during his entire career. Nonetheless, they succeeded in conferring legitimacy to the students' action. The students' success, in turn, helped fictionalize the immunity of diplomatic corps in international law.

High-level American officials, fearing harm to their diplomats, publicly apologized for US actions in Iran in the 1950s, in effect accepting the preposterous idea that the hostage-taking was justified as a response to the grievances of the "freedom-loving" revolutionaries. The publicity Khomeini gained was priceless. His every word was awaited with bated breath and endlessly analyzed. In his exile in Neauphle-le-Château, France, he had insisted that he was not after power and that he would not interfere in the governing process. Now he was the absolute ruler, commander of the armed forces, and vicar of the whole nation. He and his followers justified his complete about-face from before to after the Revolution as taqiyeh.

In a reversal of accepted journalistic practice, the Western press made no effort to check facts or require proof for the revolutionaries' wild statements and accusations. The Khomeini crowd launched absurd propaganda campaigns against the policies and actions of the previous government leaders. People inside and outside Iran seemed to believe it all. Andrew Young, the civil rights activist and US ambassador to the United Nations, said, "Khomeini will eventually be hailed as a saint"; Carter's ambassador to Iran, William Sullivan, said, "Khomeini is a Gandhi-like figure"; and Senator Ted Kennedy and others talked about the "umpteen billions" the shah had taken out of Iran and sent abroad.[1] It was said that there were hundreds of thousands of political prisoners and that most had been tortured in horrendous ways. My own stepmother once blurted out, "Gholam is on a list saying he has wired $17 million to the US."

"Are you *nuts*?" I replied.

"How do you know—maybe he didn't tell you?" she said. This happened when Gholam was in hiding in Iran while I shared a bedroom with my grandmother at my mother's house in Monterey and drove a Toyota for which my mother had cosigned the loan.

The hostage crisis also nullified the concept of political asylum. Just a year before, President Carter had praised the shah and said, "There is no leader with whom I have a deeper sense of personal gratitude and personal friendship." He was far from the only US president to consider the shah an ally: eight US presidents had considered the shah a close, reliable, and progressive ally and force in the developing world. If such a friend, who if returned to his own country would face the most egregious acts of savagery, did not qualify for asylum in the United States, then who would?

But now the shah had become a pawn in Khomeini's power game. In its desperation over the hostage crisis, the US government and others looked for ways to appease Khomeini, who continued to insist that the shah be extradited to Iran. UN secretary general Kurt Waldheim offered a proposal to form a commission of inquiry—a sort of international investigation for "the crimes" of the shah, as a way of pacifying the Ayatollah. On February 20, 1980, in the midst of these negotiations, I received an invitation to meet with the princess.

I WALKED into the ballroom at 625 Park Avenue, the princess's residence, and sat down gingerly next to the princess, at the edge of the couch, not knowing what to expect. I had been invited to a meeting, but no other details had been offered—unusual compared to my other appointments with her. The princess introduced me to two men, Robert Armao, a representative of the shah's good friend David Rockefeller and a consultant of the shah in exile, and a tall blond man, apparently a public relations expert, who sat together on the couch facing us.

The princess explained that these gentlemen were supporters of the monarchy who wanted to launch a media campaign to help us tell the truth about the Revolution to the American people. They were looking for someone credible to go on Sunday talk shows to "clear" the shah's record. He was being charged with corruption and misuse of public funds, as well as torture.

"I have told them how well you speak and how well-liked you are," the princess said.

"I am sorry, Your Highness, I don't believe I am the right person to do what you ask," I said awkwardly.

Armao, who was at the time the shah's spokesperson, thought I felt over-awed by the possibility of going on *Meet the Press* or *Face the Nation* and said, "Don't worry, we will tell you what to say."

I knew that the charges against the shah, like much of the propaganda from the Islamic Republic, were bogus and had little to do with reality. But I was neither a lawyer nor his spokesperson, nor was I in possession of specific information about the issues at hand. The undertone of sexism in Armao's comment also irked me, although he seemed oblivious to it. Had he been addressing one of my male counterparts, he would have been more respectful of their knowledge and capabilities.

Feeling guilty that I was unable to help, I turned to the princess and repeat-ed, "I am not the right person for this. I know nothing of His Majesty's finances or of the security apparatus, except for my gut feeling about the injustice of the charges. I could not present a compelling case on his behalf. I would be more than willing to speak about my work, or, if His Majesty wishes to appoint me as his spokesperson, I would be glad to speak in that capacity." I said this only in response to Armao's patronizing comment, knowing such an appointment would be totally out of the question on the shah's part as well as mine.

The meeting ended rather abruptly. I walked downstairs to the sitting room with the princess, who was visibly upset.

"I am sorry I can't be more helpful, Your Highness."

She turned to me with tears in her eyes, her hands shaking in her lap, her voice breaking. "All these years I have done whatever you have asked me. I have never questioned your choices or your judgment. I have supported you without reservation. You have often critiqued my choice of companions, my way of doing things, and shown little respect for what I have done. And the only thing I have ever asked you to do for me, you refuse."

I looked at the frail woman in her delicate chiffon blouse, sitting on the oversized couch, shaking and nearly sobbing to a penniless, powerless exile over twenty years her junior, and I wished with all my heart that there was something I could do to make things different. But "things" were what they were, and life was what it was, and there was nothing either of us could do to change them. I took her hand, held it for a moment, brought it to my lips, and murmured, "I am sorry."

After the Revolution, I saw glimpses of her courage and loyalty in her sus-tained faith in her brother and her love for him. She focused on the shah's excru-ciating journey as he sought asylum while dealing with his terminal cancer, offering support and shelter to his family. In one of the more embarrassing historical decisions by an American president, the shah was refused asylum in the United States and forced to move from Egypt to Morocco to the Bahamas, where his cancer flared, then to Mexico, where he had peace for a short time after the worsening of his cancer forced the United States to admit him for treatment, then to Panama while the Carter administration negotiated with the Islamic Republic the terms of his expulsion to Iran, and finally, thanks to his loyal friend President Anwar Sadat of Egypt, he arrived in Cairo on March 24, 1980. There, that July, two and a half years after hosting the American president in Tehran on New Year's Eve, the shah passed away at the age of sixty. Princess Ashraf attended her brother's state funeral in Cairo organized by President Sadat. For ten years she wore only total black in mourning.

DURING THIS period the home front in Iran grew daily more violent, politically more extremist, and culturally more retrograde. Ad hoc revolutionary groups roamed the streets. Homes were raided to search for any sign of alcohol, playing cards, chess sets, photographs of unveiled women, and books of poetry, including the major literature classics such as the *Shahnameh* (the *Book of Kings*) and the sonnets of Hafez, Iran's most beloved poet. Iranians left the country by the tens of thousands.

Those Iranians who came to America, including thousands of US university alumni whose education had been sponsored by the government, clamored for what was lost or quite suddenly forbidden in Iran. News related to the US embassy hostages, as well as the wildness and violence displayed on the streets of the cities, was ever-present in the media. The new exiles were vexed at the negative image of Iran and Iranians taking shape in the minds of Americans and subtly taking root in their own minds as well.

Dealing with my own identity as an exile made it necessary to counter the Islamic Republic's narrative of my homeland. For the Iranian community, I felt it was important to present the authentic culture of Iran to ourselves and our children as well as to our new country. I knew from experience that a sense of self—an understanding of one's identity—is the foundation for building a new life. The Revolution's sudden and drastic revision of the core cultural values that defined what it meant to be "Persian" damaged our sense of self. Everything we had cherished of the ancient and the modern in our culture was vilified. Any connections with our pre-Islamic history, art, and culture, as well as our modern values, were banned. We felt like broken vessels that needed to be put back together gently and expertly, so that even though we would never be what we had been, we would at least bear a close resemblance to our former selves. I began to see my personal and civic mission as one to initiate an effort to set up a center that would provide what Iranians inside and outside the country seemed to cry out for as they shaped their new identity in exile—access to their arts, history, and culture.

This effort brought together the two strands of my past life. One was the connection to literature and the arts, the other, the experience of working with women and helping to strengthen and expand the movement for equal rights. Several of our younger former colleagues were enthusiastic about the project and helped shape the concept, among them Akbar Etemad, formerly head of the Atomic Energy Commission of Iran; Abdol Samii, former minister of higher education; Ahmad Ghoreishi, former chancellor of the National University of Iran; Jalal Matini, former chancellor of Mashhad University; Amin Alimard, former editor of the journal *Jahan-e Now* and head of Organization for State Administration and Employment; and my husband, Gholam, former deputy minister of interior and head of the National Institute for Adult Literacy. They agreed to serve on the board of the planned institution.

Affluent Iranian industrialists and financiers, like those in most other non-Western countries, were not yet familiar with the American philanthropic tradition. Their notion of philanthropy was contributing to charitable causes, especially religious institutions that promised divine appreciation and a place in heaven. I wrote a simple plan and traveled to New York to present it to Princess Ashraf, the only source I could count on. She was at that time under extraordinary pressure to use her resources to support counterrevolutionary efforts. She contributed to newspapers, networks, and projects provided by former generals, prime ministers, and even some who had worked for the opposition before being expelled by the Islamic Republic. Knowing her, I was certain she would come to realize that I had been justified in refusing to participate in the poorly thought-out media campaign to defend the shah. It helped that the press had soundly criticized the absurd negotiations between the UN secretary general and the Khomeini government.

Her longing for intellectual ventures, stifled in her youth when she was kept at home while her brother was sent to Switzerland for schooling, was awakened by this purely academic, cultural, and educational endeavor. She liked my suggestion to create a foundation that would provide a safe space for objective research by scholars with a wide array of opinions and positions, in areas such as politics, sociology, and the arts that were banned in the Islamic Republic. The four specific projects were the creation of an Oral History Archive that would record the eyewitness account of Iran's contemporary history in areas such as politics, education, economics, women, labor, the arts, foreign relations, and opposition groups, among others; the publication of a quarterly journal of literature, history, and the humanities; the organization of conferences, lectures, concerts, and exhibitions—especially those that would not be allowed in Iran; and finally, the publication of literature classics that were banned in Iran, as well as the reprinting of Persian school books free of the new fundamentalist jargon being taught in the Islamic Republic, for use by the children of Iranian exiles in America and elsewhere. A crosscutting focus in all areas of research and activity was the evolving status of women in twentieth-century Iran.

Later at dinner the princess spoke with enthusiasm and energy about the project. Members of her entourage, which included a former ambassador, her chief of staff, two former ladies-in-waiting, and assorted relations who lived elsewhere but visited regularly, were unenthusiastic and remained so throughout the years. Keeping her interest and support was not easy; she was pressured from all sides to support political activities focused on reestablishing the monarchy in Iran. In the meantime, her primary preoccupation was her brother, who, dying of cancer for the last two years of his life, was forced to travel from country to country, unable to settle in one place or receive proper medical care. The financial contribution I asked of her was miniscule by comparison. But this was one venture that she found exciting. After a few meetings she signed on to the project and provided funding for the Foundation for Iranian Studies (FIS). Registered in New York in 1981 with an endowment of $2 million, the proceeds from which allowed us to begin our work, FIS relied heavily on joint projects with academic institutions, universities, and museums interested in Persian arts, literature, history, and culture.

But the funding was only a small part of the challenge. A divided and defeated diaspora community that had lost so much and encompassed widely diverse views, each holding the other responsible for their predicament, was not easy to bring together. Princess Ashraf's outsized negative image among the Iranian opposition and some Westerners was another challenge. Like other powerful women of her generation, especially those who focused on equality for women, she was demonized by the Far Right as well as the Left. But in the prerevolutionary period, the proportions gained by the myths were absurd—such as that she had set an opposition journalist on fire or that she was engaged in smuggling opium. Women of power in positions of leadership were—and still are—subjected to horrific negative propaganda of absurd proportions. A similar example would be the rumors about Hillary Clinton, among them, that she murdered Vince Foster (the White House lawyer who had committed suicide) or that she led a child-trafficking ring from the basement of a pizza restaurant on Connecticut Avenue in Washington, D.C. I had experienced a milder version of this when a postrevolutionary article stated that I had worn a see-through blouse and knee-high boots, drunk whisky, and spoken English on a cabinet trip to Baluchestan province.

I had decided from the beginning to claim my own actions and decisions, past and present, no matter how they were portrayed by others. Unlike many of my former colleagues in the prerevolution government, I did not undervalue or minimize my role in the cabinet in Iran. Neither did I edit out the narrative of my personal and career connections with the royal women. I was proud of them and their work and of what I had accomplished not *through* them but with their tacit support. I did not know what would happen with FIS, an organization openly funded by the princess. But I hoped that transparency and walking the talk with regards to tolerance and openness would win the day.

MARION JAVITS kindly offered me her apartment in Washington to stay in as I searched for an apartment of our own. Jack Javits gave Babak a Senate internship, which, important as it was as a learning experience, was also reassuring for us as we tried to find our place in our new country after yet another move following the Revolution. In January 1981, Gholam and Babak drove from California to our new home in Washington. Gholam considered it a "rediscovering of America and reintroducing Babak to his country of birth."

I was fortunate to have Ezzat Aghevli, my capable deputy from the WOI, with me to help set up the Foundation for Iranian Studies. Her calm, dignified presence was especially helpful at the beginning when we were dealing with such preliminary issues as renting a suitable office and registering as a non-profit, tax-exempt organization in Washington. Because the Islamic Republic's extrajudicial murders were reported so often in the media, we had difficulty convincing landlords to lease office space to us. When we identified our past positions to convince them we were not Islamic extremists, they worried that the extremists would come to murder us and ruin the reputation of their buildings as safe spaces.

If these challenges were not enough as we were forming FIS, my first appearances in the Middle East Studies Association (MESA) and Society for Iranian Studies conferences, where my compatriot scholars came to connect and to present their work, were marked with unexpected ups and downs. The young Iranian professors and graduate students who participated in these professional conferences had lived their scholarly life mainly in the 1960s and 1970s, when the West, especially the United States, had been radicalized by the Vietnam War and leftist movements. Many Iranian students whose schooling was subsidized by the Iranian government to train for their country's development plans were immersed in these movements—ranging from Leninism and Maoism to

Enver Hoxha's Albanian communism. At the time of the Iranian Revolution some—like my sister, Farah, and her group—went back to Iran to participate in it. Many of those who survived the new regime came back as exiles to the West. Those who stayed abroad had not experienced the evolution of Iranian society and the changes that had happened in their country during the 1960s and 1970s. The media focus on Iran and the growing propaganda from far right and far left ideologues was a powerful influence.

In my case as an exile, I had Farah and her friends to deal with at home and the scholarly community whose collaboration I sought for FIS projects at work. But the amazing support of the exile community, especially women writers, artists, politicians, and scholars, was a powerful source of optimism. All in all, the offer of a safe space for dialogue among a divided community and the opportunity to present the best in Iranian history and literature in events, lectures, and writings won the day. In one of the early meetings, a woman colleague asked, "How can you throw yourself like a sparrow flying into a window of glass, again and again? It must hurt—the act of shattering." I smiled and quoted Forough Farokhzad, my favorite poet:

> It's not about anxious whispers in the dark.
> It's about sunlight, open windows, and fresh air
> And a furnace wherein useless things are burned
> And a world pregnant with new seedlings
> And birth and ripening and pride.[2]

ONE OF the devastating outcomes of the Revolution was the destruction of records and the rewriting of history. I had lost my own diaries, notes, photos, and documents when our house in Tehran was confiscated after the Revolution. The WOI's records were destroyed when Azam Taleghani, Ayatollah Taleghani's daughter, took over the WOI's offices. During my travels to New York in the early 1970s I had learned about the growing field of oral history and had become familiar with the archives at Columbia University, the forerunner in the field. I became personally focused on learning more about the field and on establishing an Oral History Archive at FIS. Roland Grele, director of the Oral History Research Office at Columbia, and Elizabeth Mason, president of the newly created Oral History Association, were very supportive.

We selected the individuals who were to be trained to conduct the interviews from a pool of highly educated Iranian men and women in the United States and Europe. Of the ten interviewers selected for the first phase of the program, eight had PhDs in the social sciences, including political science, history, literature, economics, and communication. Elizabeth Mason came to Washington, D.C., trained our team of interviewers for two weeks, and helped create the framework for conducting, transcribing, and cataloging the interviews. Later, in the foreword she wrote for the program catalog, she reflected,

> Although I had taught a course in oral history methodology at Columbia University for the previous ten years, I had never dealt with students like these now seeking guidance. For one thing, they were mature and experienced professionals of the highest rank in their fields, a far cry from the typical graduate student. For another, they had themselves known the anguish and dislocation of political exile; the stories they would record would resonate with deep emotional echoes from their own lives. Could they learn to be honest and dispassionate interviewers, willing to probe sensitive episodes in which they too might have been participants?
>
> The more I considered the invitation, the more I was tempted by it: what a challenge, to develop a methodology with scholars of this calibre; what an opportunity to examine and apply oral history theories to recording contemporary political crises. . . . It did not take me long to accept.
>
> The week I spent in Washington that summer was an extraordinary one. . . . I rejoiced in the response, the commitment, the excitement which I felt from everyone. At the end of the initial training period, I believed wholeheartedly in the project.[3]

I visited a number of major archives, including at the Library of Congress and the University of California, and spoke with Iranians in a variety of fields to help create a roster of interviewees. It took us a decade to create an archive of more than a thousand hours of recordings with 180 scholars, writers, artists, and leaders in government, civic organizations, women's groups, labor unions, and opposition parties. Forty years later, many of these men and women are gone, and their recollections provide a unique and invaluable resource for scholars.

FIS's other primary project was *Iran Nameh*, the foundation's journal of Iranian studies. Given the divisions among a variety of political groups in diaspora, we saw the necessity of providing a safe space where scholars could engage in research and writing without pressure. Jalal Matini, the founding editor and a respected scholar, engaged the best in the field and kept the journal above the many partisan divisions in the Iranian diaspora. The journal was well received and helped create a community among writers and scholars. The nonpartisan, even apolitical nature of the scholarship was a key factor in its broad support in Persian-speaking communities across the world. But it also created waves among political activists who wanted the journal to be a mouthpiece for their particular cause. Some criticized using the title *ayatollah* before Khomeini's name. Others resented the use of the titles of the royal family. We remained steadfast, and it worked. Throughout its publication well into the twenty-first century, *Iran Nameh* remained one of the most respected and acknowledged publications of its kind, both inside and outside of Iran. The journal soon was known, said Professor Jerry Clinton of Princeton at the annual MESA meeting, as "the foremost Persian language publication on Iranian Studies anywhere in the world." Nearly as pleasing as his statement was a letter in beautiful Persian calligraphy from a Japanese student thanking the foundation for helping his young compatriots acquire a better understanding of Persian language and literature.

Today the Foundation endures, but even in its early days, it became apparent that no one, not even the Islamic regime, could suppress Persian culture abroad or even within Iran's borders. During the Iran-Iraq War in the 1980s, to gain public support, emphasis on culture became, surprisingly, a significant part of the Khomeini government's public policy. Its attacks on our epic poet Ferdowsi, the rites of spring symbolized in Norooz, and the iconic pre-Islamic site Takht-e Jamshid (Persepolis) gradually diminished, then stopped. In time, it became clear that those inside Iran, especially women, who were most pressured by the new rules, would not abandon the "Persian" in our culture and the consciousness they had gained of their rights through decades of activism, regardless of the level of regime violence. They began to produce well-researched tracts on Iran's immediate past, novels centered on the individual and on the space that men and especially women demanded, and films that circumvented the rules applied to women's hijab or unmarried actors even sitting next to each other.

Establishing the Foundation for Iranian Studies slowly helped me regain a sense of self, and watching the developments over time in Iran offered a glimmer of hope. Progress was slow, yes, but building a new world isn't something that can be rushed. Soon, though, my family would learn that time was running out for Farah and Faramarz, still in Iran, and we would all again face upheaval and tragedy at the hands of the Islamic government.

Chapter 13

Farah

FOR NEARLY TWO YEARS after my sister returned to Iran in 1979, I did not hear from her directly. Mother told me about their phone conversations and shared her letters from Iran. Farah sounded happy. She had a baby girl named Neda. But what we heard from those who had left Iran and from the news reports was at odds with Farah's account of their life there. Her family seemed to live in a bubble—in the daytime, Farah taught English and Faramarz made beautiful wooden furniture and toys for Neda. In the evenings they watched Woody Allen films on videotape and played Scrabble with friends. For the first time during their years together, their home life was that of a normal family.

What Farah couldn't write about in her letters was her constant fear.

DURING THE first few years after the Revolution, many of those left behind in Iran were preoccupied with survival: they tried to live below the radar of the Islamic Republic. Many who had had a prominent position—in almost any field—lived with a small packed suitcase, ready for the knock on the door and the angry, bearded, armed young men who barged into homes with an air of entitlement. The suitcase came to represent transience, a state of mind suggesting readiness to face interrogation and prison. For those outside the country, the suitcase had a somewhat different meaning: it was a symbol of the temporariness of their new, alien life in a strange land. For years, a good portion of both groups continued to think that whoever had plotted this new, incomprehensible, foreign way of life in Iran would see the absurdity of it and help change things back to normal. This simply could not last. For years the suitcase would remain ready for those still in Iran and only partially unpacked for those abroad.

The first few years after the Revolution were years of real terror, rooted—as terror always is—in randomness and uncertainty. It took not only Iranians but people around the world quite some time to fully realize what the Revolution's leaders had in mind: to govern not only people's public lives but their private lives as well. After nearly a century of modernization, the urban population of Iran had developed habits and lifestyles that were suspect to the conservative clerics. The new government began to display a streak of sexual obsession. There were endless discussions of the effect on a man of sitting on a chair warmed by the body of a woman who occupied it just before. And can a woman sit on a horse? What about a bicycle? Curtains divided beaches into men and women's sections. Women were made to swim fully clothed. The president of the Islamic Republic, Mr. Bani Sadr, declared that a woman's hair gives off rays that disrupt the composure of men in their vicinity—such was the justification for the strict enforcement of the new veiling regulations. As the revolutionaries confronted the many areas of interaction between men and women in a fully integrated modern society and improvised new rules to bring them into conformity with "Islamic" criteria, they began to develop a theoretical basis for gender relations to explain their new and alarmingly specific regulations and taboos.

Those in Iran learned what would get them into trouble—a pack of cards, a chess set, music featuring a female vocalist, photos of unveiled women, the sonnets of Hafez, alcoholic beverages—and how quickly to hide such things. Life was split into outdoors and indoors. Outside in public, women were veiled and segregated. They were stopped and examined for proper hijab or any sign of makeup; items such as sunglasses were deemed Western and suspect. Indoors, people continued to live as they always had but admonished their children not to reveal what they saw at home. In school, children were often coaxed into betraying their parents.

We who were outside the country heard tales of the struggle for survival with amazement, as those visiting from the inside would tell us that the shocking and unprecedented were becoming the new normal. One of the stories we heard was about Mrs. Parsa, who like numerous other public figures thought she had nothing to fear from the Revolution. After all, what had she done other than serve her country and educate its people, especially its young women? She was proud of her work. But to the clerics, Mrs. Parsa represented the antithesis of a woman's societal role, and her trial and execution gave the revolutionaries their first major opportunity to demonstrate their view of "good" and "evil" with regards to women. She was arrested in February 1980 and thrown into Tehran's notorious Evin Prison. The charge against her was "prostitution and warring with God." The evidence against her consisted of school textbooks revised to present a positive image of working women and an internal ministry memo on the dress code for teachers and students that freed them from covering their hair at school—projects we had worked on together.

Though she was not allowed a lawyer, she tried to defend herself, but the arguments against her and her defense originated from two entirely different worldviews. Mrs. Parsa was a woman who had advanced within her society by studying, working hard, and meeting her responsibilities. Her career had made her a role model for many young women—the personification of what parents would want their girls to become. To the ayatollahs who tried her and sent her to her death, however, she was an example of what a woman in the Islamic Republic must not be.

Her execution on May 8, 1980, was carried out in the south Tehran slum area that was home to Shahr-e No—Tehran's equivalent of a red-light district. Mrs. Parsa was hanged alongside a woman charged with prostitution and a man accused of drug dealing. Before she was hanged, a sack was pulled over her head and tied at her feet, in order to rob her of her identity and to preempt exposure of any part of her body to the glance of the "believing" men on the scene. Then three bullets were shot at her heart.

Mrs. Parsa was executed not for her political role as a member of the cabinet but because, for the revolutionary government, her political role, by being public and visible, was the same as prostitution.

MEMBERS OF the general public had much to fear, too. Visiting me in the United States after the Revolution, my friend Guity told me about the time she was flogged:

I walked out of the grocery store, holding a heavy bag in both arms. I felt my scarf slipping back, but had no way of pushing it down on my forehead. I wavered between putting the bag down and rushing to my car, and I decided to wing it. From the corner of my eye I saw a white station wagon slow down and stop by the curb. These are the standard vehicles for the protectors of public morality. "Ah my god, I am done for," I thought. The Zainab sisters, as they are called, supported by a couple of young men with machine guns, stopped me and told me to get in their car. Apparently this was one of the days when a lesson had to be taught. The station wagon moved down the street, stopping every few blocks and picking up new miscreants. The girls inside the station wagon began chattering about the arrests as a way for the guards to extract money. They vowed not to pay a fine and instead to opt for flogging. I tried to argue on the side of paying the fine and being done with it, but they were adamant. They refused to allow the jailers to profit from their power.

Guity went on to describe the humiliation of "a middle-aged woman being flogged as several young men watched with a bored expression on their faces." Yet on another occasion, she was critical in her description of the imaginative ways young women covered themselves to stay within the morality code and yet be innovative and exotic. "They wear tight jeans, chiffon scarves in bright colors pushed back to the crown of their heads, red lipstick, and a lot of mascara—as if asking to be taken in. What do they expect?" she said, displaying a mild version of Stockholm syndrome.

ONE DAY, after years of silence, Farah sent me a message: Faramarz had been arrested, and she and Neda were in hiding. She couldn't go to family or friends. It would be too dangerous for all concerned. She needed a place to stay while she found a way to leave. I was shocked. I had a photograph of her little girl with sparkling blue eyes and two small front teeth showing in a smile of happy surprise. I couldn't erase that image from my mind—or the thought of what the Revolutionary Guards would do to her and to her mother were they to be captured.

I called Guity, who immediately agreed to take in Farah and Neda. Guity's beautiful garden, formerly the site of so many relaxed conversations with visiting friends, became Farah and Neda's refuge for two weeks while Farah's in-laws arranged for her—seven months pregnant and with a toddler in tow—to be led by smugglers across the Turkish border.

After two weeks of coded messages from Farah that were delivered to us by friends, and two days of total silence while she and Neda crossed the border first on horseback, sitting behind a smuggler, and then on foot, they reached the city of Van in eastern Turkey. Our brother, Hamid, met them there and helped them through a maze of hurdles, including getting a passport for Neda. Then he brought them to Washington. After nearly a decade I saw Farah. She was wearing a long, loose black dress, no makeup. Her face was drawn, but her eyes reflected her old smile. She was walking with Neda, who was hugging a stuffed pink panther a foot taller than herself. She had seen the toy in the airport shop window and said, "Palang-e surati" ("Pink panther"). Gholam had bought it for her.[1]

That night at our apartment in Washington, Farah and I put Neda to bed and stayed up talking all night—she gave a brilliant analysis of the political situation in Iran. She described the euphoria of the early days of the Revolution when the chaos allowed every group a soapbox. A spirit of optimism and enthusiasm prevailed, and everything seemed possible. In the next months, the Islamists began to solidify their power and eliminate their opponents. They identified members of various political groups and arrested them. They broke them under torture and forced them to reveal the names of others. Every day the newspapers were filled with reports of executions. The leftist groups began to realize how badly they had misinterpreted the conditions in Iran and how removed they were from the Iranian working classes. She went on,

> One day in the early months of the Revolution we were at a large demonstration of factory workers. At the end of the demonstration, a few of us stayed behind to talk about the importance of continuing the Revolution until we had achieved a true democracy. The workers listened politely, but as we turned to leave, one of them called to us, waving his hand. "Bye-Bye," he said in English, grinning with amusement. This was a powerful expression of the foreignness of our contingent to the workers whom we had thought our natural allies.

Almost every group on the left was touched by the repression, she said. Many had to disband. Others fled the country. Only the most committed recruits, the ones who allowed themselves no doubts, remained loyal to the ideology. Some thought the growing disillusion with the Revolution provided an opportunity to reverse the course of events. A group of 100 decided to take tents, food, and guns to the jungles near the small city of Amol in the north to attack the Revolutionary Guards, believing that if they held the city for a week, people would rise and join them and the rest of the country would follow. Faramarz and Farah were both against this plan, and Farah had left the group when Neda was born. Faramarz, still involved but growing apart from the group, had tried to convince the others to avoid their suicidal plan. But the more radical faction—those he had recruited and trained—shunned him, calling him reactionary. On January 25, 1982, they carried out the attack. The Guards held their position, and people supported the Guards. Many of the guerrillas were killed. Others escaped and went into hiding. Some left the country. For several months Farah and Faramarz carried out their lives as before. Listening to her, I thought of a sparrow facing a cobra—paralyzed.

On July 11, while she was shopping for the uniform covering that had become compulsory for women, Farah called home to check whether Faramarz had returned from a meeting. Her sister-in-law picked up the phone quickly. "Everything is fine, the brothers are here," she said.[2] "Yes, yes, I think you should go to your mom's with Neda."

Farah realized that Faramarz had been arrested and had been brought back to the apartment to wait for her return. "Go to your mother's"—that was the signal. She rushed to a friend's house, but she knew she couldn't stay there. The house could very well be under surveillance. There was no one she could go to. Her friends and colleagues were either vulnerable themselves or they were unwilling to risk keeping her. That's when she reached out to me. For years she had given up on her family; she had never contacted Gholam when he was in hiding in Tehran, long before she and Faramarz were in danger. It was their way. For them there was no family but the Union of Marxists. No other ties. I had thought often of E. M. Forster's "What I Believe"—an essay Farah and I had read together: "If I had to choose between betraying my country and betraying my friend I hope I should have the guts to betray my country. There lies at the back of every creed something terrible and hard for which the worshipper may one day be required to suffer." What a long way she had traveled from Forster's faith in personal relationships. But I didn't know that evening that for her still it was really love that mattered most and not the cause.

After she arrived in America, Farah, like the rest of us, took refuge in Mother's house in Monterey. Like Babak, Farah's new baby boy, Nema, was born in Carmel Hospital. In California, she began the process of exile and contemplated her choices, as I had done four years earlier. In February 1979 I had watched terrified as the images of Khomeini's return to Iran ran constantly on the news and I waited to learn Gholam's fate. The nightmare I had dreaded was now real for Farah. Faramarz was in Evin Prison awaiting trial, which began on January 8, 1983. It was an elaborate, televised mass trial: thirty defendants with no lawyers were seated on a stage while hundreds of families of the "martyrs"—Revolutionary Guards who had been killed in the uprising—shouted demands for their execution. The hall was decorated with huge banners bearing slogans condemning the defendants.

"Shall I come?" I called Farah from Washington to ask if she wanted me with her in California. This would be my fourth trip to her in as many months.

"Not just now," she said, and added, "Even if 10 percent of them are killed, he will have to be one of them."

I flew to Monterey anyway and kept vigil with Farah, who was in a state of shock but candid.

"I wonder what he feels, waiting for death," she mused.

"Probably not much worse than you feel," I said.

"Once when I said I felt sorry for a friend whose husband had just died, Faramarz told me 'Feel sorry for the one who lost his life.' I think I would've been a better prisoner waiting to be executed, and he would have been a better widow coping with life," she said.

We regularly dialed her in-laws in Iran. Each time it took half an hour before we got through. They told her Asadollah Lajevardi, the prosecutor, had asked Faramarz and another leader, Ali, if they had anything to say. Faramarz said, "I want to say for history that international Marxism has reached a dead end. It offers no solution. I was against Amol. I accept Imam Khomeini's leadership of the Revolution." Ali complained to the parents in the audience, "You didn't teach us properly and train us on the virtues of Islam. We erred."

Farah said, "I wish they could die properly."

"Many fools die stubbornly—how one dies is not a reflection on how one lives—just another isolated act," I said.

The show trial took three weeks. While we awaited the daily calls from Iran that would come at any time, day or night, given the eight-and-a-half-hour time difference, we tried to keep reality at bay. It was not all stress and sorrow. We bought colorful cushions for mom's drab beige couch. We introduced Neda to our favorite breakfast of pancakes and eggs at the diner we used to frequent before politics overwhelmed our lives. Farah kept her sense of humor. Once when she was filling out a form for a credit card, she read aloud, "Marital status," then smiled at me. "Potential widow?"

Finally, the news came. They were all convicted of treason against the Islamic Republic and of warring with God. The sentence—execution—was a foregone conclusion, but there was no indication of when it would be carried out. Farah and I talked for hours. She fell asleep on the couch, with diapers and toys everywhere. I had to leave for Washington the next day. Mother said,

"Take Farah with you. What if the execution happens after you leave? I can't deal with it. I will take care of Neda. You take the baby."

Gholam picked Farah, Nema, and me up at the airport in D.C. We were all calm, as if fear had passed—as if the threat had passed. The next day I went to work. The call came. They had all been executed. I rushed home. Farah was feeding the baby.

She looked at me. "Has there been an accident? Did something happen to Mom?" She would not think of the obvious. Then her face went blank. Gholam took the baby.

She hurled herself about. "I won't hear it, I won't believe it!" she repeated.

I brought her a glass of water and a Valium and held her in my arms. She calmed down a little. "He was my best friend, what a shame, what a shame, what a shame." She recalled the two of them driving with little Neda standing in the back and bending over to kiss each of them. She remembered kissing the back of Faramarz's neck as she held him in bed each night—again and again, as if to ward off the hour when he would be taken away. She told him, "If they take you for these silly meetings, I will really be pissed off."

Then she began to cry—not because she had lost him, but because she had lost him for nothing.

IN TIME, Farah began to figure out the kind of life she wanted for herself and her children. She moved to Washington along with Mother, who had just retired. We spent most of our free time together as a family—a strange, dysfunctional, but close family. We wrote to each other often when we were apart and sometimes when we were both in Washington, even though we saw each other regularly. In the early years of exile, Farah walked a mental tight-rope, trying to adjust to a normal life and career in the United States, working at organizations that had been demonized by her group, while maintaining her reverence for Faramarz. This required a certain refusal to deny or openly express regret for their past beliefs or activities.

As I look back to my dialogue with Farah, oral and written, it becomes increasingly clear that were it not for our love for each other, it would have been well-nigh impossible for us to have kept our anger in check, having lost, and at the time still losing, so many good friends and loved ones. In one of my early notes to her I wrote,

We are in a vicious circle. You need your past to cope with the present. Your past excludes me. I cannot be what I would wish to you. The pity of it is, when the moment comes (if it comes) that you can accept me, you wouldn't really need me anymore, and just when you need me most—when you are attempting a transition to a new life—you cannot make use of our relationship. I love you and will be there for you if and when you need anything within my power to provide, but until such a day when the situation will allow a basic transformation, there is little hope that we will be friends.

"We were active members of two opposing forces locked in a life and death struggle," she wrote back:

> I knew you and I shared many human values, but I also thought that your talents were being used to strengthen a regime that was structurally feudal, economically dependent and politically corrupt. I strongly believed in the Marxist-Leninist ideology and in all, it was the most scientifically correct philosophy and just view of human social development. During that time I genuinely thought that what I was doing was right. My basic hesitation was that in taking the road that I did take, I had to turn my back on my family, in particular you, who before Faramarz, I loved most in the world. I had to betray my family's trust in me, which was lost and . . . may never be regained. The last year I was in Iran, I began to have strong differences with my organization and with many of the Marxist principles. My views had begun to change then and Faramarz's arrest and my subsequent trip to the US let loose the full extent of my doubts. I must apologize to you and Gholam Reza for the past. I think you were civilized and noble in that you were able to put the hurt and insults aside and help and guide me through the past two years. You know very well that if you had not been by my side, I may have lived through these months, but the toll would've been so much greater. Words unfortunately often cheapen and lessen the intensity of the feelings that they are meant to portray. I know that if Faramarz were alive, he too would apologize. He may not have thought exactly as I do, but he too was going through changes. I only wish you and Gholam Reza had been able to know him as the noble and decent man that he was.

"About your past reaction to me and to Gholam, no apology is necessary," I wrote.

> Any regrets would only be due the loss of companionship all of us could have used. I, too, miss very much the chance to have known Faramarz

and to have related to him—an important factor in my bitterness against the political organization which made it impossible for us to communicate and to know one another. About your past politics, it is not the fact that we held differing views which was so disruptive. In other words, I have no problem with someone whose analysis of the world situation is based on Marxism. But the all-inclusive nature of it eliminated the possibility of interaction on other matters of life, while holding different opinions on politics.

We kept on writing to and talking and fighting with each other over several years. I think it was her love of Faramarz that kept her from giving up her special way of talking about her past.

In time, both of us learned to be more careful not to throw about slogans and political clichés in our conversations. Since Marxism still influenced her views on social questions, it was difficult for Farah to refrain from fixed opinions on certain topics. For example, she referred to USAID as a CIA front and spoke of the World Bank as a tool of American imperialism. A few years later, both of these institutions became successful workplaces for her. While I thought I was not as hampered by ideology as Farah had been, it turned out that my use of the royal family's titles, not to mention the tone of respect and affection when mentioning the queen or Princess Ashraf, had been just as jarring to Farah in the 1970s as her stories of her comrades chaining themselves below the Statue of Liberty had been to me. And she seemed to agree when I told her in jest that though it was understood that most great powers had less concern with the morality of interaction between peoples than with the extension of their own spheres of political and economic influence, to bandy about comments on US imperialism was really annoying when it happened on a regular basis.

Our family gatherings invariably followed a pattern. Farah and I went back and forth, recalling lines from scripts of vintage comedies—*Dr. Strangelove*, *The Wrong Box*—and laughed. Then we read from our favorite poets—T. S. Eliot, Emily Dickinson, Robert Frost. At some point, without warning—remembering a scene from our separate past experiences, an item in the news, almost anything—the explosion came. Babak once said, "Your discussions are like you're holding a stick of dynamite with a fuse; no matter how long the fuse, it will finally explode." Mother waited each time with the apprehension of the peacemaker worried about permanent damage. But Farah and I knew by now that we could take it all, and our relationship would survive the ordeal.

Part of our healing came through my ten-hour interview with her for my book *Women in Exile*. The book as intermediary and my role as a neutral listener helped her to reflect as she told her life story for the first time. She was candid and open. But when I sent her the story as I had written it, she struggled with the text and edited it heavily, reflecting her altered worldview. In order to make Faramarz's decisions more rational in the world of America in the 1980s, she seemed to rob him of the heroism and self-sacrifice that was part of his reality at the time. On our last review, which took several hours, she finally agreed to let Gholam decide if the narrative rang true. The experience brought us into a closer relationship than I can name—friends, sisters, progressive allies, and bicultural exiles.

Soon after, I took Farah on a holiday trip to London where we stayed with my close friends. She was comfortable and easy with them. We drove to Stratford-upon-Avon, watched a play, and visited Shakespeare's house. Then we sat on a bench eating fish and chips in the sun. The next day we visited the grave of Karl Marx. We stood in thoughtful, somber silence for a while and walked around the space.

Then she looked at me. "And now for something entirely different?" she asked.

"Marx & Spencer?" I responded.

And we laughed with the exuberance that only our past experience would justify.

Chapter 14

Sisterhood

AT THE HEIGHT OF the Iranian Revolution, I met the editor, poet, and well-known feminist activist Robin Morgan in New York. She was a small woman with short hair, bright brown eyes, a caring smile, and an uncanny talent for making those who were in her inner circle feel exuberant, empathetic, sisterly—in fact, part of a tribe. I felt this at our first meeting when she sat across from me, leaned forward, and listened in a way that was completely present and fully receptive. I found myself telling her about the call from my husband in Iran that had changed my life. It seemed important that I tell her the exact words of the conversation. As I finished, I glanced at my lap and noticed I had twisted my paper napkin to shreds. I gathered the pieces and looked up, surprised to see tears in her eyes. Before we parted, she asked me to write the Iran chapter for a book she was working on, called *Sisterhood Is Global: An Anthology of the International Women's Movement*.

Writing that chapter was my first attempt to review my work in Iran. It was painful to speak of the WOI in the past tense, but I needed to begin to look back, to reflect, to evaluate our work, and to make some sense of what had happened. After *Sisterhood Is Global* was published in 1984, Robin asked the contributing writers their thoughts on creating an institute that would allow us to continue our work together. The seventy women who had written, each about their country, agreed and contributed their honoraria as seed money to set up the Sisterhood Is Global Institute (SIGI), the first global feminist think tank, whose members included prominent feminists from around the world—from Simone de Beauvoir of France to Fatema Mernissi of Morocco, Ama Ata Aidoo of Ghana, Peggy Antrobus of Jamaica, and Devaki Jain of India, among others.

I visited Robin whenever I went to New York, first from California and later from Washington, D.C., where I managed the newly established Foundation for Iranian Studies (FIS). Her apartment, with its pleasant roof garden, was the meeting place for the SIGI steering committee. A few of us who were in exile in the United States, a few who worked at the United Nations, and any member who happened to be in New York on travel would gather there once or twice a year for a glass of wine and to talk about the situation of women around the world.

At this time FIS was primarily a man's world, and these conversations with the SIGI steering committee led me to begin thinking of expanding FIS's work to include more women—their paintings, films, writings. I began to combine my passion for literature and my preoccupation with women as "the other"— inside in their homeland and outside in exile—as I worked with a group of talented women in diaspora to shape the foundation's projects. Among these were exhibitions of Iranian women's art, presentations by scholars and literary figures, and screening of films by women directors. Special issues of *Iran Nameh* focused on women's history brought together major scholars in the field and made possible events at the Middle East Studies Association (MESA) conferences and at universities and museums. Three issues focused on the work of the most revered literary figures—Simin Daneshvar, Simin Behnahani, and Forough Farokhzad—were especially valued.

In time, FIS established its Women's Center. Designed to facilitate and encourage research on the past, present, and future of Iranian women, it compiled a rich collection of material, including oral history interviews with women leaders and activists from many walks of life. The Women's Center became the venue through which we organized lectures by scholars and activists from Iran to present at international conferences and to publish their research on Iranian women. This also helped convince the FIS board to provide office space and support for SIGI. The local-to-global planning helped make SIGI's growth possible and gave me an opportunity to test what I had learned from my work in Iran in my discussions with leaders from around the world. In the mid-1980s, when I was still putting myself back together and figuring out who I would be in exile, a group of powerful, smart women believed I could contribute great value to the global conversation about women's rights. Just maybe, I thought, they could be right.

IN THE spring of 1987 several SIGI members, including myself, were invited to Rutgers University for a brainstorming meeting about the global women's movement. The participants were mostly academics, but some had UN, civil society, or government experience. For the past few years, I had concentrated on FIS, and now, nine years after the phone call that began my exile, talking to the women activists and scholars from around the world, I felt like a fish that had just been thrown back into the stream—it was a bit of a bumpy swim, but wonderfully refreshing. Still, I felt little real connection to anything or anyone there. The few women from the developing world were at times resentful of the Western feminists' condescending comments that betrayed the unconscious presuppositions in their worldview. The Westerners talked about diversity and respect for difference but with the kind of certainty that spoke not to an inaccurate perception of others' contexts so much as a total lack of awareness that others might have different concerns. Those from the Global South realized this but nevertheless bent an ear toward the "white folks" rather than those of backgrounds similar to their own. I felt strangely orphaned. All that I had learned in the decade of my work in Iran—all that I had heard from the women of Iran and considered to be the truth of things—had become suspect due to the long shadow of the Islamic Revolution. I did not question what I had seen and heard, but I had little faith in myself as a proper conduit for its message. I took in the dialogue as the person I had been. But the person I had become was above all, uncertain. I felt shy and hesitant, nevertheless thrilled to be part of this conversation on topics that were significant to me.

As I learned to expect in many meetings in the years to come, Bella Abzug, the former congresswoman from New York, in her red outfits and broad-brimmed hats, claimed the center of attention. Robin and her partner, Marilyn Waring, were exuberant and mischievous. They sometimes sat on the floor, legs outstretched, and often spoke as if they intended to be subversive. I didn't know enough about the women present to understand the undercurrents of tension or sense the personal chemistry between them. I felt that as much as Robin liked some of the people with official résumés, such as Maria de Lourdes Pintasilgo, the socialist former prime minister of Portugal who was then president of SIGI, Gwendoline Konie, Zambian ambassador to Germany and a member of the SIGI steering committee, and me, she preferred her role as the "radical" antiestablishment feminist—especially now that she had a supportive partner in Marilyn.

That 1987 brainstorming session was a precursor to the founding of the Center for Women's Global Leadership (CWGL) at Rutgers University in 1989, with Charlotte Bunch, the well-known activist, author, and organizer in the women's and human rights movements, as its founding executive director. I worked closely with Charlotte for the next two decades. Some of the themes discussed during that meeting later reemerged in the work of Charlotte and her colleagues at the CWGL and were reflected in the themes that the center would advance a few years later at the 1993 UN Conference on Human Rights in Vienna. The CWGL, supported by the UN Development Fund for Women (UNIFEM), played an important role in the preparations for the nongovernmental forum at that conference and afterward. Among the themes and outcomes were the idea that women's rights are human rights, the consensus that violence against women is a serious global issue whether it takes place at home or in public, and the brilliant advocacy campaign, "16 Days of Activism against Gender-Based Violence," that still takes place every year between November 25 and December 10. During those days, thousands of organizations around the world focus on advocacy to eliminate violence against women in ways that suit each group's local conditions.

IN DECEMBER 1991, during her tenure as editor in chief of *Ms.* magazine, Robin asked me to meet her at her office. She showed me to a chair facing her office door, and she and Marilyn Waring, SIGI's executive director, took their places facing me.

"Our seating arrangement is not accidental," she said with a smile, pointing to the door that was blocked by their chairs. "We come to you with a proposal and want to make sure you won't bolt! You said you've been thinking of setting up an organization for Third World women. You know we've been talking about possibly closing the Institute after Marilyn's term is over. Why don't you take over SIGI's management and see what you can make of it?"

This was unexpected. I felt puzzled, confronted with a choice that could be an exciting opportunity or a quagmire. I smiled and said, "May I leave the room if I promise I will think about it seriously?"

I did think about it for months—not only how it would fit with my life plans and responsibilities but also how to make a success of an organization that had already been around for several years with various leadership arrangements and in two quite different locations—New York and New Zealand—without resolving the basic issue of its identity. There was no clear goal, no agreed-upon set of activities, and no funding.

After over a decade of exile, my professional life was beginning to take shape. On October 5, 1991, two months before the meeting at *Ms.*, I had organized a conference at the George Washington University, in collaboration with the University of Pennsylvania, the first conference since the Iranian Revolution where scholars presented research on the condition of women in postrevolutionary Iran, at which Robin gave a rousing keynote presentation. Then, in November at the MESA conference in Washington, I helped organize an exhibition of portraits of contemporary Iranian writers by Maryam Zandi. Both events were met with enthusiasm. These were followed by collaborative projects at the Smithsonian's National Museum of Asian Art, the Film Institute, the Textile Museum, and several universities across the United States. One of my favorites was "Voices and Visions: Iranian Women Artists, Directors, and Writers," which included an exhibition of well-known Iranian women painters, readings by Iran's beloved novelist Goli Taraghi, and the screening of an award-winning film directed by Rakhshan Bani Etemad.

I weighed the strong position I had gained in the Iranian academic community and the important work we were doing for Iranian women as I considered Robin's offer. I had decided once before in Iran that although academic work was an important venue on its own, it would not be sufficient to bring about change in the lives of women. But to make SIGI a successful organization that would bring systemic change in the status of women, I needed serious and thoughtful advice. Months of regular discussion with several women with deep experience in women's and human rights, including May Rihani of Lebanon, Fereshteh Noorai of Iran, and Sima Wali of Afghanistan, among others, gave me hope. The risk I had taken in 1970 when I accepted the position of secretary general of the WOI had begun for me not as a job or a mission so much as an interesting experiment. That experiment succeeded beyond my wildest dreams and turned into a lifelong mission for me. I began to think I should give SIGI a try. It helped that Gholam, who had opposed the earlier decision, was now more enthusiastic than I was. He saw it as an expansion of my work for Iranian women—from local to global.

SIGI WAS originally vaguely defined as "a global women's think tank." But a think tank needs either institutional support or enough funding to set up the facilities and infrastructure to support the writing and knowledge production of its members. When I took the position of executive director, SIGI had obtained a two-year grant from Canada's International Center for Human

Rights and Democratic Development. The first year's grant had been spent, and only $18,000 was reserved for the second year. The think tank idea seemed to be a nonstarter.

Our ongoing discussions with several scholars and activists quickly taught me that any level of success would require carving out a focused mission and credible strategies to bring moral and financial support for the organization. SIGI's structure would have to evolve to accommodate the global challenges of the organization's new mission, which was yet to be identified.

In the meantime, box after box sent from SIGI arrived at the Foundation for Iranian Studies, where I was then working. For years I had made sure that every aspect of the FIS work, most especially the Oral History Archives, integrated women's presence and perspective, and I made sure that projects related to women had a special place in the foundation's site. Now I could again expand my work to include women's rights on a global scale. The FIS board had agreed to house SIGI and give staff support to it; in return SIGI would prepare Persian adaptations of their learning and advocacy material and would focus on Iran as an area of concern. But my satisfaction wavered as I opened all those boxes containing press clippings, copies of articles written by SIGI members, old biographies, and the like. What the boxes did *not* contain was any specific project proposal, action plan, brochure, minutes of meetings, financial records, or other documents that might have suggested a road map for the future. This wasn't a complete surprise given SIGI's limited resources: Marilyn Waring had been working as SIGI executive director on a volunteer basis with an intern as an assistant. There was no other way to work at SIGI at that time.

Our main resource at SIGI was the name recognition associated with its roster of leading members. Had the organization appeared two decades later, technology would have made it possible to connect these leaders and create a functioning communication and knowledge production network. But at the time, with "members" who had little or no connection to each other, no funding, and no specific projects, creating an international organization embodying the aspirations and goals of women from such disparate backgrounds was a challenging task.

What we lacked at the outset in planning materials, we had in high-level management experience: Ezzat Aghevli, a distinguished civil servant who had been deputy minister of rural development in Iran and served as my deputy at the WOI during my years in the cabinet, had been with me at the foundation for years. Together, and with the resources provided by FIS, we would find a way through.

THE 1993 UN World Conference on Human Rights in Vienna seemed a natural place to launch SIGI's new phase, discuss ideas for new projects, and network with other organizations. But Marilyn and Robin were against it. This was a time when the United Nations was somewhat suspect among some US feminists, since the more radical activists believed governments were not where the work for women's rights should take place. They thought, not without justification, that governmental conferences were spaces largely occupied by men. But we had defined SIGI as a human rights organization. I believed if we were not present in some way at the second world conference on human rights,[1] we would be out of touch with events and actors that could impact our mission.

We have come to take for granted some of the developments that were the outcomes of the UN conferences. Strangely enough, this is particularly true in the United States, the country that led the world in the global effort to create the United Nations. Eleanor Roosevelt played a leading role in the drafting of the UN Charter and in building its founding structures, yet in the United States there is a surprisingly low level of public awareness and support for the institution's activities. This has led to the United States being the only UN-member nation not to have ratified major treaties such as the Convention on Elimination of All Forms of Discrimination against Women (CEDAW) and the Convention on the Rights of the Child.

I prepared for the Vienna conference with excitement and trepidation. My position at this conference was a far cry from the one I had in Mexico City in 1975 as one of the leaders of the Iranian delegation. At the Vienna conference, I was neither a delegate nor a representative of an active NGO. I had been invited by Alicia Partnoy, who served on the board of Amnesty International and invited me to speak on a panel called "Survivors of State Violence," whose keynote speaker was the Dalai Lama. I was excited to participate in this important gathering, but now my safety as I traveled internationally couldn't be guaranteed. Concern had developed among the Iranian diaspora about the government's plans to assassinate its enemies abroad—a malicious scheme that had already taken the lives of more than thirty opposition leaders in Europe. This campaign had accelerated early in the presidency of Akbar Hashemi Rafsanjani (1989–97), one of Khomeini's close confidantes. Most notable among the victims was Shapour Bakhtiar, the shah's last prime minister and a member of the National Front, a centrist opposition group that had sought speedier democratization of the monarchy. In August 1991, Bakhtiar's house in the Paris suburb of Suresnes, supposedly heavily guarded by the French authorities, was nonetheless easily entered by the Islamic regime's executioners, who savagely decapitated him.

Abdorrahman Boroumand, another leader of the National Front, was stabbed
to death as he stepped into the elevator to his Paris apartment.[2]

The most consequential case of the extrajudicial murder committed abroad
during Rafsanjani's presidency was the mass murder of Kurdish dissidents at
the Mykonos Restaurant in Berlin in 1992.[3] The case was tried at the International Criminal Court, which held several top leaders from Iran's governing
bodies, including Rafsanjani and the Supreme Leader Ali Khamenei, responsible for the crimes. The Mykonos case significantly altered Europeans' attitude
toward the Islamic government.

As for those of us who had worked to promote the rights of women, two
cases of political assassination, those of university professors Cyrus Elahi and
Reza Mazlouman, were particularly painful. Cyrus had conducted extensive
research on women and work. In October 1990, he was assassinated at his home
in Paris. Reza, an enlightened and passionate defender of women's rights, had
conducted pathbreaking research on the causes and consequences of "honor"
killings, which the WOI published under the title *Murder in the Name of Honor*.
In May 1996, he was shot dead in his apartment in Paris. For those of us on
the Islamic Republic's original "warriors against God" list in 1979, no place
seemed safe.

But before I had a chance to worry too much about the hypothetical dangers
of my speaking out in the public Vienna venue, the government of China, worried about its control over Tibet, strong-armed the conference into refusing to
allow the Dalai Lama to enter the conference premises. Meeting plans were all
disrupted, so we moved our program to the open space outside the conference
complex, where the Dalai Lama spoke to a mesmerized audience of hundreds
under the pouring rain. The rest of us decided that he was too hard an act to
follow, so that day I did not have to choose between personal safety and my
duty to tell my story as a survivor.

I had tried to pull together a group of SIGI members to participate in a
panel titled "Third World Women and Global Feminism," but the only SIGI
members who made it to the conference were Sima Wali of Afghanistan, Hilkka
Pietilä of Finland, and Gertrude Mongella of Tanzania, who had recently been
appointed secretary general of the Fourth UN World Conference on Women to
be held in Beijing in 1995. Dorothy Thomas, director of the Women's Division
of Human Rights Watch, with whom I had worked since its founding, also
joined the panel. I was surprised to see Ayatollah Taleghani's daughter, Azam
Taleghani, in the audience. Ayatollah Taleghani had been a long-standing Khomeini ally. His thinking had inspired and shaped the People's Mujaheddin, the
Islamic Marxist terrorist organization that was despised by Iranians because

during the Iran-Iraq War it sided with Iraq. Azam Taleghani and a daughter of Mehdi Bazargan, the first revolutionary prime minister, had taken over the WOI and settled in my office after the Revolution to oversee the WOI dissolution. Shortly before the conference, Azam Taleghani had implored Muslim women around the world to help capture and deliver me to Iran to stand trial for being "a corruptor of the earth and a warrior against God." Now she sat in the front row in full hijab—a heavy black scarf that covered her hair and neck—over which she wore a long black chador. Next to her, a tall dark woman in a white scarf and the alternative uniform prescribed by the Islamic government, a long overcoat and looser head-scarf, offered whispered translation. As Azam listened to me speak, nodding to the translation, I wondered what she was thinking. Did she still believe in the ideology of the Islamic Republic, and if she did, what was she doing at this conference—the entire purpose of which was in conflict with that ideology?

Azam Taleghani's presence didn't prevent our panel from providing the audience with an excellent opportunity to test some of my ideas on the global women's movement from the vantage point of women from the Global South. An important issue was to expose the recently popular concept of cultural relativism of rights used by some fundamentalist activists to gloss over or ignore harmful cultural practices, such as female genital mutilation, and in effect weaken the growing belief in universality of human rights.

Later, walking by the "Rights Place," where activists posted photos and announcements, I noticed the Iranian government had posted propaganda material showing pictures of women in chadors, with ambiguous statements about "the dignity of women" and their "special revered role of mother." The pamphlets were stamped with the insignia of the Islamic Ministry of Information, the entity tasked with censorship. I brought this to the attention of the coordinator of the "Rights Place," who stepped in to remove them. As I watched the photos being taken down, I noticed a young Iranian exiled journalist in jeans carrying a camera following the "Survivors" team on their way to their next event. She reminded me of the camerawomen in prerevolutionary Iran. "I am afraid that's the best I can do for your colleagues back home just now," I thought to myself and smiled and waved to her with disproportionate satisfaction at causing the removal of the Islamic Republic's propaganda—a small act of subversion.

While there were many successes at the Vienna conference, for the first time in my life I understood what it feels like to be a child bullied at school. The other feminists were unfriendly. Not only were they unwelcoming, but some went so far as to not tell Sima Wali and me when or where one of the side meetings was to take place. I was puzzled. At one point I asked Dorothy if she noticed this. She told me that SIGI, with its single, well-known representative from each country, was considered an elitist organization. Charlotte Bunch told me years later that there was a joke going around calling SIGI members "Miss Canada," "Miss Morocco," and so on. Dorothy added, "Not only did you serve in government, but an unpopular one at that. Don't worry about it. There's a lot of tension among all of us and a lot of issues are surfacing. Just ignore it. Your work will speak for itself."

One great benefit of the Vienna conference was that I met Margaret Schink. For our first conversation, Mudge and I had tea at a corner table in a cafeteria. Everything about her tended to make her inconspicuous. She was neither short nor tall, her hair was neither blonde nor dark, her eyes were neither blue nor brown. The feature that made her unforgettable was her soft voice and the aura of kindness and empathy that surrounded her like a halo. The woman drinking tea with me had no sharp edges in her appearance or in her speech. She seemed the personification of the Sufi spirit. It didn't matter what we talked about; we were like two instruments softly playing a harmonious, quiet tune. In the years that followed, Mudge and I worked and traveled together, supported each other, and shared our energy and our thoughts. She steadily supported my work through her organization, the Shaler Adams Foundation, the first partner for SIGI's human rights education program. Her support was also instrumental in saving several exceptional women and helping them blossom in exile. Yet the two of us never discussed the details of the work together. That conversation didn't fit into the spirit of our connection. Our relationship reminded me of my once-Sufi friend Tahereh Saffarzadeh with one difference: I know that had there not been a revolution, Tahereh would have remained the person I loved and admired. But Mudge would be Mudge no matter what happened around her.

AFTER SEVERAL years on SIGI's steering committee, over a year as its executive director, and after a series of brainstorming sessions with activists, donors, NGO leaders, and scholars, I found that it was finally the UN Human Rights Conference that provided the ideas, connections, and opportunities to form a viable conceptual framework and a set of practical and workable strategies to help move SIGI forward. The Vienna Declaration reaffirmed the universality of human rights, placed special emphasis on women's rights as human rights, and created the Office of the UN High Commissioner for Human Rights and that of the Rapporteur on Violence against Women. Article 18 of the Declaration articulated the noble goals that had drawn many of us to Vienna: "The human rights of women and of the girl-child are an inalienable, integral and indivisible part of universal human rights" and "Gender-based violence and all forms of sexual harassment and exploitation, including those resulting from cultural prejudice and international trafficking, are incompatible with the dignity and worth of the human person, and must be eliminated."[4]

Soon after the Vienna conference, Miriam Cook of Duke University, who was chairing the organizing committee of MESA's annual meeting, invited me to speak at the first and only plenary session on women in MESA's history. This was an exceptional moment. Our chair was Deniz Kandiyoti, originally from Turkey. Fatema Mernissi from Morocco, Nawal El Saadawi from Egypt, and I from Iran each had a story to tell. We spoke from experience, and each of us was very aware that this was a chance of a lifetime to do two things: one, address the core issue of our struggle to an audience of 1,200 scholars of Middle Eastern studies from around the world, and two, to bring a feminist perspective on the role of women in understanding and living with or without Islam in Muslim societies. My paper became the basis for much of SIGI's work on human rights and helped me conceptualize the framework and methodology for our women's human rights education program in the Muslim world.

IN PREPARATION for the UN Fourth World Conference on Women in Beijing in 1995, SIGI organized three "Women-to-Women Dialogues" in the fall of 1994. The dialogue that changed SIGI's focus was the third, "Religion, Culture, and Women's Human Rights in the Muslim World," which took place at the American University in Washington, D.C., against the backdrop of opposition to women's reproductive rights at the UN International Conference on Population and Development held in Cairo in early September 1994, where Saudi Arabia, Iran, and the Vatican led the conservative bloc to fight women's rights to contraception, reproductive health education, and abortion.

The D.C. conference brought together more than 200 scholars and activists from 50 countries to discuss the status of women in Muslim-majority societies, and explore the role of religion in shaping the values, cultures, and laws relating to the role of women in the family and society. The discussion pointed out the similarities between the three Abrahamic religions and the exclusion of women in the higher echelons of churches, mosques, and synagogues. It was a novel experience to hear feminist scholars discuss the significance of religion in the lives of the majority of the people of the earth and the urgency of dealing with religious reform while working on strategies for women's empowerment.

There were many other meetings in preparation for the Beijing conference. One of the more consequential was the "Women's Global Strategies Meeting," organized by the Women's Environment and Development Organization

(WEDO), which had been founded by Bella Abzug. The four-day meeting resulted in a series of suggestions for women's activism across the globe to be shared at Beijing. Our SIGI group, mindful of Robin's unique poetic talent, was tasked with preparing "A Woman's Creed," which would encompass the highlights of the deliberations but also express the ideas in rousing language. For several hours our group filled a white board with a long list of challenges and aspirations of women. Late on the final evening, Robin sent us to bed and promised she would sum it all up for us by early morning. At the conclusion of the next day's program, she read the poem to a hushed crowd and received a standing ovation. The poem began with these lines:

> We are female human beings poised on the edge of the new millennium. We are the majority of our species, yet we have dwelt in the shadows. We are the invisible, the illiterate, the laborers, the refugees, the poor.
> And we vow: *No more.*
> We are the women who hunger—for rice, home, freedom, each other, ourselves.
> We are the women who thirst—for clean water and laughter, literacy, love.[5]

And ended with

> Bread. A clean sky. Active peace. A woman's voice singing somewhere, melody drifting like smoke from the cook fires. The army disbanded, the harvest abundant. The wound healed, the child wanted, the prisoner freed, the body's integrity honored, the lover returned. The magical skill that reads marks into meaning. The labor equal, fair, valued. Delight in the challenge for consensus to solve problems. No hand raised in any gesture but greeting. Secure interiors—of heart, home, land—so firm as to make secure borders irrelevant at last. And everywhere laughter, care, celebration, dancing, contentment. A humble, early paradise, in the now.
> We will make it real, make it our own, make policy, history, peace, make it available, make mischief, a difference, love, the connections, the miracle, ready.
> Believe it.
> We are the women who will transform the world.

Chapter 15

SIGI Comes Into Its Own

W HEN I ARRIVED IN Beijing in 1995 for the UN Fourth World Conference on Women, China was undergoing a rapid and messy transition. The throngs of men and women in gray uniforms that I had seen riding bicycles in 1973 had been replaced by people in colorful Western-style clothes and by honking cars of every color and manufacture. Formerly quiet streets devoid of stores or restaurants were now lined with shops and street vendors of all sorts. One could hardly purchase an item without haggling, and some of us took a perverse pleasure testing the Chinese vendors' negotiation skills, much to the annoyance of our Western friends. One day in Huairou, walking back with Robin in torrential rain to find a taxi that would take us to Beijing, we passed by a vendor with a single umbrella for sale. I asked him how much it was, and he said ten dollars.

I began the ceremony of haggling: "TEN dollars?!"

He shook his head, "Yes."

"It doesn't seem big enough—do you have any others?" I asked.

"Come on," Robin interjected, wiping rain from her forehead.

"No, only this," said the vendor. "Will you pay seven?"

"For heaven's sake, take the damned thing!" Robin exclaimed.

I smiled and gave the fellow ten dollars, both relieved and disappointed at the abrupt termination of the dialogue.

The Fourth World Conference on Women in Beijing was the largest of its kind in history. More than 30,000 women from 180 nations and 5,000 individuals representing 185 government delegations gathered to attend the official conference and the parallel nongovernmental forum. Although the official conference was well organized and comfortably situated, the NGO forum was a nightmare on both fronts. The government of China at the time, under the impression that NGOs were its mortal enemies, resisted the nongovernmental portion of the conference at every turn. Shortly before the conference, it suddenly discovered structural problems in the building in Beijing where the NGO forum was to take place, close to the site of the governmental conference. The new designated space for the NGO forum was in the village of Huairou, north of Beijing, where an unfinished sports complex was to house the participants as well as the events. Traveling between the main conference in Beijing and the NGO forum in Huairou took an hour and a half, effectively making interaction between them impossible. The plenary hall where Hillary Clinton and other high-profile speakers were to speak held only 1,500 people—this for a conference with 30,000 registered participants. Other rooms were haphazardly assigned to events and changed without notice or assistance available for reorganizing. Over 30,000 women milled around trying to find scheduled panels that may or may not have been moved to other locations. Beijing was one of the most painful and yet most exhilarating experiences of my life.

Chaos reigned in the village itself, too—its streets were mostly unpaved, and incessant rain created mud puddles everywhere. In a country with one of the most distinguished cuisines in the world, the food stands in Huairou regularly offered a miserable version of a McDonald's hamburger, the only edible part of which was a lettuce leaf we had been warned not to eat. Bottled water was sold at prices exorbitant for most of the Global South grassroots participants. But even those from the North who could afford the bottles chose to endure thirst for fear of having to search for and then use the temporary toilets that were no more than holes in the ground.

Life in Huairou was a continuous battle, but somehow the frustration was almost invariably followed by the euphoria of positive outcomes. Our session "Religion, Culture, and Women's Human Rights" was assigned a room on the third floor of a building, which my Lebanese colleague Afifa Dirani Arsanios and I had checked out prior to the event, only to find a group of Nordic ministers engaged in intense conversation. They informed us they had booked the room for the whole week. Back in the huge tent for organizers, we were told a computer was needed to locate an alternate space and that it would take an hour to walk to the place where a computer *might* be available. Hungry and exhausted, we waited for the young woman assistant to return, kept ourselves busy purchasing markers, pens, and tapes, and confiscated some loose paper from a table. On the assistant's return we walked all the way back to the Nordic ministers' meeting to make and post signs with directions to the new site, and then we walked to the new location. But once our panel began, the room filled with feisty, energetic, interested women activists, some of whom had no idea what the panel would be about but were looking for an occasion to engage in dialogue and discussion. It made us forget our aching feet and our thirst. I was ecstatic to receive enthusiastic support for commitment to the universality of rights as the foundation for culture-conscious policies for achieving rights—a view that was to become the basis for SIGI's human rights education program in the years to come.

Another day of difficulty combined with progress happened when I was scheduled to speak at a key afternoon session that Bella Abzug's organization, WEDO, had organized. Earlier in the day I had to be in Beijing, and when it was time to head to the session, I tried in vain to convince cab drivers to take me to Huairou. At last I found one who was willing to take me and seemed to be going in the right direction. The cabbie inexplicably dropped me a mile away from the venue on a muddy roadway in pouring rain, oblivious to my abject pleas and thunderous threats. By the time I arrived, the session was about to close. Bella took one look at my mud-covered shoes and drenched hair and clothes, graciously stopped the wrap-up, and asked me to present my talk. I have no idea what I said, but I was energized by a wave of sisterly support and compassion.

A bright highlight in Beijing was the splendid reception in the plush ballroom of the luxurious Kempinski Hotel that Margaret Schink's Shaler Adams Foundation had organized for the launch of *Faith and Freedom: Women's Human Rights in the Muslim World*, a book I had edited based on the papers from the "Religion, Culture, and Women's Human Rights in the Muslim World" dialogue that SIGI had held at the American University. Some 300 women leaders of the human rights community attended the reception and were warmly supportive. There had been an agreeable change of attitude among the feminists in the two years since Vienna. The conference, the book, and the meetings in Beijing launched a new discourse in feminist circles on religion, culture, and women's human rights.

IN MANY of the meetings and conferences we organized at SIGI, both before and after the Beijing conference, the idea of a human rights education project for women in Muslim societies was identified as a priority. We talked about the alienation caused by shaping human rights discussions in ways that had nothing to do with the reality of women's lives. Invariably they focused on the lack of culturally relevant language to convey the message of international human rights documents to Muslim women and the need to develop models that used indigenous ideas, myths, and idioms to explain the rights contained in international documents.

During these conversations I often recalled our work in Iran, especially that of Shamsi Amiri, the WOI's secretary in Khorasan province who was to me the role model for working with the grassroots. She merged the values personified by the women heroines of Islam—among them Zeinab, the symbol of courage and sacrifice, and Khadija, the Prophet's wife, who was a successful businesswoman. This helped young women who were searching for connection between their community's values and women's human rights.

With my young colleague Haleh Vaziri, a scholar and researcher, we wrote a manual that would bring together human values embedded in the religious texts as well as the international documents of rights and, more important, provide a learning method that would empower women to believe in their own capability to understand and decipher ideas and relate them to their life decisions. The manual presented personal stories about Leila, a fictitious middle-class, educated Muslim woman. Each story focused on a topic related to her life as she made decisions about courtship, marriage, family planning, economic independence, education, fair compensation, freedom of religion, bodily integrity, and violence. The stories were followed by exercises that included quotes from relevant human rights documents, literature and myth, and the Quran and Hadith, around which women discussed religion and culture and their interpretation of secular and religious texts. Workshop participants discussed Leila's choices and the relevance of the texts to the given issue, and then made decisions about the choice *they* would have made. The manual served as a catalyst for dialogue among women about their human rights priorities.

Claiming Our Rights: A Manual for Women's Human Rights Education in Muslim Societies,[1] was tested in five countries in the Middle East and in South and Central Asia in 1996. Within two years it was translated into eleven languages and culturally adapted for use in workshops in Azerbaijan, Bangladesh, Egypt, India, Iran, Jordan, Lebanon, Malaysia, Pakistan, Syria, and Uzbekistan.[2] *Claiming Our Rights* became a phenomenon. In addition to acclaim from newspapers such as the *New York Times* and coverage on various television and radio stations, such diverse personalities as the scholar of Islam and professor of law at Emory University Abdullahi Ahmed An-Na'im, feminist leader Gloria Steinem, Amnesty International's curriculum coordinator Nancy Flowers, and Moroccan philosopher Fatema Mernissi praised it, validating the concept and methodology used to introduce human rights principles in connection with religion, focusing on empowering women to trust their own right and capability to make choices. Madhavi Sunder, professor of law at the University of San Diego, wrote an article for the Yale Law Journal in which she introduced the idea that reform in Islam was now being led by women, "contemporary agents of enlightenment who are doing the work of philosophers who in the 19th century [in Europe] brought ideas of tolerance and defined the place of religious and civic agents in modern life."[3] For the first time since the early days of radical feminism, the role of religion in shaping and sustaining the status of women became an acceptable subject of discussion.

Almost overnight, SIGI became a well-known international human rights organization and demonstrated how an NGO with modest financial support could bring together a shared vision that would help women effect change in their own countries.[4] We helped Asma Khader, a brilliant Jordanian lawyer who had just lost her position as the head of the National Council of Jordanian Women, set up an organization as an offshoot of SIGI. Although Asma was a lawyer, she was too valuable an activist and leader to be limited to her legal practice. Mudge Schink came to our aid once more and made it possible to help Asma set up SIGI/Jordan to carry out human rights workshops based on *Claiming Our Rights* and to engage in human rights advocacy. In time SIGI/Jordan grew to be a strong force for civic activism and women's rights in the region. Asma was later appointed as Jordan's minister of culture; subsequently she was a senator and then headed Jordan's National Election Committee. Thanks to Asma's efforts, Jordan became the hub for SIGI's work in the MENA region.

Another recipient of Mudge's timely support was Sakena Yacoobi, an Afghan woman who had graduated from the University of Michigan and was at the time a refugee from the Taliban living and working in Pakistan. I was impressed by Sakena's energy and commitment, and we became allies easily and quickly. She told me about her ideas for helping Afghan women refugees by organizing literacy classes and health care and capacity building: "With as little as $15,000 I could start a network and do so much good work." Mudge came through for her and increased her assistance over the years.

I invited Sakena to join SIGI and introduced her to the Persian version of *Claiming Our Rights*, which she took back to Pakistan with some ambivalence. But in a few months she returned with glowing reports from her trainees in the refugee camps. She described the impact of connecting universal human rights to the values of Islam and of introducing the heroines of Islam as role models. She described the impact on women of finding out, often for the first time, that the Prophet's first wife, Khadija, was his employer and was the first to believe in him as God's messenger—and as such was the first Muslim.

When the refugees were able to return to Afghanistan, I was invited to participate in a video conference organized by the World Bank with Habiba Sarabi, then minister of women in Afghanistan, along with the Afghan minister of foreign affairs. Before our conversation started, Habiba began telling me in Persian how excited she had been when as the executive director of the Afghan Institute of Learning, the organization Sakena had established, she facilitated the workshops on *Claiming Our Rights* for Afghan refugees in Pakistan. She spoke excitedly about the impact she witnessed initially on the girls and women in the refugee camps and later in Afghanistan as they were introduced to human rights through material that spoke to their own values and concerns.

An exceptional leader, Habiba went on to become the first governor of Bamyan, one of the most challenging positions in Afghanistan, especially for a woman. I met her again in Beirut at a conference of the UN Economic and Social Commission for Western Asia (ESCWA) during one of the most trying moments of my life. As I landed in Beirut, I heard about my sister's surgery, which had revealed the spread of the cancer Farah had been fighting valiantly. I will always remember standing on the balcony at our hotel with Habiba, beginning to tell her about the news, thinking I would be able to handle it, and bursting into tears, finding I could not. Habiba embraced me, spoke to me kindly in a soothing voice, and stayed with me to get me through that trying moment.

Chapter 16

Women in Iran

T HE TENSIONS AND CONFLICTS within the Iranian system during
Rafsanjani's presidency (1989–97) opened the way for the election
by a large majority of Mohammad Khatami, who became the "good
cop" face of the Islamic Republic. Even though little changed internally in
Iran, his softer, gentler approach to social issues and foreign relations made
some interaction in and with Iran possible. Secular activists for women's rights
were able to join the religious women's groups that enjoyed the approval of
the regime. An unexpected result of this was the consciousness raising that
took place through the two groups' dialogue. Prior to the Revolution, largely
because religious leaders had disapproved of the presence of veiled women
in integrated public spaces alongside unveiled women, contact between the
two groups had been limited. Now that segregated spaces were available and
all women were veiled in one fashion or another, conservative women felt
comfortable in the public space. This allowed an ongoing dialogue between
the secular and the religious groups, as well as the emergence of an ever-more

outspoken and assertive population of women from conservative religious backgrounds.

Among the secular activists and groups were Noushin Ahmadi Khorasani and Parvin Ardalan, cofounders of the Women's Cultural Center, and Shadi Sadr, lawyer and activist in the Stop Stoning Campaign. Important figures who lent their support to the women activists were Shirin Ebadi, one of the first prerevolutionary lawyers to be appointed as a judge (and who later won the Nobel Peace Prize); the journalist and lawyer Mehrangiz Kar; and the poet Simin Behbahani. Those from religious backgrounds who joined the movement were Mahboubeh Abbasgholizadeh, editor in chief of the journal *Farzaneh* (*Wise*), who worked on Quranic studies from a feminist perspective, and Shahla Sherkat, the founder and editor of *Zanan* (*Women*).

Shahla Sherkat, a religious revolutionary who veiled herself in a full-length black chador when she founded *Zanan*, slowly changed as she interacted with secular writers and activists. She moved gradually toward topics and themes that were clearly feminist, and she became more outspoken and included news items and articles in her journal that, if not against, were clearly not in tune with government policy. From Washington I followed the journal's progress and Sherkat's evolving role with great interest and hope. In one issue I was surprised to see a piece with extensive quotes from an article published in one of the last issues of the prerevolutionary journal *Zan-e Rooz* (*Today's Woman*), at the height of the upheaval. The article had attacked the WOI as both corrupt and nonexistent, and reported that I had been "drinking whisky while wearing fancy boots and a transparent blouse and speaking English to Baluchi women" during a cabinet visit to Baluchestan, one of the least developed of Iran's provinces in the extreme southeast of the country. When I first read the reprint in Sherkat's *Zanan*, I was saddened that a promising women's journal would republish such antifeminist propaganda and lies. It brought back memories of my frustration and anger when the article was first published in 1978. Back then, Zohreh, the WOI press officer, called the *Zan-e Rooz* editor, with whom we had courteous relations, to ask what it all meant. The editor, Majid Davami, told her, "I'm sorry. SAVAK sent us this article and explained that this is the first signal of the new government policy to attack women activists and organizations in order to appease the Islamic opposition."

At that time, Zohreh and my other WOI colleagues pressed me to contact the prime minister to check the truth of this. I called Prime Minister Sharif-Emami's office and was told by his secretary that he was visiting the National Iranian Television studios to speak to the rebellious employees. The prime minister called back shortly after, sounding exhausted and rattled. I was sorry to bother him, but it was too late to back out. I said, "An article appeared in *Today's Woman*, replete with falsehoods about the WOI and insulting to me personally. The editor tells us this is government policy."

He responded in an even more agitated voice, "Ma'am, could you please repeat *which* woman has insulted you?"

My frustration and anger gave way to an almost uncontrollable fit of laughter while I searched for an appropriate response. Finally, I was able to communicate my query to the beleaguered prime minister, who responded, "I can assure you there is no such government policy."

The new prime minister had been chosen because of his reputed close ties to the clerics, with the understanding that he might be able to negotiate with the Islamist revolutionaries. It looked as if SAVAK, always critical of the WOI—even more so now that we were one of the revolutionaries' main targets—was eager to throw us to the wolves. This was especially worrisome. It indicated that the government departments were at odds with each other, that there was no clear line of resistance to the revolutionary upheaval, and that the radical Islamists would likely succeed in forcing other factions to follow their rhetoric and goals—all the way to self-annihilation.

As I looked at that issue of *Zanan* with the reprint of an article I had first read in my office at the WOI a decade before, and as I recalled the conversation with Prime Minister Sharif-Emami, I decided the time had come to test the situation in Iran, or more accurately to test the mood of its activists. I wrote to Shahla Sherkat expressing shock and disappointment to find reprinted in her journal a propaganda piece reviling the WOI that had been commissioned by SAVAK at the height of the Revolution. She printed my response exactly as written in the next issue, doubtless at considerable risk to herself. My past as Iran's only minister for women, and worse, my present work as president of an international women's organization that focused on raising Muslim women's consciousness of their rights, meant that I remained a regular topic for the government propaganda machine. But in spite of all that, it was apparent that Sherkat's group was ready for a dialogue with the past.

SHORTLY AFTER my exchange with Sherkat, I began a series of initiatives to provide opportunities for prerevolutionary women activists and newly minted feminists in Iran to participate in the global dialogue on women's rights. Although it was impossible to register secular NGOs in Iran, after the dissolution of the WOI my former colleagues continued their connections to informal networks of activists. They were able to facilitate the process of selecting and briefing leading feminists from diverse disciplines and groups to participate in international meetings. As executive director of the Foundation for Iranian Studies, which was an institutional member of MESA, I had an active role in MESA's annual conferences and sponsored panels and presentations. My FIS colleagues and I regularly supported the participation in these meetings of several speakers from Iran. Sometimes the effort was successful and sometimes not; there were impediments on both sides. Among the obstacles were passports, which Iran might or might not issue or renew, and visas, which the United States might or might not provide. And, once the speakers returned to Iran, there were the unpredictable after-effects of participation in an international forum. But there were always a few courageous souls who braved the consequences. Among those who came to the United States several times to give lectures were Mehrangiz Kar and Azar Nafisi.

COMING FROM a family with limited educational background, Mehrangiz overcame difficult personal circumstances and went on to study at the university, gain a journalism and law degree from Tehran University, and work as a successful journalist and lawyer in Iran during the 1960s and 1970s. She had helped the WOI create and publish a simplified curriculum for classes on legal literacy for grassroots women, including workshops on labor laws affecting women. After the Revolution, Mehrangiz tried to adjust to the new circumstances in Iran by using her skills to support and defend women where there was no legal precedent except for remnants of the old laws. I invited her to speak at a special Persian session at the 1996 MESA annual meeting held in San Francisco. She was one of the first Iranian lawyers to risk speaking about the deterioration of the legal status of women after the Revolution. At the end of that trip and again on future trips she joked, "If you see me on Iranian television calling all of you disciples of the Great Satan and corrupt spies of the CIA, remember, it's because I have no tolerance for pain. A mere threat of torture will make me sing like a nightingale—or a crow."

Mehrangiz's lecture on the Islamic Penal Code helped us understand the Islamic Republic's idea of justice. She explained that under Iran's new Shari'a-based legal system, crimes such as murder are considered as against the family of the victim and not the state. The murderer must pay the victim's family "blood money," and the amount is to be negotiated between the families. A woman's life is worth half that of a man's. If the murderer is a man and his guilt is established, and he is condemned to execution, the family of the murdered woman must pay half of the blood money to the murderer's family to make up for the difference in the price between a man's and a woman's life. At some point in her talk Mehrangiz referred to camels lined up outside the courtroom.

When she was asked to explain whether she was using "camels" metaphorically, she replied, "No, this is a real manner of payment. Since the penal code is drawn from ancient texts such as the Hadith, they actually mention payment in livestock rather than money." The audience was aghast that at the close of the twentieth century a modern nation had regressed a century or more.

Mehrangiz also told us how hard it was for a woman to gain acceptance as a professional and a lawyer, as the law left little recourse for women. The 1975 Family Protection Law, which had given women equal rights to divorce and marriage and limited polygamy, had been annulled by Ayatollah Khomeini. Women judges, such as Shirin Ebadi, had been banned from courtrooms.

On one of her later trips to the United States, I discussed with Mehrangiz the possibility of her taking a consulting position with SIGI and suggested a comparative study of the status of women in Iranian law with the articles of the United Nations' CEDAW, known as the Women's Convention. This approach, which we had used at the WOI, had made criticism of the laws less controversial inside Iran in prerevolutionary times. Perhaps Mehrangiz could do the same to avoid retribution by the government. She agreed and produced two major works: one provided a full exposition of the shortcomings of the laws of the Islamic Republic with regards to women's rights, using CEDAW as the standard; the other focused on violence against women—a theme not banned in the Islamic Republic and therefore blessed with a permit to publish.

I asked Mehrangiz whether it would be safe to gather a small group of women in an informal workshop to test the Persian version of the *Claiming Our Rights* manual. The manual's exercises were meant to encourage participants to think for themselves, to engage one another in discussion to build consensus around their decisions, and, if consensus was not possible, to respect that others could come to different legitimate conclusions. Most important, the goal was to dispel the mystery around the contents of the Quran and challenge the clerics' hegemony on interpretation of the message of God. Mehrangiz said, "I know just the right person to help with the religious texts. There is a bright young cleric who can help us navigate them."

The workshop was very successful, but the bright young cleric, Mohsen Saidzadeh, was imprisoned and defrocked for this effort. While Mehrangiz was spared at that time, in 2000 she was arrested for her participation in a conference in Berlin, where several intellectuals had discussed the political conditions in Iran—a program that had been tacitly approved by the regime. The vagaries of the political power struggle in Iran sometimes caused devastating consequences for ordinary people, when the green light given by one group in the power elite unexpectedly turned red through interference from a rival faction. Mehrangiz was imprisoned along with several others, tried, and sentenced to four years in prison. While in Evin Prison, she was diagnosed with cancer and allowed to leave Iran for medical treatment. She was subsequently given a longer sentence in absentia, and her husband, Siamak Pourzand, was arrested in Tehran and tried for treason.[1]

Since then, Mehrangiz has lived with courage and great perseverance in the United States. Unlike some of us in the first group of exiles, who had studied in the West, she struggled to adjust to an alien language and culture, in addition to facing the economic challenges of survival. She supported herself and her two daughters through their university studies while continuing her work as a human rights defender.

I REDISCOVERED my cousin Azar Nafisi in January 1991 at a conference on one of Iran's foremost novelists, Sadegh Hedayat, at the University of Texas at Austin. We bonded immediately, even though we hadn't seen each other since childhood and despite the fact that she, like my sister, Farah, had been active in the Confederation of Iranian Students, a Marxist opposition group. Her husband, like Farah's, had been a comrade in arms. Azar, in contrast, was at heart what her colleagues in the confederation would consider bourgeois. Like me, she was a student and teacher of English literature, and this tended to bring with it substantially more delineation and nuance in analyzing human relations than the confederation's brand of Marxism allowed. We delighted in recalling that we were related on both of our parents' sides. She came to Washington after the conference in Texas, and we spent some time together with my mother and Farah. We talked of literature and spent hours, as was our custom, reciting poetry at the dinner table with Gholam and Hamid. Mother was elated. She smiled, astonished that after all these years of strife her children were sitting around a table, talking and laughing with no sign of political discord.

An exuberant and effective speaker, Azar impressed audiences with her intimate immersion in two cultures, moving seamlessly from Rumi to Eliot, from Attar to Henry James, reaching for similarities and unities. I invited her to various conferences in the next several years, including one SIGI cosponsored with the Aspen Institute in Berlin, where we came together with a number of interesting women, including my friend the erudite and spirited feminist philosopher Fatema Mernissi. When we met in 1993, Fatema and I had connected instantly, and for the next two decades we would be kindred spirits. We each could surmise what the other was thinking or feeling with regard to an event, a political situation, or a work of literature. We both regretted that there were so few Muslim women visible in international debates. We found it incomprehensible that in these debates religion was nearly completely neglected, despite its being such a powerful factor in shaping the values that impacted women's lives around the world.

Fatema also helped conceptualize the framework for the September 1994 conference "Religion, Culture, and Women's Human Rights in the Muslim World" in Washington. At a long lunch at Sequoia in Georgetown overlooking the Potomac, we talked of many things, including our friend and agent, Edite Kroll, who was puzzled that we spent—in Edite's term, "wasted"—so much time on advocacy work for and with women of our region. As I drove Fatema home, I told her I planned an anthology based on the conference papers that focused on the themes we had discussed and that I would need one from her.

"I have decided I will not do papers for anthologies," she said.

"But you must. You have to, as they say here, 'put your money where your mouth is.'"

She wondered over the expression for a while and tried it in French and Arabic and finally replied, "Okay, ten pages."

"I need twenty pages," I responded, adding, "Do you see the pattern in this conversation—I mean 'the haggling'?"

"Yes," she said. "In that spirit, we will settle for fifteen pages!"

The conference was a great success and the book *Faith and Freedom: Women's Human Rights in the Muslim World* was published in record time for the Beijing conference the following year. The next year we organized a conference at the George Washington University, "Muslim Women and the Politics of Participation: Implementing the Beijing Platform for Action." This led to another anthology published in time for the conference's second anniversary.

Azar fell into an easy and pleasant relationship with Fatema and me almost from the start. One afternoon during the Berlin conference, sitting at an outdoor café, Azar and I sipping Baileys Irish Cream and Fatema drinking her favorite champagne, I bought three long-stemmed roses from a young Bangladeshi vendor who gave us a wide-mouthed smile while his eyes registered a mild indifference.

As we talked we played with our flowers, each in her own way. By the time we left, Azar had shorn the leaves from her flower's long stem, keeping only the bud; Fatema had cut hers and trimmed the leaves, keeping a short stem that she tried unsuccessfully to place behind her ear; I cut my stem shorter but kept all my green leaves. We laughed at how different our roses looked and mused about what our ministrations meant and what they said about each of our personalities.

Not long after, Fatema suggested an event at the Smithsonian's National Museum of Asian Art focused on the myth of Shaherezade, the storyteller who saved her own life and the king's through the ongoing narratives that came to be known as *The Thousand and One Nights*. I mentioned to her that the museum's programs are decided at least a year prior to the event. She shrugged, "I think it's worth a try." I did try, and the event at the museum with Azar, Fatema, and me turned out to be an interesting and lively learning experience that helped us bring about an enthusiastic conversation with a savvy audience on the many aspects of the power of storytelling. Fatema also ask me to organize a meeting with Madeleine Albright, who was then US secretary of state, and another meeting with well-known women journalists. Both meetings were helpful in making influential groups familiar with the ideas of women leaders in the MENA region.

On a later visit to Georgetown University in Washington, D.C., wearing the uniform and scarf she was obligated to wear at home, Azar spoke eloquently about the symbolism of forced veiling. At the end of her lecture, she tore the scarf from her head, spontaneously declaring her freedom through that simple but potentially dangerous gesture. Later that evening after dinner, when everyone else had left or gone to bed, we sat sipping our Baileys and worrying.

"What do you think will happen?" she asked. "They say there are spies everywhere . . ."

It was a difficult question, which I would face time and again in the years to come. I couldn't tell her, "Don't worry, nothing will happen," even though that often turned out to be the case. It would be as if sitting comfortably in Washington I was undervaluing her courage and underestimating the reality of the danger she faced on her return to a state governed by terror. Azar had been through these agonizing experiences before, during, and after every trip, continuing to prove that courage is not the *absence* of fear, it is giving yourself and others the gift of freedom *in spite of* fear.

On her travel back to Iran she called from London. "People here are talking about rumors circulating in Iran that you are working with the CIA to recruit agents among scholars working in Iran."

"Who cares about rumors," I replied.

"*I* do. They're saying *I* am the one you are recruiting!"

After her return to Iran, we continued our calls and correspondence but used my American name "Leah" as a thin disguise.

As I prepared several events for the NGO forum at the Fourth UN World Conference on Women in Beijing in 1995, I decided to invite Azar to join us at a session on women's studies to speak about the experience of teaching in

Iran. Margaret Schink, my good friend and supporter since our first meeting in Vienna in 1993, was helping a group of young women from around the world to travel to Beijing, and Azar could join them. With her usual generosity, Mudge hosted them at the Beijing's luxurious Kempinski Hotel so that, as she explained to me, "They would have respite from their struggles—even if for a short time—in comfort and safety."

During the conference, over a cup of coffee and pastry at a student cafeteria, Azar and I talked about her situation in Iran. Ironically, in Beijing of all places, she was able to speak openly and without fear. She told me that the atmosphere was truly oppressive at the university, where she was constantly watched. Her students passed through inspection at the entrance every day and were punished for such things as laughing "in a giggling manner."

"Why won't you just quit?" I asked her.

"Because I love teaching," she said. "The dialogue with the students is the only buffer between me and insanity." As an afterthought she added, "Besides, I need the money!"

She told me she was paid around 100,000 tomans a year, less than $10,000 at the time. It wouldn't be difficult to raise that amount, I thought, and perhaps we could create the kind of consulting arrangement we had been able to work out with Mehrangiz. I asked Azar what she thought about setting up in her home the private class she had always wished—a kind of workshop—with several of her women students.

"Since discussions based on English fiction are actually about intercultural dialogue and human rights, if you and the students were free to explore these topics you would provide a valuable learning experience for them, and you could prepare a culturally relevant version of Claiming Our Rights based on literature," I said.

We were excited, but both of us had to think about the feasibility of our project and to find our way through the maze that each of us outside and inside Iran was forced to navigate. Margaret Schink, as always, responded with excitement and provided the funds, all the while trying to make me feel as if we were doing her a favor.

Azar's workshop in Tehran grew at a fast pace. She sent me the stories, charts, drawings, paintings, and poems that poured out of her students as if a dam had broken within them. The painting of a torn drawing of a rose next to a broken vase still hangs in my office, reminding me that my young compatriots are still far from living a life they would have freely chosen.

The following year I invited Azar and one of her students, Naghmeh, to San Francisco to take part in the annual State of the World Forum and to give visibility to the condition of Iranian women. At a plenary session Naghmeh was given an appropriately powerful audience to hear her read the poem she had written during the Tehran human rights workshop led by Azar. That poem now graces the Persian adaptation of the *Claiming Our Rights* manual:

> I'm not invisible.
> I touch the russet fall of the leaves and feel the scent of the last light in the sky.
> The crushed sound of bygone leaves, I hear.
> The last song of sparrows in the depth of sycamores, I see.
> The breeze, taking the lifeless leaves, I taste.
>
> I'm not invisible.
> The night hears me, engulfing my voice.
> The shadow of a cypress sees through me, covering my gaze.
> The gray of a cloud cloaks my skin.
> The veiled sound of a cricket bears my breath; the silence of the dark carries my cry.
>
> Stretch out your hands . . . I'm in the wind
> Call me . . . I'm in the echo of the waves
> Follow me . . . I'm in the last vanishing notes of a seagull.

Later, Azar moved to America and told the story of Naghmeh Zarbafian and her friends in the workshop. That book became her powerful international bestseller *Reading Lolita in Tehran,* which brought Iranian women's voices to an audience of millions around the world.

Chapter 17

Endings and Beginnings

A S SIGI GREW IN stature and reach, more funders became aware of our concepts and strategies and supported the organization's programs. In turn, I learned how to build an international organization in the West—how to develop a vision, a work plan, and a message, and how to mobilize financial and moral support. But more important, I learned that to work effectively for sustainable global change, one needs to work with organizations that have deep roots in their societies. Intelligent, well-educated individuals can study change and even offer formulas to bring it about, but they cannot *make* change happen. SIGI's success in human rights education for women in Muslim societies was due to the work of leaders in those societies who led viable organizations and were connected to active networks. They believed in people's shared aspiration for human rights and knew that rights can be realized only when groups within communities and societies develop their own vision and strategies in dialogue with each other.

But a few SIGI members—including Greta Hofmann Nemiroff, a professor of women's studies and English literature in Montreal, but especially SIGI's founder, Robin—did not share my view of how sustainable change happens and what is needed to reach a global audience and speak to them effectively. This more practical, slow work in the field often meant two steps forward, one step back, and it lacked the glamour and excitement of the radical feminist culture of the 1960s and 1970s. In essence, the difference was focused on our ideas about the place of men, the family, religion, and culture in the global women's movement.

In 1998, when our disagreements at SIGI escalated, the emails I received from Greta and Robin stated repeatedly that "Sisterhood is global. Sisterhood is not Muslim." There was also pressure to focus on issues such as sexual orientation, more constructively advocated in parts of the West at that time. To those of us who worked in the developing world, it was obvious that areas of emphasis and related activities must reflect the priorities of the grassroots if they were to appeal to people, to mobilize them, and to make a difference. For women who are subject to violence of all sorts, have little power over their bodies and their lives, struggle just to put bread on the table for their children, and regularly are forced to choose between giving their children a piece of bread or getting them vaccinated, sexuality is often not a priority.

I was intrigued by the similarity between the Religious Far Right's and the radical feminists' fixation on women's bodies and their sexual orientation and preferences. It reminded me of our trip to the Soviet Union in the early 1970s and the minister of health's concern with the "domestic economy"—when our translator couldn't think of "reproductive health," she pointed to the area below her waist and said, "The Minister is talking about 'this *here* domestic economy'!" Back at the WOI in Iran, the phrase had become a humorous reference in discussions about the Iranian fundamentalists' preoccupation with women's sexuality. The radical feminist passion for the topic of women's sexuality was an issue in the 1970s, continued into the era of *The Vagina Monologues*, and perseveres to this day. Needless to say, these functions are of vital importance, but one would think that the role we have been denied and want to take on for the sake of our collective survival as the human race demands the whole female person—our heads, hearts, and all the rest.

I preferred Robin's uncompromising position on rights to that of some academics in Western universities, especially those in the diaspora who focused on Muslim-majority societies. These self-defined "Islamic" feminists welcomed the new respectability of religious discourse but seemed to miss the central point with regard to women and religion—that women are secondary actors in *all* faith systems. Women, with the ability and intellect to decipher the fundamentals of their religion and to adapt them to their lives, are not recognized as agents in their own lives. Freedom of religion is significant as one of the rights enumerated in the UN Declaration of Human Rights. But this right does not nullify other human rights. Above all, the only way freedom of religion can be guaranteed in multicultural, multifaith, modern societies is to separate religion from governance. As Christ said, "Render to Caesar the things that are Caesar's and to God the things that are God's" and "My kingdom is not of this world."[1]

TO AVOID a barrage of emails to me, and letters addressed to members— communications that in their tone even more than the topics threatened to damage the budding alliances being built around the world—I thought I would draw upon SIGI's original concept: periodic rotation of the institute to a new location, which SIGI had exercised earlier. I tried to interest some of the stellar SIGI members, such as my good friend, Leticia Ramos-Shahani of the Philippines (the secretary general of the UN World Conference on Women in Nairobi and former senator), or Thais Corral of Brazil (cofounder and then vice president of WEDO), to stand for leadership of the organization. After at first expressing interest, both soon gave up, predicting they would not have the needed autonomy. Perhaps a more pressing factor was the flawed structure of the institute as originally envisaged. There was, at that time in the late 1990s and in the absence of today's communications technologies, no way to establish meaningful communication between individual members, most of whom had little connection with each other beyond having written an article for the SIGI anthology.

Just as challenging as finding someone new to steer SIGI was finding the resources to gather SIGI's large general membership, an event necessary to ensure a smooth leadership transition. I recalled that Ismail Serageldin, the World Bank vice president who chaired the World Water Commission (WWC), had expressed interest in convening a meeting to discuss how women's needs and concerns could be most effectively incorporated into WWC programs. I called Ismail and suggested that he invite several SIGI members, some of whom were especially interested in this issue. It seemed like a great opportunity to schedule our own meeting in conjunction with the WWC consultation and ensure that we brought the leadership and experience of our members, especially those from the Global South, to this global issue.

Our plans went forward, and SIGI members participated in a vigorous discussion on inclusion of gender perspectives in water-related policies and helped plan the next consultation in Stockholm a few months later. But another wrinkle was introduced into the smooth and open discussion of choice of the next leader when it was asked that a transition committee be appointed to evaluate the volunteers and report its decision at the September 1999 meeting of the steering committee. By the time of the meeting, only one candidate remained. Greta Hofmann Nemiroff became the new president of SIGI.

The following months my two brilliant young colleagues Ann Eisenberg, a lawyer and writer, and Rakhee Goyal, a technology engineer, helped me organize the transfer of the SIGI office to Canada.[2] Rakhee and Ann copied every document we had accumulated over six years; packed up books, computers, publications, even office supplies; and sent them all north. SIGI also moved to Canada with $400,000 in grant money, which covered a full year's budget and a curriculum that included the manuals *Claiming Our Rights* and *Safe and Secure*, the first already translated, tested, and adapted in ten languages and in use in workshops in seven countries, and the latter, published the previous year, available in four languages. The SIGI anthologies *Faith and Freedom: Women's Human Rights in the Muslim World* and *Muslim Women and the Politics of Participation: Implementing the Beijing Platform* were in use in women's studies courses at several colleges and universities. A number of funders were committed to SIGI's programs and had come to believe in its track record. I thought the organization had every opportunity to survive and flourish, and I encouraged the members who were worried about the prospects for the organization to stay on at SIGI and continue their good work. At the same time, I felt relief bordering on euphoria that I would soon be free to continue the work that I had come to believe exciting and useful through a more viable venue.

Greta shifted SIGI's areas of interest, which had been largely focused on human rights education—especially in the Middle East, North Africa, and East and Central Asia—to unpaid work and fisheries. However, after another rift in the leadership and once the funds were depleted, SIGI moved back to New York under Robin Morgan, the original founder.

THE BATTLES of the last few months at SIGI, senseless as they were, had left me feeling battered. I had to keep reminding myself that the discord over SIGI's transition was a tempest in a teapot. But there was an uncanny similarity to what I had gone through during and after the 1979 Revolution. In each case a group of women had worked hard under difficult circumstances to think of ways to bring positive and empowering culture change and had achieved heartening results. The attacks against the work had similar characteristics. In the WOI scenario, the women were considered not "Muslim enough." In the SIGI version, they were too Muslim. The new battle employed a milder version of the Islamic Republic's charge against me of "corruptor of the earth," even though the Republic's other charge of "fighting against God" was mercifully absent. The second experience was a miniscule version of the first but more devastating because it was personal and came from allies, not enemies.

Strangely enough, under these challenging circumstances and after more than two decades of living in exile, I came to feel "settled" in Washington. My family had adjusted to America as well. Gholam had undertaken the monumental task of documenting the history of Iran under the two Pahlavi rulers in a book titled *The Life and Times of the Shah*. It took him more than eight years—not counting the time it took him to produce the ten volumes of edited and published oral histories of the leading officials of the Pahlavi era that provided the foundation for the work. He was relaxed and content. One Valentine's Day during this time, Gholam came home from the Library of Congress, where he was fact-checking his manuscript, with nine white roses he had bought from the fellow selling flowers in the tunnel leading to Metro's Bethesda station. Gholam had only $15 cash, so he spent $14 on the roses and $1 to buy me a lottery ticket for Valentine's Day. Uncertain about his choice, he said, "If you win, it will be the most unforgettable gift you ever received." I didn't win, but somehow it did become an unforgettable gift.

Babak was working in finance at Merrill Lynch in New York. He had married Parisa, an Iranian woman who, like himself, was born in the United States and had completed graduate school at Columbia. Farah had found a balance between keeping her relationships with her former comrades who had adjusted to life under capitalism—a transition she had helped make easier for them—and her new life with her second husband, Habib Ladjevardi, a member of a highly successful Iranian industrialist family. Her children had grown into charming and lovable adolescents. She was working at the World Bank and traveled to Iran on a working journey, where she met with representatives of the Islamic Republic's financial and banking leadership; she walked through the entrance to the building alongside her male team members and did not wear the full black chador as expected.

But what would truly turn my life around would be the arrival of my grandchild, Saphora, whose birth in 2002 I described in my diary in rather giddy terms as "the highlight of my whole life—a joy, a blessing, a window on a new life, new pleasure in life—renewal. Her chubby, smiling person is the most precious thing in my life and Gholam's. I thank God for her wonderful presence."

Chapter 18

Women's Learning Partnership

WHEN I LEFT THE Sisterhood Is Global Institute in 1999, I encouraged the women I worked with from the MENA region during my time with the organization to continue their work with Greta Hofmann Nemiroff, but within months, the shift in SIGI focus from women's rights to unpaid work and fisheries made this impossible. These women were leaders of grassroots organizations and not contributors to the *Sisterhood Is Global* anthology that had morphed into the institute. Rather, they had joined the organization to help design, test, and adapt *Claiming Our Rights*, our incredibly successful manual. These new collaborators—among them Asma Khader of Jordan, Afifa Dirani Arsanios of Lebanon, and Sharifah Tahir of Malaysia—wanted to build an inclusive grassroots-focused civic space. An atmosphere of energy and enthusiasm prevailed with a new approach to women's agency in all areas, including the right to study and understand the basic tenets of their faith. They felt they were on the threshold of creating a new movement.

My friend Fatema Mernissi thought the United States would be the perfect place for the secretariat of the emerging institution that came to be called the

Women's Learning Partnership (WLP). "Whether we like it or not," she said, "this is where the major media is, and it is also, often unfortunately, where decisions are made that impact all our lives." She cajoled, argued, and encouraged me to arrange meetings, press conferences, and briefings with significant women policy makers and reporters. I would normally not have followed that route. I wasn't even sure I could make those things happen. But Fatema pushed, I acted, and they did happen.

Our most pleasant and interesting meeting was with the then first lady, Hillary Clinton, in April 1999 at the White House. Fatema and I didn't know that we would be the only guests from outside the administration. Also joining us was Hillary's closest colleague and chief of staff, Melanne Verveer, and Theresa Loar, executive director of the President's Interagency Council on Women. The conversation focused on our view of women's status in the Muslim world. We stressed how important the separation of religion and state was for the development of both democracy and religion in Muslim societies, as it had been in societies that had already gone through the secular phase. The first lady was positive, optimistic, and supportive. At the end she asked us an unexpected question: What did we think would be a good role for her when she was no longer first lady? There were rumors about her running for the Senate. We suggested, maybe more bluntly than protocol directed, that if she wanted to eventually end up where she was just then—in the White House— she should run for the Senate. If not, then we believed that the international women's movement would benefit greatly from her support. When we walked out, Fatema said, "You see, it's not so hard. If you have something to say, there's always someone who will listen."

She was right. Over the years, many who had ignored culture and religion began to listen carefully. Emphasis on human rights based on an individual's humanity rather than her identity related to racial, gender, religion, nationality, or any other category became the entry point for our theoretical context and strategic work. In effect we returned to the universality of rights expressed in the UN Declaration of Human Rights. This helped us point to the similarity of the condition of women within the family and in the community, in the private as well as the public sphere, and the structure of the relationships between men and women across the world and across history. We were able to emphasize the importance of solidarity across all divisions—real and imagined—to help us change what I called "the architecture of human relationships."

At the turn of the millennium, five exceptional leaders decided to walk with me on the journey to create a new, more inclusive, grassroots-focused international women's organization—Marian Wright Edelman, the civil rights leader and founder of the Children's Defense Fund; Jacqueline Pitanguy, an academic and NGO leader involved in Brazil's political transition to democracy; Zenebeworke Tadesse of Ethiopia, a founding member of the Association of African Women for Research and Development; Khadija Haq, cofounder of the Foundation for Human Security in Pakistan; and Hafsat Abiola, just graduated from Harvard, whose parents had given their lives to the cause of freedom in her country, Nigeria. Together, these women made up the board that helped establish the new initiative's parameters: we would choose community-based women's rights *organizations* to partner with rather than *individuals*. We would select these partner organizations from four regions of the world on the basis of their capability to think locally, to act locally as well as regionally or globally, and to communicate what we learned together to a wide constituency in their countries and regions. We would make no theoretical assumptions but base our knowledge on actual experience, moving from experience to theory rather than the reverse. Most important, we would "walk the talk," meaning we would be truly participatory in our decision-making and we would deeply respect the views, outlook, challenges, and constraints of our partners in communicating and mobilizing a diverse cross section of women in their societies. At the threshold of the twenty-first century, we believed that the new communication technologies would make possible an ease and accessibility of connection across continents that was unprecedented in human history, and that this would, for the first time, make it possible to have interactive and dialogue-based decision-making at the organizational level, in spite of the initial challenges of lack of infrastructure, skills, and broad availability of technology.

Two of these leaders in particular—Marian Wright Edelman and Jacqueline Pitanguy—have sustained me with their wisdom and friendship over several decades, and our vision for the global women's movement would not have come together without their support and leadership.

I met Marian in 1997 through Mudge Schink, who had asked me to organize participation of women leaders from across the world in the State of the World Forum, an annual gathering of several hundred world leaders from political, economic, scholarly, and cultural communities to engage in dialogue on how to shape our institutions to best serve humanity in the new millennium. A well-known civil rights lawyer and the founder of the Children's Defense Fund, Marian always reflected a winning demeanor of dignity and humility, and I liked her immediately. During the difficult transition period between my leaving Sisterhood Is Global and the creation of WLP, her support helped me through some very dark days. I could not have been more overjoyed when she spontaneously agreed to serve on the board of the new organization. But then something happened that showed me I had much more to learn from her than I had originally thought.

During our first year of building WLP, we held board meetings and housed members who came from abroad at the Cosmos Club;[1] it seemed to me that everyone enjoyed the atmosphere.

"Would you like to join the club?" I asked Marian.

She looked at me with a strange, blank look I had never seen in her eyes before. "No, I don't," she said. "The first time I came to the club I was sent to enter through the back door."

My stomach churned. Being shocked by something I should have known awakened me to my own ignorance of the suffering and humiliation she had experienced. In some ways, it led me to understand my colleague Naser Yeganeh, Iran's prerevolutionary chief justice, who did not mention the mock execution, the suffocating cell, or the torture he endured after the Revolution but repeated the innocuous-sounding sentence, "They insulted us." I began to understand not only the pain and violence but also the very denial of one's human dignity that is at stake in racism.

I knew of Marian's work as a disciple of the Rev. Dr. Martin Luther King Jr. and as a mentor of Hillary Clinton, and her amazing work as an advocate for the rights of children. But I was most impressed by the way she brought young civil rights leaders like Susan Rice together with revered elders like Dorothy Height in a wonderfully smooth and rewarding dialogue. At the conferences Marian initiated, I came to learn about the spirituality that made the passion, creativity, and energy of Black women in America even more compelling, and I had the opportunity to view the United States from a different vantage point. I gained not only a better understanding of the horrific history of oppression but also the realization that so much of what the world celebrates as specifically American in music, dance, art, and culture as well as peaceful resistance is owed to Black Americans.

My work with Marian over the years has been strengthened by her spontaneous acts of kindness. One day when I was home with the flu, she called me about a book of children's stories for which she wanted an inspiring narrative from the Middle East. Soon after our conversation, she came to my house with a beautiful orchid and a lovely ornamental box. She said, "This box was a gift from Yasser Arafat when he was here negotiating for peace." That box is still here on my desk.

I met Jacqueline Pitanguy, a Brazilian sociologist and political scientist, briefly during my first years as president of SIGI, when she was on the organization's advisory board, but we got to know each other better at the same place where I got to know Marian: the 1997 State of the World Forum in San Francisco. From the start of our acquaintance, I was drawn to Jacqueline by our tendency to end up on the same side of nearly every discussion—as well as by the similarities in our backgrounds. Jacqueline and I shared the experience of serving in the government at an important moment in our country's history. She was the first to connect the women's movement to the government in Brazil and to bring a strong feminist voice to the debates shaping Brazil's new constitution. She was also closely connected to the academic world as well as to international institutions. We both had experienced the significant role that government needs to play in achieving inclusive decision-making and most urgently in protecting women from domestic violence and the impact of war. We had learned that we need women in positions of leadership if we are to guarantee them full rights to professional engagement as well as the full involvement of both parents in raising their children. We were both skeptical of radical feminists' harsh views about government and international entities, as well as their aversion to religion.

Over the years, on most work trips after our long days of meetings, we ended up taking walks, buying souvenirs, and talking about our experiences. In New York for a parallel event of the UN Commission on the Status of Women, I discovered another side of Jacqueline's life when I went with her to St. Patrick's Cathedral on Easter Sunday. Her reaction to the setting, the music, and the psalms reminded me of my own during my trip to Mecca in 1974. There, the ceremonies and repeating the prayers whispered to me by my guide had a soothing effect. But what made the experience unique for me came at the end of the routine rituals and chants, when the guide whispered, "Now you can ask for whatever you most desire in your life." In that particular moment, I felt sure that whatever I would ask for I would get. I wanted nothing.

Jacqueline and I continued to bond through a similar spirituality related to our two faiths, based on the impact of their positive values not only on ourselves but also on a vast majority of people around the world. The emphasis on ceremony that our good friend Frances Kissling fondly called "bells and smells" we considered beautiful and uplifting. We both believed in secularism that respects both faith and civic law as two separate but interrelated aspects of our lives.

ONCE THE WLP board had been established, Ann and Rakhee helped put together the signs and symbols that would birth a new organization—name, registration, logo.[2] We started with the name: Women's Learning Partnership for Rights, Development, and Peace (WLP). It replicated the Beijing conference subtitle, "Action for Equality, Development and Peace," with a slight change—we chose "rights" instead of "equality." We were already aware that equality within a flawed system would not suffice. We chose "learning" to emphasize that we all are learning individuals, seeking to create learning organizations and societies.

Once we had the board and the organizational principles in place, we gathered the key women and institutions that would help us launch the new organization. My friend Farhad Kazemi, the vice provost of New York University, led me to Shiva Balaghi, associate director of the Hagop Kevorkian Center for Near Eastern Studies at NYU. She helped us organize a conference titled "Cultural Boundaries and Cyber Spaces: Women's Voices on Empowerment, Leadership, and Technology."[3] The rather awkward title was chosen to recognize the two elements crucial to the success of the new organization: cultural boundaries that must be learned and accommodated in order to create a shared vision for change, and new technologies that make possible continuous and affordable communication, an essential requirement for collective decision-making and experience-sharing. Margaret Schink, whose belief in me strengthened my belief in myself, was as usual the first to help support the initiative. Noeleen Heyzer, executive director of UNIFEM, and Thoraya Obaid, director of the Division for Arab States and Europe, UN Population Fund (UNFPA), provided funds for the conference as well as their friendship, wisdom, and experience.

I met Thoraya Obaid in 1998 through my friend Afifa Dirani Arsanios, a generous and kind woman who set up the first affiliated organization of SIGI in Lebanon. At the time, Thoraya was chief of the Social Development and Population Division of the UN Economic and Social Commission for Western Asia (ESCWA), stationed in Lebanon. Thoraya and I liked each other immediately. Our love of English literature, the focus of our graduate studies in the United States, was an interesting addition to our shared Middle Eastern background. The combined impact of the two cultural contexts brought us closer together in our struggle to advance women's rights across the globe.

Not long after we met, I invited Thoraya to participate in a panel I organized on violence against women at the MESA conference. She was an eloquent and thoughtful speaker with a nonconfrontational demeanor that would make her a skillful negotiator in her next role, as director of the Division for Arab States and Europe at UNFPA. We saw each other regularly after she moved to New York when I traveled there or when she visited Washington. At dinner in Washington one evening, we introduced our husbands to each other, and we were very pleased that they were immediately on the same wavelength.

Thoraya and I moved about Washington, D.C., and New York, feeling ourselves—me a Shi'ite from Iran and she a Sunni from Saudi Arabia—as loving "enemies." In a store or elevator or at a conference, we often introduced ourselves in those terms, wishing there were more people who could feel as we did. I discussed with her my belief that the women's movement must be global and comprehensive, and to make that happen, we need visibility and empowerment for women from the Global South and respect and inclusion from the North. Having worked at the United Nations for so long, she knew that the universal vision expressed in the UN declarations needed to be ratified not with exceptions based on religion or culture but with full discussion and agreement of the whole text. To achieve that, we needed dialogue at every level and contextualization of the generally shared vision.

In 2000, when she was nominated to replace Nafis Sadik, the director of UNFPA, I invited Thoraya to meet Theresa Loar, executive director of the President's Interagency Council on Women, and Melanne Verveer, Hillary Clinton's chief of staff, to reassure them of her positions on reproductive rights and women's status. We had a pleasant lunch and good rapport. In 2001 Thoraya was appointed head of UNFPA and undersecretary general of the United Nations, the highest position any woman has held at the organization and the first Saudi to hold the top position at any UN agency.

Thoraya supported my work at WLP from the very beginning, helping fund the opening conference in 2000 and several other events in the years to come. These were symbolic gestures that, although helpful at the time, were not the most consequential. Her most important contribution to my professional life would come later, after her tenure at UNFPA ended and she joined the board of WLP as chair. She would alter and expand our discussions at our board and partners' meetings with in-depth presentations of regional issues in the opening sessions of WLP's annual meetings that we called "State of the World." These statements became useful and important essays about the political, economic, and cultural developments from the regions that complemented the grassroots experience of the partners as we planned WLP activities for each coming year.

But on June 2, 2000, all of that was still in the future. It was the day of "Cultural Boundaries and Cyber Spaces: Women's Voices on Empowerment, Leadership, and Technology," the conference that would launch WLP, and euphoria filled the air. The new millennium had raised expectations for change: the collapse of the Soviet Union promised a cessation of great power hostilities and the resulting tensions around the world; the United States had managed to eliminate its budget deficit; innovations in communications technologies offered exciting new opportunities. All these developments created an atmosphere that promised real possibilities for the expansion of development resources. There was a new boldness in analyses of the status of women and strategies and timelines for change—it seemed like the beginning of a new era, when women would speak of themselves in terms of their capabilities to bring about positive change for all. They stressed their victimization as one of the *outcomes* of the dysfunctional social structures—that is, a symptom, not the disease.

I walked into the conference hall at New York University excited and hopeful, but uncertain. Since WLP's goal was to focus on women of the Global South and to ensure their participation in the international dialogue, the majority of the nearly 200 participants in the conference were from non-Western societies. Many women in the audience were also in New York to take part in the discussions around the fifth anniversary of the UN Beijing conference. On hundreds of occasions—at the United Nations, the State of the World Forum, and the National Cathedral, to name but a few—I had spoken at much scarier places to more powerful and demanding audiences. But this was happening right after a painful transition. And, for the first time, I was initiating a project to set up a new international organization focusing on the same issues for which I had been attacked. But as I began to speak, I felt the enthusiasm and warmth of the participants and their earnest interest in sharing ideas. I felt for the first time the feeling I often had before the Revolution—tiny, happy bubbles rising in my chest, as those in a glass of champagne.

In a conference organized and focused on women, the participants demonstrated an exceptionally broad and inclusive tone and approach. As Noeleen Heyzer said about the Beijing conference, "It was not a conference about women of the world, but a conference on women *and* the world." On the first day several knowledgeable and experienced women leaders from around the globe offered new definitions of power and leadership and described strategies to achieve individual and institutional transformation. There were spirited discussions about the pros and cons of globalization and intense dialogue between the more optimistic and the more cautious participants.

As the day progressed, our words began to draw a road map for the new organization. The partnership was not to be built as a central international organization with partners at the periphery. Rather, collectively, the various independent, autonomous organizations were the institution. They would share a common vision achieved through communication and dialogue, work together to define the foundational concepts, and adapt them to each of their areas of priority and focus. WLP International, the secretariat, would convene regular regional meetings and once a year bring all partner organizations together to exchange experiences of their work at the grassroots as well as national levels and to draw up the work plan for the following year. The secretariat, located in Washington, D.C., would help sustain dialogue among partners, ensure their participation and voices in the global dialogue and gatherings, and bring the most innovative ideas in the West to the partners. It would also help normalize and expand the use of communications technology for skills building and knowledge sharing. We ended the day exuberant and hopeful, with plenty of ideas to work on, and, most important, with a sense of unity and harmony.

The second day was devoted to a meeting of representatives of the countries we were considering as the founding partners as well as those we had chosen to be part of WLP's advisory group. The founding organizations of the partnership—the Association Démocratique des Femmes du Maroc (ADFM) of Morocco, BAOBAB for Women's Human Rights of Nigeria, and the Women's Affairs Technical Committee (WATC) of Palestine—were joined within a year by Sisterhood Is Global/Jordan (SIGI/Jordan) and the Afghan Institute of Learning (AIL). Each partner organization would remain independent and autonomous as a national organization but represent the partnership locally and identify itself as such in regional and international settings. The structure allowed full local engagement, adding substantial diversity and richness to the international vision and concept. It also brought the full force of international presence and broad knowledge to the national advocacy efforts.

At that first WLP conference, the groups discussed their experiences in the field. Since WLP was committed to basing its knowledge on actual experience, rather than theory, this was critical.

ONE YEAR later, in June 2001, we invited some of our allies from among leading civil society activists to review and evaluate a draft manual we had prepared with Haleh Vaziri and Ann Eisenberg and based on concepts agreed upon with our new partners. The participants were leaders of major human rights and women's rights organizations and scholars who dealt with civic organizing and democratic leadership.

The central concept for the WLP leadership model is that leadership is not inherent in special personalities, nor is it based on charisma. Rather, good leadership—leadership that serves both women and men, poor and rich, and the powerless and powerful—is inclusive, participatory, and horizontal. Everyone can be and sometimes is a leader and sometimes a follower. But, above all, the basis of leadership is effective communication. For a leader to mobilize others, there needs to be a message, and the message is most effective if it is designed and articulated through deep, respectful dialogue that values others and their ideas. The new draft training manual, *Leading to Choices: A Leadership Training Handbook for Women*, put these principles into practice. Our objective was to create a tool, adaptable for any community, to enhance women's participation and leadership in various spheres of social interaction and decision-making. The manual consisted of twelve sessions. Each contained a short narrative that briefly described a person facing an important decision and several exercises that helped small groups to discuss the positive and negative aspects of the choice described. As in many of the sessions of later WLP curricula, the stories on which the workshops were built came from the real experiences of partners and allies. For example, the first session, "One Woman Can Make a Difference," appropriately identified the central agent of change: the individual woman. The dialogues created an atmosphere of active listening, respect for the opinion of others, and learning from each other. The goal was to reach consensus among the group if possible, but if that was not possible, then we wanted at least to understand and respect each other's perspectives.

Because the narratives in the manual were about people from a variety of backgrounds and cultures living in diverse communities, we thought that once the material was translated and discussed in a test workshop, various countries would choose to use local personalities and topics from within their own cultures. While in each community two or three new stories and exercises were added to reflect issues specific to the society and culture, the partner organizations decided to keep most of the original stories to show the universality of women's conditions and issues across the world. One story that was added showed how one woman can make a difference. Asma Khader, attorney, human rights advocate, and former president of the Jordanian Women's Union, recounted how she decided to spearheaded campaigns to eliminate honor crimes and violence against women and girls in Jordan:

> About twenty years ago, a frightened and grief-stricken young woman came to my office requesting my help. She recounted how her husband had murdered their fifteen-year-old daughter, who was pregnant as the result of a rape. He was sentenced to only six months in jail, claiming that he killed the girl to vindicate the family's honor. Yet this woman, determined to honor her daughter's memory, revealed the truth to me—that her husband was in fact the rapist, and that she suspected him of murdering their daughter because the pregnancy had begun to show. The court readily believed her husband and did not bother to investigate the crime.

Although this woman came to my office only once and then disappeared, thanks to her, I learned a great deal about how women and girls suffer due to specific laws. I realized that I could not be an effective lawyer if I did not do my best to change laws that cover up and even sanction crimes against women. This woman challenged me to address a problem that I could not ignore—crimes of honor.

And so it happened that I became one of the leaders in the campaign to eradicate honor crimes. Yet I think that this woman who trusted me, who was brave enough to visit my office and inform me about this reality, she was the leader. She overcame her own fears to expose her husband's crime and seek my assistance. People like her challenge us to examine issues that we had not previously considered. We must follow such people and try to serve.[4]

In just six years, with a small secretariat of fewer than ten staff, WLP grew to twenty grassroots organizations in four regions of the world. The organization represented a variety of cultures and religions and adapted and published its curriculum in twenty languages. One evening at dinner, Amina Lemrini of Morocco, Sengül Akçar of Turkey, Jacqueline Pitanguy of Brazil, and I marveled about how we had expanded so fast.

"If we grow at this rate, we can have a hundred countries!" Sengül said.

"And perhaps eighty languages and cultural adaptations in the next ten years," Amina mused.

"But would we be able to have our regular meetings?" Jacqueline wondered. "Even if we got the funding, would they be as intense and interactive as we are now?"

"Tomorrow, let's discuss how we can grow without growing!" I laughed.

We didn't find our answer that evening or the next day, but we understood our experiment in movement building would require learning how to expand our reach while avoiding entangling ourselves in a large bureaucracy and thus losing the intimacy and trust that had become the driving force of our work together. We joked about "how to grow without growing," and chuckled about applying the formula—once we found it—to other areas, such as weight control. But by the next annual meeting, our years together led us to the solution: we would keep the institutional partners at twenty but grow by expanding the partners nationally and regionally—replicating WLP International's model whereby each partner created a national or regional partnership with like-minded organizations in its country or region. We eventually increased our leadership training to sixty countries in thirty languages while keeping our interactive and dialogue-based decision-making manageable, and without growing into a large bureaucracy.

Aside from the days of discussion and planning, our annual partners meetings, which consisted of leaders and staff of all twenty partners, usually ended with a celebratory dinner. One evening at an outdoor restaurant close to our conference center near Washington, D.C., we began singing, as was our custom. The manager said that was okay until the other tables were filled. Then we began dancing to our music—a mix of Middle Eastern, Indian, and American songs.

I turned to the group at the next table and asked, "I hope we are not disturbing you?"

They reassured me we were not and turned their chairs around to face us, as in confirmation. After a while the waiter, an Algerian, joined the dancing. Soon shouts of different countries' names brought dancers of various levels of expertise from each partner country. Eventually there was a call for "heads," the word we used for the leaders, and Asma, Amina, and I began dancing, albeit not nearly as well as the young trainers we called the "hearts" had done.

"Perhaps it is time to pass the torch to a new generation!" I called out.

The other tables responded to that with applause, to which I laughed, "Thanks, but you don't have to be so adamant about it!"

A woman and her friend who had been seated inside the restaurant came to us, said they were celebrating her birthday, and asked could she join us. We sang "Happy Birthday" to her in multiple languages. Wherever we held our meeting's final dinner, there were others who joined and enjoyed our uneven, largely mediocre dancing and singing. At an end of one work meeting in Petra, Jordan, the situation turned around: a group of men in long robes decided to dance, and we sat clapping and singing, enjoying the role reversal.

As our work continued, some of the concepts and terms new to the movement, like *learning organizations* and *participatory leadership*, became familiar to other activists around the world. Sylvia Borren, director of Oxfam Novib and an early WLP supporter, held several meetings in the Netherlands to discuss these concepts and practices. Rakhee conducted a training for some of the Oxfam Novib personnel on our inclusive, dialogue-based concept; Oxfam Novib then adopted it and in later years it became one of the pillars of Oxfam International's shared vision.[5] At a dinner, Sylvia said, "Who would've thought that after so many years of trying to find a democratic leadership structure that would suit our feminist ideals, the concept would emerge from the part of the world that has the least experience with it!"

Sylvia's words made me feel I had finally achieved what I had hoped for, though coming from a woman and a feminist, her remarks still left a slight uncertainty. After all, we understood each other and our joint work with a generosity that was not as easily replicated in other groups. My feeling of triumph came after a session we organized and that I moderated at the National Endowment for Democracy (NED), an independent, nonprofit foundation dedicated to the growth and strengthening of democratic institutions around the world, with Sakena, Asma, and Rakhee speaking about WLP's work on democracy development through the use of technology. Carl Gershman, the founding president of NED, introduced me as "not only the leading voice on the World Movement for Democracy's steering committee but one of the leading democrats internationally." I was deeply touched and flattered.

Chapter 19

The War on Terror

ON SEPTEMBER 11, 2001, I was on a conference call with WLP's Palestinian partners when excited voices on their side interrupted our conversation.

"Something terrible is happening in New York," they said. "Turn on your television."

I rushed to the conference room and saw images that would become burned into the world's memories: a plane flying into a tall building, smoke billowing behind it. Then, a second plane. Bodies falling through the air to escape the hellfire. On the street below, people running in panic, some barely visible through the smoke and dust. In Washington, D.C., another plane flew into the Pentagon. Over rural Pennsylvania, passengers in a fourth plane gave their lives to thwart an attack that would otherwise have claimed the US Capitol.

The horrific violence killed almost 3,000 people, from some 90 countries. Many of our partners knew someone who had perished, and almost all of them had lost a compatriot. There was a worldwide outpouring of support for the United States, as well as strong feelings of solidarity. Demonstrators across the world carried placards that read, "We are all Americans today." But the initial global reaction of sympathy and support for the United States soon gave way to concern. Many of those in other countries who had stood with lighted candles and signs of support began to wonder why the actions of nineteen terrorists, fifteen of whom were citizens of Saudi Arabia, all of whom died with their victims, did not warrant investigating that country's possible role. Instead, the US response morphed into a global war on terror—in practical terms, a war on Muslims. Our WLP allies and partners from around the world at first grieved, then, with the escalating rhetoric from the United States and its military allies,[1] began to worry about the emerging global conditions and how they would impact their communities and lives. The effect on our own lives here in the United States was horrific. The daily rhetoric of danger, the signs on highways warning us of the level of impending danger, the ever-tightening security measures at airports, the tapping of phone conversations all gave one the feeling we were living in a police state, without any impact on actual security. Soon bombs were dropped on Afghanistan, then Iraq. At WLP, we decided to put our heads together, search for a shared understanding of the events and their ramifications, and determine our position and the appropriate reaction to the changed circumstances.

From September 24 to 27 WLP held a series of dialogues with Feminist International Radio Endeavor and Women's International News Gathering Services.[2] Some dozen women leaders from among our allies around the world participated in family conversation-style radio broadcasts, as if the discussions could have happened around a living room in any of the cities where the speakers lived—from India to Canada, from Jordan to Brazil. The speakers all had surprisingly similar reactions: sorrow for the victims and their friends and families; sympathy for the cities that were subject of the attacks; and worries about the consequences. I felt gratified at our unanimity about the way forward: the act was criminal; such actions must be prevented by dealing with the extremist ideology that had been indoctrinated in the murderers' minds; those who taught this behavior or encouraged it should be held responsible; interfaith dialogue should become part of education and civil interaction around the world; women should teach their children tolerance and understanding at home; and women's organizations should integrate interfaith and intercultural dialogue into their global movement building.

Shortly after, WLP held a public interfaith dialogue in which women leaders from the three Abrahamic faiths—Marian Wright Edelman, Blu Greenberg, Azza Karam, and I—spoke about terror, war, and peace.[3] That conversation brought out the basic unity of vision among the three faiths, all originating in a limited area in the Middle East, and all believing in monotheism, in one eternal god who created the universe, that god guides humanity through revelation to prophets, and that humans have a choice between good and evil. The speakers were surprised at how little they had thought about or knew of each other's faiths—even such simple things as the numbers of believers in each faith. They came to the conclusion that they should explore and encourage their communities to learn about the other faiths that so closely resemble their own. The conversation ended in sharing our belief in the values of peace, charity, and civility and our common goal to work to avoid violence and war. I felt validation of all that I had been learning from my previous experiences. There was something essentially wrong in the way decisions were being made in our world—the way that war was considered a normal activity, almost inevitable. Nations, like individual leaders, felt they had to flex their muscles, build military capacity, threaten each other, and from time to time engage in activities that would justify the rhetoric and pump up the individual as well as the national ego. One of the most thoughtful and important, yet seldom remembered, statements about this state of affairs was President Dwight D. Eisenhower's farewell address:

> Until the latest of our world conflicts, the United States had no armaments industry. American makers of plowshares could, with time and as required, make swords as well. But now we . . . have been compelled to create a permanent armaments industry of vast proportions. . . . We annually spend on military security more than the net income of all United States corporations.
>
> This conjunction of an immense military establishment and a large arms industry is new in the American experience. The total influence—economic, political, even spiritual—is felt in every city, every State house, every office of the Federal government. We recognize the imperative need for this development. Yet we must not fail to comprehend its grave implications. Our toil, resources and livelihood are all involved; so is the very structure of our society. . . .
>
> Down the long lane of the history yet to be written America knows that this world of ours, ever growing smaller must avoid becoming a community of dreadful fear and hate, and be instead a proud confederation of mutual trust and respect.
>
> Such a confederation must be one of equals. The weakest must come to the table with the same confidence as do we, protected as we are by our moral, economic, and military strength. That table, though scarred

by many past frustrations, cannot be abandoned for the certain agony of the battlefield.

Disarmament, with mutual honor and confidence, is a continuing imperative. Together we must learn how to compose differences, not with arms, but with intellect and decent purpose.[4]

Since Eisenhower's speech on January 17, 1961, the Soviet Union has dissolved and new opportunities for peace have appeared. But unfortunately we searched for a new enemy and the fifteen extremist Saudis and their four cohorts created an opportunity to imagine a new global threat. The longest war in US history has finally ended after twenty years, and Osama bin Laden, the leader of the extremists, has been destroyed, but the many thousands of Afghans and Americans killed in the process don't seem to have made much of a difference to our security or that of the Afghans. The essential points made by President Eisenhower are more valid than ever. For me, personally, the vision reflected in his statement embodies all that the women's movement hopes for. And it shows that inspiration and support for our struggle for peace and rights can come from places where we would least expect—a man who spent his whole professional life in the armed forces, leading major battles, speaks words that describe the culture change we seek.

But on October 7, 2001, the United States attacked Afghanistan, and on October 26, Congress passed the PATRIOT Act, which expanded the government's powers to use surveillance and to wiretap domestic and international phones, increased the government's ability to obtain search warrants, and gave more law enforcement and investigative power to the US attorney general and to the Immigration and Naturalization Service, among other provisions. Although there were conversations about the nature of the attacks and questions about the legality and usefulness of aspects of the PATRIOT Act, support in the United States for a war with Al Qa'eda and its leader, Osama bin Laden, was strong. But the increasing focus on the dangers of terrorism soon led to paranoia and a deepening Islamophobia.[5] Americans wondered, "Why do they hate us?" and the answer they received was "Our democratic values." The chilling narrative that emerged was one of a country besieged by savage enemies who were against foundational American values and beliefs. The Cold War seemed almost tame in comparison.

The success of the US government's messaging showed itself in how easily citizens accepted its new elaborate security apparatus, especially at airports. But the civic reaction had a downside: not only there was no resistance to or questioning of the increased state security at the outset, when the country was in the thick of grief and fear, but there seemed to be no serious examination of its implications even two decades later. No one seemed to demand analysis of the efficiency, feasibility, or cost of the measures. No one questioned the nature of the "enemy" and its capabilities. One might anticipate that the many think tanks, universities, or media would ask about the actual nature of the potential threats to public safety: the numbers involved, the probability of reoccurrence. But we have seen few or no extensive comparative studies regarding this, as there have been for other public safety and security issues such as those related to cars, water, trains, guns, addictions, and pollution.

Events would continue to unfold unexpectedly: a young man from Nigeria, whose father had already alerted Nigerian and US embassy officials about his son's abnormal behavior, was caught on a plane with liquid that could be used as an explosive. From then on, every airline passenger was searched and any liquids—from water to perfume and moisturizer—were confiscated. After a man in Paris tried to board a plane with a potential explosive in his shoe, all airline passengers throughout the United States patiently removed their shoes and walked through X-ray machines. In a country where gun violence kills more than 20,000 innocent people a year and car accidents almost 40,000, and which has had no subsequent terrorist attacks on airlines, these reactions seem excessive at best, absurd at worst. Yet we all have complied meekly and carefully, knowing what could happen if we didn't. After September 11 I was especially careful, since my passport revealed my birth place as Kerman, Iran. I have lived fifty years of my adult life in the United States; I am American enough to vote, but not quite American enough to leave and enter the country without arousing suspicion. I hold my arms above my head as I stand facing the X-ray, a line ahead of me and one behind, and wonder what a science fiction writer would have made of this scene a decade earlier.

What was my great adopted country coming to? The PATRIOT Act had done away with habeas corpus—the right to protection against illegal imprisonment. It allowed my phone—like that of every other American—to be tapped. If I, who had been wary of the intelligence organizations in Iran before and after the Revolution, was petrified now, knowing how much more efficient this law and those who were expected to implement it were, why was it that my compatriots in America seemed so complacent about this?

As a result of the attacks and the US response to them, the formerly robust dialogue and language on human rights from governments and in international gatherings gave way to an emphasis on democracy defined mainly as "elections" and as military security to promote peace or guarantee national or individual safety.[6] I watched as the United States in March 2003 began a second war in

Iraq, based on weak and faulty intelligence that only tangentially linked that country to the September 11 attacks and on the threadbare claim that Iraq was building "weapons of mass destruction." Baghdad went up in flames under merciless bombardment, the goal of which was proudly described by the US president to create "shock and awe." Soon afterward, former ambassador Paul Bremer, a man who had never traveled to any part of the Middle East, spoke little to no Arabic, and had little to no knowledge of the history or culture of the region, was appointed "Governor of Iraq." I was amazed—even the British colonialists had tried to employ people who had at least some basic knowledge about the people and country they were sent to rule.

At WLP, our partners, especially those in the Arab world, were shocked. They could not fathom the US position; for decades previously, the country had been known as a reliable supporter of international law. I was deeply depressed to see the world that just eighteen months ago on September 11 had shown so much admiration and sympathy for the United States now viewed it as a danger to world peace.[7] As an American I had no answer to the US-led invasion of Iraq, let alone a convincing rationale to offer our WLP partners.

A shadow fell over the Middle East as 150,000 members of the Iraqi civil service who had been members of the Ba'ath Party—the leftist political party that civil servants had been required to join—and nearly the same number from the armed forces were summarily dismissed. Overnight, the young men who had been drafted for Iraq's compulsory military service, along with those in the professional army, suddenly became untouchable—Paul Bremer's first order in May 2003 was to exclude from the new Iraq government any members of the Ba'ath Party. No one seemed to have thought about the consequences of these decisions. The unemployed young men provided a potential constituency for the radical Islamists, soon became the foundation for Al Qa'eda in Iraq, and shortly thereafter created ISIS. In an equally inexplicable decision, 15,000 Shi'a activist Islamists and their leader, Ayatollah Sistani, who had fled to Iran to escape Saddam Hussein's Sunni-led rule, were allowed to return to Iraq, and Sistani became the leading voice of the Shi'ite population in Iraq. The Islamic Republic of Iran's leadership gloated over their unexpected good fortune. The United States had replaced their enemy Saddam with a friendly and supportive group of trained activists exported from Iran and had replaced a substantial army with a crumbling society enmeshed in chaos and discord.

Most important of all, the United States sank in its international reputation and moral influence, and the experience of Afghanistan and Iraq chilled the euphoria that had prevailed in the global women's rights community for a few short years after the fall of the Soviet Union. The terrible wars and destruction brought anger and discord in the Middle East, and the war that was perceived to be against Muslims became a major challenge to WLP's vision of a global movement based on inclusiveness and dialogue. Just as devastating was the loss of strong US support for the UN declarations and agreements on human rights and democracy; this weakened the foundations of civil society organizations, especially those related to women's rights. The challenge was no longer one of movement building—in itself a tremendous task—but instead simply sustaining the partnership and adapting the activities to what might be possible. I tried to view what seemed a near impossibility as a test of WLP's resilience to adapt and evolve in response to the changing circumstances. Our MENA partners most impacted by the wars, those in Lebanon, Afghanistan, and Jordan, added new programs to empower internally displaced and refugee women and girls, especially those at risk of being trafficked into forced prostitution and sexual exploitation. They also provided shelters for refugee women and children and helped bring physical and emotional healing services to those displaced by war.

Invariably, though, the challenges grew as the wars extended to other arenas. Much of what we saw seemed the result of a combination of hypermasculine thinking and uncontrolled greed and ambition. As we saw images of young Americans who had died in war-torn countries and as we confronted the senseless destruction of those countries' cities and inhabitants, we wondered why these shocking costs were tolerated. What was the point of creating "shock and awe"? It was obvious that a new way of thinking and a new set of values needed to be presented to the world. Asma Khader said, only half-joking, "The world needs a mom!"

IN THE fall of 2003, in the same year that the United States invaded Iraq and WLP was struggling to adjust to the difficult new global situation, Hojatoleslam Hussein Khomeini, grandson of the ayatollah whose regime had placed me under a death warrant, came to my house for dinner.

It all began when our colleague Hormoz Hekmat, editor of *Iran Nameh*, acted as interpreter for a speech Hussein Khomeini gave at the American Enterprise Institute in Washington. Hormoz was very impressed with the young man and suggested we meet with him. I asked Hormoz to call him and invite him to have dinner with us, but then the family negotiations about where to have such a dinner began. Farah said she would be pleased to have him at her house, but then called to say Habib's (her second husband's) first reaction was, "Over my dead body this guy comes to our house," but Habib did indicate interest in meeting him at *our* house. Gholam was hesitant as well. He didn't want to go to a restaurant, fearing we might run into someone we knew. He also felt uncomfortable inviting him to our house. I decided to ignore all this and began preparing for dinner. I stopped by the local Iranian restaurant and got some rice with herbs, chicken with walnut and pomegranate sauce, and sweets for dessert.

Habib and Farah arrived early, and, in a gesture of defiance, both Habib and Gholam poured themselves generous glasses of vodka. I brewed some tea for the guests. Hormoz arrived with Hussein Khomeini and an Iraqi supporter—both of whom were dressed in slacks and T-shirts. They seemed a bit shy but quite nice and friendly. We began the conversation talking about Iraq. The Iraqi fellow was handsome and rather fierce. Farah mused later, "The guy could well be a suicide bomber, regardless of his looks." He was completely prowar, pro-US, and down on all of the Middle East. He said, "They have to come and run our country, since we can't do it ourselves." Later, however, when he listened to us and sensed our attitude, he said, "I wouldn't accept Bush as my servant, let alone my master!" Hussein Khomeini was quieter and more studied. He talked about the separation of mosque and state and about his own position vis-à-vis the Revolutionary Guards and Hezbollah, saying that he had a place among them and was listened to with interest. He also said he was able to use his notoriety and name recognition; the Islamists allowed him to say things that people would not tolerate coming from others. All in all, it was a friendly and interesting conversation, and everyone was quite pleased with the experience. Farah was especially excited about the evening and considered it a lesson in unexpected possibilities.

The next day I called Carl Gershman, the president of NED, saying, "Guess who came to dinner last right . . ." and asked whether he would want to meet Hussein Khomeini. He said he would very much like to. After going back and forth with Khomeini's handlers, Hormoz, and NED, we finally settled on a time. Hormoz didn't know whether Khomeini would be at the hotel, or if, as his handler had said, he would be doing interviews on the Hill and would come directly to NED. Hormoz was a bit upset that the arrangements he had made were now uncertain.

"I will go to the hotel, but if he is not there, he's on his own," he said.

It is interesting how even the kindest of men become so tied up in this sort of thing, I thought. The guy is outside of the Middle East for the first time in his life. He doesn't know the language and has no idea what these people are arranging for him. He makes dates, but then his hosts take him elsewhere. There is no telling what they say to him and whether he understands any of it. It is a wonder he seems so cool and collected and so in possession of his identity.

Hussein Khomeini was wearing his black wool *abba* and turban and looked appropriately exotic when I saw him get out of the black limo for the meeting at NED. Carl, Mark Platner (editor of *Democracy Journal*), and a NED program officer joined us. I ended up translating for Khomeini. He spoke well as he explained the differences between the two major sects of Islam. He said Shi'ites believe in freedom of religious practice, as well as separation of religion from civic authority. The Sunnis, on the other hand, believe in the unity of mosque and state, and throughout history they have connected religion and government under a caliph, who in his person embodies both religious and secular authority. "Ayatollah Khomeini," he said, "had tried to bring Shi'ism close to Sunni ways. There are others who are trying to bring the Sunni ways closer to Shi'a tradition."

He described his potential constituency of students and reformists, his doctrine of separation of religion from the state, and his prospects. Carl told him about NED and said they would like to help him with his projects. Hussein Khomeini explained that he wanted to work in the Iraqi cities of Karbala and Najaf, sites that are holy to Shi'a Muslims. He wanted to open a traditional *madrassa* (school) with classrooms and rooms for students around the courtyard and *talabe* (students) sitting on the floor, listening and discussing religion, secularism, and democracy. He said that many would come from Iran and many from Iraq and that they would be the change makers. He promised to send a proposal to NED.

We spoke a couple of times before he left for New York; on our last call he said, "Khanom, man o shoma dindar hasteem, vali in araba ba ma farq darand" ("Ma'am, you and I are believing people, but some of these Arabs have different ideas").

I would never have thought that one day I would be sitting in Chevy Chase, Maryland, talking with Khomeini's grandson about religion and state and how we can bring change to the Islamic Republic of Iran. I don't know what the results of our meetings were for him, but the experience confirmed my belief in giving dialogue a chance without presuppositions—especially during the war on terror, which in so many other ways had fractured what I believed to be true.

Chapter 20

Iranian Feminism and the Green Revolution

A S WLP GREW, I looked for ways, as I had done with SIGI, to engage with Iranian feminists. Mohammad Khatami's tenure as president of Iran (1997–2005) had opened the country's civic space considerably, and it seemed a good time—or at least less risky than before—to open dialogue with the people trying to advance women's rights while living under the Islamic government. A key opportunity arose in October 2005, when WLP was set to hold its annual partnership meeting in Bangkok to coincide with the Association for Women's Rights in Development (AWID) Forum, which would bring together more than a thousand women from around the world. The forum offered an occasion to showcase WLP's work and to seek comment and feedback; it also gave WLP an opportunity to provide visibility to our partners from Muslim-majority countries in the Middle East, North Africa, and South, East, and Central Asia, who were almost always excluded from international gatherings. Hoping for the best, WLP decided to invite ten activists and leaders from Iran to join us at the meeting and take part in a weeklong training workshop, offered in Persian, on participatory leadership and advocacy strategies in closed societies. Since they did not need visas to enter Thailand, their travel would not attract Iranian government interest. It seemed like a safe place for them, and the AWID conference could be used as a cover, if necessary.

Layla, an Iranian American woman who had recently returned to Iran, helped us select the participants and handled the logistics. If all went well, this would be an exceptional opportunity for budding Iranian activists, who were for the most part isolated, to share their experiences and hear from WLP's partners. At the conference we were set to launch the English translation of *Guide to Equality in the Family in the Maghreb*,[1] a meticulous documentation of the campaign that led to reform of legislation on the status of women in Morocco, which we hoped the Iranian women might see as an inspiration.

Once I arrived in Bangkok, I realized that for the first time since the Revolution, I was working face-to-face with a group of feminist organizers from Iran. The group included a psychologist, a journalist, a Kurdish leader, an attorney, a computer engineer, a professor of women's studies, and several NGO leaders. They were sharp, receptive, outspoken, and adept at working in groups. It was exhilarating to realize that all the work of my generation had lived on in the independent spirit of these young women. But some things had changed: their attitude was noticeably different from that of women I had worked with in the 1970s. These women seemed more defiant even here in Thailand, where they were not being challenged or restricted. It took me a while to realize that what they were saying, with their short, choppy hair, their jeans, and their power posture: "We are not what they want us to be. We haven't given up. We are nobody's victims." Speaking with them, I was surprised to hear the new developments in the use of the Persian language—a language that had remained nearly unchanged for centuries. When I was working on my dissertation on *The Rubaiyat of Omar Khayyam* in 1967, I was perplexed by the ease with which I could read and comprehend the eleventh-century Persian text, while the English of Chaucer's *Canterbury Tales*, written 300 years later, was almost a foreign language even to native English speakers. But in just two and a half decades, Persian had suddenly undergone a dynamic transformation, as though it had been so rocked by the apocalyptic events in politics and society that people required a new vocabulary that would speak to their experiences.

The young Iranian women were as excited to be there as I was, and they enjoyed a smooth, easy rapport with the WLP partners. They worked hard and put in long hours, eager to learn and to master the techniques we taught them for facilitating workshops and building successful networks. They also partied energetically in the evenings, some drinking, some dancing, all of them connecting with women from other countries and relishing every moment of their simple freedoms—to dress, speak, move, and dance without fear and anxiety.

Several months later, Shahla, one of the Iranian women in Thailand, came to see me in Washington. The night before her visit we had been working on a human rights alert about her sentence in absentia—four years for "crimes against national security." She looked different now, free of the scarf she had worn in Thailand. She wore a beige linen blouse over slacks, no makeup, and her highlighted hair was pulled back. But it was an air about her—a loosening up of her joints, rather than her physical appearance—that most impressed me.

She hugged me tight, and when she sat down, I noticed she had tears in her eyes.

She said, "On my way here I was thinking, 'What shall I tell you, where would I begin?'" I smiled and said, "Begin from where we left each other in Thailand. What happened when you returned to Iran?"

I listened as Shahla poured out her story:

> When we returned to Tehran, I was the only one of the group who was called in for questioning. When the man from security called and asked me to meet him for an informal conversation, I asked him to write to me and tell me what it was I was being called in for. He said, "If I write, this will become more formal and in the end it will be more difficult for you." So I agreed to meet him. I went to the Sabet Pasal house in Shemiran—you remember that big mansion?[2] Now it is a place for intelligence work. The guy kept asking me why I was in Thailand. I had written an article describing the Forum—not the work of our team, of course. I told him, "Look, I don't remember the details. The work of the AWID Forum is transparent. Everything is on their website. You will see, there were people from all over the world and workshops about all sorts of things." Finally, they let me go.

She paused and wiped her eyes. "I don't know how to proceed. There is so much to say." She stared out of the window intently, as if reading something on a blackboard.

> There is my personal life. My husband and I have lived together for twenty-five years. I married him when I was sixteen. I come from an entirely different family from his: my father was an army officer before the Revolution and my uncle was a diplomat. My husband's family is

very religious. The first day after we were married I mentioned to him a film I had seen about the life of the prophet Mohammad. He asked incredulously, "Did you go to the cinema?" I said, "Yes, I did." He said, "That's the last time you will do something like that!"

For many years I lived a lie. I covered my face and kept my black chador tightly closed under my nose and kept my voice low and moved quietly. I wanted to appease him so that I would be allowed to go to college and to do some of the things I was interested in. But it was very difficult.

The trouble with the situation in Iran is that everyone is terrified. None of us is Che Guevara. We are all afraid of the ever-recurring call for questioning and of going to jail. The last time I was in prison I was put next to women of all sorts—from the age of nine onward. Some were drug addicts, some smugglers, some prostitutes, and mixed among them were political prisoners. Some of the women cut themselves all across their chest, neck, and arms, to show they were tough. Some did it because of the agony of the addict with no access to drugs or treatment. Anyway, it's not easy to spend time in prison. But I am ready to do it if I have to. Right now I am confused. I am doing interviews with Voice of America and Radio Liberty. It will be hell to answer for when I go home, especially with my husband's situation and the divorce hanging over my head. But I have to go back. If I don't, the others will be demoralized. They will think, "There goes another one." Everyone who leaves weakens the budding movement. It's true that we are supposed to be leaderless. It's true that we have learned collective decision-making and participatory leadership. It is also true that these days the young especially would not stand for someone telling them what they need to do. But in the end there are a few whose activism and understanding drive the movement. Each one who leaves damages the group. There are differences among us, but we love and respect each other. We have a shortage of love in Iran. We have hated for so long and have been angry at each other for so long that now we want to love, to respect, to give permission to each other to be who we want to be. But there is one big dividing point that affects how people behave in the end—whether they think the Islamic Republic is capable of reform or not. Layla, for instance, thinks it is. Roya thinks it is not. We talk to all sorts of people. We negotiate. But in the end it matters which view you hold and it makes all the difference in the choices you make, including whether to leave or to stay.[3]

Shahla stayed in Washington and became a full-time exiled opponent of the regime. Yet with the memory of the Revolution and the death and destruction it had brought to the country still fresh in the national consciousness, many of the Iranian women in the Thailand group decided to stay in Iran and adopt "reform" rather than revolution as their goal. Some went on to add what they had learned in Thailand from women from other countries to the strategies they had developed at home in Iran. For example, they used ideas from the advocacy campaign the Moroccan activists had designed to reform their country's laws on the status of women in the family to work toward their goals in Iran. This learning reemphasized to me the importance of enabling women from the Global South to attend international meetings. It also demonstrated the viral nature of ideas and strategies, as well as the need for a global response to the challenge of patriarchy.

In the following years we invited small groups of the Iranian women leaders who had gone to Thailand to our WLP annual partners' meetings. Although the Iranian activists had held participatory leadership workshops in Tehran and in Kish Island, they felt it was not safe to do any more formal trainings in Iran. But they had come up with ingenious ways to approximate the workshop experience in ordinary situations. Taraneh, a journalist, told the WLP partners how she and others had adapted the "fish bowl" exercise, in which two participants take opposite positions on a controversial issue, such as veiling, and each vigorously argues the case she is representing; in the presence of other workshop participants, each tries to convince the other. The audience then discusses and evaluates the two women's advocacy skills. Since the law in Iran does not allow more than three people to gather in public spaces, Taraneh and her colleagues took advantage of any occasion where groups of people were gathered "legitimately," such as at a bus stop. She and a friend would act out an argument along the lines of, "Should women be banned from the night shift at work for their own safety and to benefit the family?" Soon other passengers waiting for the bus would get involved in the argument, taking sides. Taraneh said with glee, "The bus arrived and my friend and I got on. When we looked back at the heated discussion between the spectators who had now become participants, we saw that the policeman who stopped to check what was going on had joined the discussion as well. We felt quite proud of our work!"

This was even more creative than the success that Tolekan Ismailova (director general of WLP's partner in Kyrgyzstan, Bir Duino) had in Kyrgyzstan in convincing a TV station to include workshop sessions from *Leading to Choices* on a call-in show, where not only the guests in the studio but the audience across the whole country could respond to the questions in the workshop exercises.

WHEN PARVIN Ardalan and Noushin Ahmadi Khorasani launched the One
Million Signatures Campaign for Reform of Discriminatory Family Laws in
Iran in 2006, their goal was to mobilize 1 million activists by gathering 1 million
signatures. Inspired by work of the Moroccan family law reform campaigners,
which they knew from the Persian translation of the *Moroccan Guide to Equality
in the Family in the Maghreb*, they added digital outreach and social networking
to the traditional methods; they knocked on doors and spoke to women about
the unfairness of laws that treat women as minors or like the insane, always in
need of protection and never independent human beings. They outlined the
articles of Iran's family law and the consequence of violating them for a woman,
a wife, a mother, or a professional. Finally, they asked the many women they
spoke with to sign the petition to reform the unjust law. They went to grocery
stores, hair salons, and dress shops—anywhere where women congregate—to
engage women of all ages in dialogue. If they collected a signature, fine; if not,
they left the reading material, asked the woman to think about the laws, and
provided contact information for a neighborhood group she might wish to
join. Through all of this, Ardalan, Khorasani, and their activist friends honed
their consensus-building and negotiation skills.

The campaign reached out to men, to persuade them that reforming family
laws was about them as well, that women and men share the cost of the unfair
treatment of half of the population. Ultimately, men comprised one out of every
three signatures the campaign gathered, much to the chagrin of the authorities who simply could not understand the movement's appeal to men. The
campaign was also exceptionally adept at using social media both to mobilize
local young men and women and to bring awareness and support to the Iranian
diaspora and the international human rights community. The campaigners
studied the experience of political activists in Iran and other countries and
adapted what they learned to their own political situation. They mobilized
large and diverse constituencies by approaching other groups, including those
with religious backgrounds, to discuss collaboration specifically on women's
issues and not close collaboration on organizational vision and methods. The
strategy was strengthened when the women's coalition contacted the three
major candidates for president, all of whom had in the past rejected CEDAW.
Two candidates, Mir-Hossein Mousavi, a former prime minister, and Mehdi
Karroubi, former Speaker of Parliament, agreed to the movement's demands
and included ratification of CEDAW as part of their platforms.

MEANWHILE, AHEAD of the Iranian election, WLP translated Noushin
Ahmadi Khorasani's book on the One Million Signatures Campaign into

English and launched it at an event in Washington in 2009,[4] well aware that the new movement's ideas and strategies were fast taking shape in other closed or semiclosed societies in the Middle East and North Africa. Our long-time partner Zainah Anwar, who had cofounded Sisters in Islam in Malaysia, was a speaker at the book launch, along with Rabéa Naciri, an architect of the Moroccan advocacy effort and coauthor of *The Guide to Equality in the Family in the Maghreb*, whose Persian translation had inspired the work of the Iranian activists—showing the viral nature of ideas and strategies. Zainah was fascinated by the interaction between the Moroccan and the Iranian movements and talked about initiating a similar movement in Asia, an idea that before long blossomed into the international network for women's rights in Islam, Musawah (Equality). In her words, Musawah suggested "a rich and diverse collection of interpretations, juristic opinions and principles that makes it possible to read equality and justice in Islam ... [and] a vital contribution at a time when democracy, human rights and women's rights constitute the modern ethical paradigm of today's world." Zainah invited Rabéa Naciri and Amina Lemrini, founding members of WLP's Moroccan partner organization, ADFM, to join an advisory board to guide the new network, and we all met at the conference that launched Musawah in Kuala Lumpur in February 2009.

While in Kuala Lumpur, several Iranian participants asked me to talk to prominent Iranian exiled women in Europe and the United States, "the outsiders," to help encourage women inside Iran to participate actively in the upcoming presidential election. Our conversations convinced me that the talented, resourceful, well-connected Iranian diaspora in the West could play an important role in shaping social and political movements in Iran. But this had to be done together with the "insiders." The vision is similar across the world: freedom, equality, justice, and political participation. But the tangible realities of the life inside—the constraints, the evolving needs and ways to articulate messages that resonate at any given moment—have to come from them.

At the conclusion of the Musawah conference, WLP held its own wrap-up session for partners. Many practicing Muslims in our group thought one could find the solution for reform within Islam itself, in the concept of ijtihad, a practice that allows and often requires the ulama to reinterpret or adjust our understanding of the meaning of the scriptures to the conditions of changing times.[5] We all agreed that reinterpretation is a useful tool for communicating with a large part of our constituency, especially if it is tied to comparative interfaith studies that show the similarities between the three monotheistic faiths. These religions and cultures share concepts that nourish and support the best inclinations of human beings. However, they also represent injunctions about women, slavery, and homosexuality, among others, that are not only morally abhorrent but also no longer realistic or practical.

I believe from personal experience that Christians, Jews, Muslims, and believers of all religions can be feminists and at the same time uphold the basic tenets of their religion. Feminism, like human rights in general, cannot be placed within the framework of any particular religion. Some of us are Muslim feminists. But we are not "Islamic feminists," a term coined by Western academics, picked up by the diaspora, and reflected back into academic circles in the Muslim world, much to the delight of the more sophisticated fundamentalists, who use it as a way of derailing the energy and resources of some women's groups into textual analysis of statements that, no matter how they are reinterpreted, are a strong impediment to women's rights. The Musawah meeting helped us clarify and strengthen our position on religion, culture, and rights and led us to focus on reframing secularism correctly defined not as atheism but as the separation of civic law from any specific belief system.

ON ELECTION day in June 2009, over 39 million Iranians, representing about 85 percent of eligible voters, cast their votes. The government claimed that Mahmoud Ahmadinejad, the only one of the three candidates who had not supported the activists' demand for ratification of CEDAW, had received 62.6 percent of the votes and was chosen for a second term. Mousavi and Karroubi both demanded nullification of the elections. Hundreds of thousands of voters filled the streets in Tehran and other major cities across Iran, shouting, "Where is my vote?"

As a response to the fraudulent election, the Green Movement was born; it evolved from the mass of angry voters to a nationwide force that demanded the democratic rights originally sought in the 1979 Revolution. The protests continued for more than a week, and the women's coalition staged huge demonstrations against election fraud, with hundreds of thousands of marchers chanting, "Down with the dictator!" "Death to the dictator!" and "Give us our votes back!" Perhaps not surprisingly, the government and the paramilitary forces used ruthless violence to quickly put an end to the demonstrations and arrested and interrogated hundreds of people, including prominent reformist politicians, university students, and human rights activists.

Ultimately, the Green Movement was an extraordinary phenomenon that brought unprecedented civic awareness and political mobilization across the nation. Iranian women, who were at the forefront of the demonstrations and have fought the theocracy on every item of the state's agenda, proved that once rights are ingrained in the psyche of a population, they cannot be erased, no matter the amount of state pressure and violence. More than four decades of force have kept Iranian women from playing the leading role they had earned for themselves in their country's politics, economics, and culture and in the international arena; however, they continue to be a productive and dynamic force in the country's literature, arts, and entrepreneurial work—anything that does not require positive governmental support or legal sanction. Substantial change in family laws may appear to be impossible in a theocracy, but Iranian women have pushed back against the government's original draconian measures meant to segregate and exclude women and have succeeded in keeping their demands and aspirations at the center of national dialogue. Unfortunately, the Green Movement also resulted in a second wave of feminist exiles to Europe, Asia, and the United States.

The massive participation of women, their lead role in the use of social networking for mobilization, and their slogans of inclusion, freedom, and equality leading up to and throughout the 2009 Green Movement would soon be replicated in the "Arab Spring" 2011 uprisings in the MENA region. But once again, as in the 1979 Islamic Revolution in Iran, when no organized civic bodies were behind the people's uprising, the collapse of the old regimes was followed by reactionary, authoritarian government takeovers. The Islamists' access to the vast network of mosques and their ready constituency, as well as the substantial funds available to them through *vaqf* (charitable donations) often make them the most likely political victors.

IN 2010, the annual WLP partners' meeting, to be held in Indonesia during the World Movement for Democracy conference,[6] came at a terrible time for me. Farah, who had been battling cancer with amazing courage and zest for life the past five years, was moving toward her last days. I spent time keeping her company every day, taking her for a walk, driving with her and Hamid for an ice cream cone. I didn't want to leave her, but when I was deciding whether to attend the Jakarta meeting, Farah insisted I should go. The day before my flight, I sat with her and made her take a bite of her favorite snack: feta cheese, lavash bread, and walnuts. She took it but said, "You have to get ready to let me go."

I spent the longest trip of my life dazed and mute. As I entered the hotel in Jakarta, Hamid called to let me know that Farah was gone. Rakhee met me at the front desk and checked me in. I have no recollection of how I got to the room, of the doctor Rakhee had called to prescribe a calming medication for me, or how she reserved a seat for me on the next flight back to Washington. She cared for me as Farah would have.

Farah's memorial was a fitting celebration of her spirit and her joy of life. Two hundred loving friends, including her colleagues at the World Bank, the key figures in the Marxist organization that she had represented as spokesperson so many years ago, and members of the ruling elite of the prerevolutionary government of Iran joined family to celebrate her life. Her favorite music, Antonín Dvořák's Cello Concerto in B minor, was performed, and I added to Farah's eulogy her favorite short poem, by Edna St. Vincent Millay:

> My candle burns at both ends;
>   It will not last the night;
> But ah, my foes, and oh, my friends—
>   It gives a lovely light![7]

"Are you very sad Aunti Farah is dead?" asked my eight-year-old granddaughter Saphora, who had come from New York to take part in Farah's remembrance.

"Yes, my dear, I am very sad," I answered.

"Maybe we should make a story together."

"That's a good idea."

For the next several weeks Saphora and I worked on a story she called "Jessica and the Dancing Parrot." The theme was, you can do whatever you really want to do if you try hard enough. We spent a lot of time on the phone at all hours on the weekends and sometimes at night. One night when we were interrupted at her bedtime, she called telling me she was holding a flashlight under the covers, since her mom had turned off the light. We went through the story of our imaginary Jessica and her struggles with her parrot, Lexi, to help the bird stand on tiptoe and replicate Jessica's ballet moves. Through their joint efforts she finally succeeded. Lexi was allowed to join the ballet class and became a successful ballerina.

Saphora wanted to include a variety of exciting adventures. I argued for focus—no detours on boat trips and ball games. She asked, "Why not?"

"Focus, my dear," I responded, thinking about the reader's attention span, while Saphora was thinking of all the things Jessica wanted to do with Lexi. We settled on including a conversation over a breakfast of waffles for Jessica and Cheerios for her toddler brother when her mom finally agreed that Jessica could take Lexi to the ballet class. Lexi was given a standing ovation, and both parrot and Jessica were praised for their accomplishment.

But Saphora still had difficulty seeing the book as more than a conversation between the two of us. I shared our story with Rakhee, who decided she wanted to be the publisher. Rakhee soon added drawings and photos of ballet classes and parrots. I picked up an album with a pale pink cover. Rakhee printed our narrative on dark pink paper and we glued those on the pages of the album. By then Saphora had caught writer's fever. "Mamani, can we have our book in the stores where we buy our story books?"

"Not quite yet, my dear," I said. "Maybe with the next one."

During this period I relived my childhood experience with Farah, when I took her to my Zoroastrian school in Kerman during our parents' divorce to register her for first grade and helped her learn how to read. This project with Saphora was just what I needed to pass the initial period of mourning for Farah, until I learned that my sister has never really left me. It also helped me realize how the idea of empowerment can take root in a child's mind.

Chapter 21

Changing the Architecture
of Human Relationships

THE WLP PARTNERSHIP WAS severely handicapped by the wars in Iraq and Afghanistan, the first supposedly ending in 2011, the other continuing for another decade, both spreading in the MENA region and replicated by outside engagement and interference, causing endless death and destruction. A few short periods, such as Iran's Green Movement in 2009 followed by the Arab Spring in 2011, brought exhilaration and hope. But I was less optimistic than our partners in the region. The experience of the Iranian Revolution had proved to me that demonstrations, uprisings, and slogans, helpful as they may be in giving expression to the needs of populations involved, will not improve systems of governance unless responsible civic leadership is already in place.

I was happy to see that my emphasis on building NGOs as "learning organizations," constantly evolving and responding and adapting to changes in the environment, proved useful for us during these difficult times. The WLP partners came up with ways to help the Syrian, Iraqi, and Afghan refugees, such as informing the responsible UN and government entities about the needs of the women, training women to advocate for themselves and to learn marketable skills, and helping with legal issues they and their children faced.

I was proud to see the effectiveness of the "grow without growing" plan we at WLP had created together with the partners earlier. Now, as the partnership grew, conducting trainings in sixty countries in thirty languages, we had succeeded in keeping the international WLP secretariat small while growing in four regions of the globe as each of the twenty partners expanded their reach in turn by partnering with other independent organizations at the national and regional levels. I was happy to see that successful women who had participated in our trainings were increasing their numbers among elected and appointed political leaders, while leading in an inclusive, dialogue-based style of leadership and decision-making—showing none of the usual "I win, you lose" attitude.

During WLP's second decade, 2010–20, as a member of the steering committee of the World Movement for Democracy (WMD), I had the opportunity to ensure that our WLP partners played an important role in making women's participation in democracy development not a "matter of concern" but the central issue. I made sure that the annual WLP partners meeting took place in conjunction with the WMD. It seemed amazing to me that women—the majority of the population of the earth, who almost everywhere are responsible for bringing up and educating both genders of the next generation—are generally seen as just another minority. It was hard to see why the democracy movements, not unlike Marxist movements of earlier times, seemed to believe that once their formula of liberation is achieved, the issue of women's participation would automatically be solved. I had seen the horrific failure of this formula in the Soviet Union and China. I also experienced the continuing challenge of inequality in democratic societies of Europe and the United States. Having seen the similarity of the basic structure of human institutions beginning in the family—society's basic unit—and replicated in schools, religious establishments, the arts, and politics, it seemed obvious to me that to create a healthy, successful, truly democratic society, it is necessary to change the architecture of human relations.

Because educational establishments, from high schools to universities, are already committed to civic education, and institutions of research on politics are where the idea of defining and sharing the theoretical aspects of democracy development is in principle accepted, I thought WLP's leadership model, which we had successfully adapted to a variety of languages and cultures around the globe, could prove a useful additional arena to provide the skills necessary for participatory, democratic decision-making. Two powerful areas often ignored by those who engage in democracy development and human rights are religious establishments and the arts. Since I was a child listening to Naneh Fatemeh's stories, I have known the power of narrative. As I grew to adolescence and adulthood, literature became more and more vital in shaping my worldview. I saw the impact not only on myself but also on my young students, and later in the emotional reaction of the crowds on all sides of the political arena during the Revolution in Iran. I will never forget the "Ten Nights of Poetry" reading series in Tehran at the German Embassy's cultural arm, the Goethe Institute, in 1977, and its importance in glamorizing the coming Revolution. Night after night, to growing audiences, beloved poets read their passionate and exquisite poems in praise of liberty, freedom, and the iconic landscapes of the country they loved. There were no harsh discussions of any program, political agenda, or challenge, just lovely, inspiring words. Iranians came to identify the revolutionaries with these words and sentiments—which partially explains the revolutionaries' popularity, as well as the shock and disbelief when the Revolution's leading figures actually gained power and showed their true intent. Since that time I have tried to help provide a setting where the positive and humane ideas of the women's movement can be communicated through the arts, especially poetry and storytelling. In my work in the global women's movement and throughout my experience with FIS, SIGI, and WLP, I have tried to connect feminist activism with the arts—painting exhibits, film screenings, and storytelling. One of the most popular events we held was "Lifelines: The Literature of Human Rights."[1] The series began in collaboration with the Library of Congress in Washington and later in New York at the New School for Social Research in conjunction with the annual meeting of the UN Commission on the Status of Women. It featured a diverse group of distinguished writers and poets such as Fatema Mernissi, Grace Paley, Elizabeth Alexander, Robin Morgan, and Ama Ata Aidoo. After the poet Abena Busia joined the WLP board in 2013, she choreographed "Lifelines" as an exciting intergenerational dialogue among activist poets. Over the last two decades, these sessions have brought a new level of passionate engagement to our discussions.

During my work with the WOI in Iran, I had learned the power of religious institutions, and the important role they played through their regular community gatherings—both faith-related and social. Given that the positive messages of the texts of all religions are inspiring and the negative messages are products of the exigencies of ancient cultural history, it seemed important that as democrats we try to help implement an important article of the Declaration of Human Rights on freedom of belief, which, if fully exercised, would leave this area to individual choice, and civic governance to elected representatives.

In Iran, women activists emphasized the holy texts' positive dictates of kindness, justice, and caring, as well as the recommendation to adapt to the changing times. At the WOI, we stayed connected to the more enlightened religious leaders, who were often ahead of their communities. In exile I continued this effort. In April 2008, a multiyear initiative called Women, Faith, and Development launched a global effort at the Washington National Cathedral supported by Mary Robinson (the first female president of Ireland), Madeleine Albright (the first female US secretary of state), Kim Campbell (the first and so far only woman prime minister of Canada), and others to bring together governments, women's organizations, faith-based organizations, UNFPA, and others to raise funds and work together to advance peace, eliminate poverty, end violence against women, and promote gender equality.[2] Thoraya Obaid and I spoke at that first event, she on behalf of UNFPA and I on behalf of women's NGOs. Mary and Kim each presented powerful statements on the positive role that religious organizations must play to support gender justice if they are to reach their stated goal of eliminating poverty and injustice and promoting peace. The April event was highly successful, raising $3 billion in commitments for the cause. Since then, the idea of interfaith connection and conversation has expanded, and women have become more visible in the leadership of these efforts. The latest advance in this important collaboration is the appointment in 2019 of Azza Karam as secretary general of Religions for Peace (RfP).[3] Her work to promote interfaith dialogue and mutual support between women activists and religious groups will be enhanced by her new position.[4] Since RfP identifies itself as "not an organization but a movement," the possibilities of mutual benefit to women's NGOs are enormous.

I HAD worked with Mary Robinson on several initiatives over the years and had felt privileged to be included in the formation of some of them. At a casual get-together in New York in March 2019, a little more than ten years after our collaboration on "Women, Faith, and Development," she told me she wished to work closely with WLP. I was euphoric, imagining the new avenues of action her guidance and presence would open up for women's leadership. Our conversation, as always with Mary, softly opened a window on the broader possibilities for the partnership we had built.

"I share your vision for a global women's movement that represents the views and values of women in the Global South and I support the idea that we need to change the structure of human relations to reflect a new egalitarian decision-making process in the family, replicated at all levels of society," she said, speaking in her soothing voice and with a sparkle in her eyes. "You and I know how long that effort has taken and how much longer it will take for it to become real." She took a sip of her wine and added, "But we have only eleven years to save our planet."

"Tell me what you are thinking," I asked.

"I think we should mobilize women to be serious actors both in the process of saving the planet and in advocating for climate justice." She continued, "If we don't act, women, especially the most underprivileged women, will suffer most, even though they have contributed least to the destruction."

Like many other feminist activists, I had thought about the environmental devastation we are witnessing. In my weekly phone calls to friends and family in my hometown of Kerman, they told me how water, always a precious commodity, had all but disappeared in many parts of the province. Pistachio trees that we referred to "as camels of vegetation," because they needed so little water and persevered on the driest lands, were dying. Others sent me photos of the parched riverbed of the beautiful Zayanderood in Isfahan. I was also familiar with the worsening global environmental degradation and felt anger and frustration when in 2017 the US president announced his plan to pull out of the Paris climate accord. But in my mind it seemed I had relegated that struggle to others.

Mary recalled her history as a wakeup call:

I felt I had to apologize for being rather late to the table. I realized that during my term as President of Ireland, then as UN High Commissioner for Human Rights, I never made a speech about the planet. Afterwards, as Honorary President of Oxfam, everywhere I went in Africa women would say to me, "We just don't know what's happening, the long periods of drought and the flash flooding and the rainy season that doesn't come or comes too late—we don't have schools, we don't have a hospital, we don't have access to clean water, we don't have supermarkets, the trees are our super markets, they are our pharmacies." I realized that food insecurity and scarcity of clean water in particular and so much else related to the environment was affecting women more than anyone.

Listening to Mary, I was embarrassed to think that the women's movement I was envisioning—global, holistic, and inclusive of all aspects of the human condition—had no real focus on the survival of life on our planet. We were dozing off in our own silo while the earth was fast changing, to the detriment of all living things.

I immediately switched to active mode. "I promise to educate myself on climate justice and share the information with our partners," I said. "We will focus on bringing together some of our allied organizations to connect climate activists with those working on refugees, poverty, human rights, and political leadership. We will organize a series of 'Feminist Climate Justice' seminars with leading organizations beginning in September, and if you join us at our WLP annual meeting in early November, we will bring it to the partners and board."

Mary's presentation at WLP's Climate Justice seminar on September 20, 2019, was an eloquent call to action. She referred to the millions of children who were marching throughout the world that day, united in a global general strike and demanding that the adults in charge do something to address climate change. "They are calling us out," she said. "I have a lovely text this morning from my two-year old grandchild, holding a placard that said, 'Don't burn my future.' It was written by somebody else, but she had scribbled all over it. I thought to myself, that's what it's about—that's a wake-up call and that's really why we need a Feminist Forum and a feminist solution."

The thirty women leaders present at the Climate Justice seminar were moved by her words, and each wanted to know more and to offer what role her organization could play. They spoke about the connection between water scarcity and health as well as nutrition, the loss of livable space and livelihood, and the increase in the number of refugees. Many had the same feeling I had when Mary first reached out to me. They were puzzled by how little involvement we had with the movement that was so closely connected to the groups and issues that were the focus of our work, as well as our collective survival. Mary added, "Climate change is a man-made problem and what it requires is a feminist solution, and a feminist solution definitely includes men."

At the 2019 WLP partners meeting, Mary was gratified by the partners' openness to new ideas and by each regional session's specific solutions. Moroccans who had worked successfully helping to gain land rights for rural Soualiyates women decided to make environmental protection a focus of their advocacy. The Lebanese partners who trained Syrian refugees in income-generating skills suggested expanding the project of cleaning the seashore of plastic. They gathered, cut into strips, and dyed the discarded plastic to make beautiful purses to provide income for themselves while helping improve water quality and fish survival. Our Senegalese partner, active in the Kilimanjaro Initiative, would work with parliamentarians to support women's work at the intersection of income generation and environmental protection.

Mary spent three days working with the WLP partners. She emphasized the importance of starting at the individual level, the root of all global change. This had been our belief and we each committed to three specific changes in our own behavior. Then we planned several advocacy and fundraising initiatives and events. WLP partners have since held multiday trainings in Brazil, Central Asia, Jordan, and Nigeria focusing on intergenerational advocacy and action for environmental preservation and climate justice. In 2021 alone, youth leaders from seventeen countries around the world participated in three regional youth institutes hosted by WLP partners, using the experience gained by our Jordan partner that originated the youth program in 2008.[5] These youth institutes, held annually, are developing the skills of hundreds of young leaders who are working on multimedia campaigns, websites, and apps to address many of the most pressing human rights issues, now focusing on climate justice. The youth trainings are important not just for imparting new skill sets but also for showing young people the value of empowering individuals to work together. As one participant in the 2021 Brazil institute said, "I learned that as much as it seems that we are fighting alone for a specific cause, there are other people who think and fight like us. In other words, my main learning was to believe in the strength of collective initiatives."

AS I write this chapter in August 2021, the globe is in the eighteenth month of the COVID-19 pandemic, and our experience of this devastating virus supports the understanding that, in the final analysis, our destiny is inescapably interconnected.

In conversations with women leaders, I have become increasingly aware that demanding equal rights in a world that is structured to perpetuate violence, poverty, and insecurity was in itself neither effective nor desirable. Our goal cannot be summed up in seeking the same rights as the other half of the population. A new system has to be put in place, and for that we have to make certain that women create a movement based on their collective power as the majority of the world's population. The most important aspect of this movement is not only that we are more than half of the world's population but that we have a primary role in educating both genders and that we contain within our numbers all the other minorities of the oppressed as well as the powerful.

WLP's second decade brought to us a blossoming of our partnership that confirmed the validity of our shared vision and the necessity of communicating that vision in ways that are in tune with particular communities and cultures across the globe. We learned what would work and what would not, how to define our issues, where to look for solutions and how to identify our allies within a cross section of disciplines and capabilities. We became adept at finding how to pass on the knowledge we gained to others across borders of language and culture and how to make our material local and native— seamlessly adapted and comfortably assimilated. We used the new methods of communication to realize our goal of ongoing connection and exchange. Every year we came closer to our goal of a shared vision of the future we wished to build through a renewed version of our diverse cultures, keeping what is good and in harmony with our aspirations and changing what time and awareness had made cruel and ugly.

Epilogue

I N RECENT YEARS A new level of awareness among women has emerged across the world. It is as if curtains are falling down all around us, revealing scenes of incomprehensible cruelty and violence—events that do not make sense and for which there is no rational explanation. For me, the first shock happened decades ago on a sight-seeing bus going around Berlin in 1989, shortly after the Wall fell. Looking at the devastated buildings that seemed to be talking to me, I was reminded of the events that had led to these scenes. Peoples who had been friends had become foes, only to become friends again. More than 80 million killed in World War II—only a small part of the enormous toll of misery and suffering that was endured by people around the world. I was reminded of scenes of the young soldiers up to their waists in the waves at Normandy, mowed down by other young men in planes who could not distinguish the faces of the ones who fell, one from another—and other horrific images, such as the naked young girl running on the dirt road in Vietnam, her face a mask of terror; babies whose arms were bones covered by mere skin, eyes barely seeing, dying of starvation in a war without a cause in

Yemen that no one understood or explained and no country tried to stop; and the latest—tens of thousands of Afghan men, women, and children pushing against the barriers around Kabul International Airport, some hanging on to the wings and undersides of American military planes in their horror and fear of being left behind.

After the fall of Kabul, it was heartbreaking for me to speak with Habiba Sarabi, the wonderful Afghan minister of women and the only woman who had ever served as governor in Afghanistan. With her husband in hiding and her family scattered, I was reminded of my own exile, my fear for my husband's fate, and the horrors of losing all that we had worked for and believed in. I was back inside the mind and body of the young woman I had been who expected so much of the country that was host to her youthful self and that served as a model for what she had wished to achieve in Iran.

We have seen these images and experienced these situations and many more throughout the years—nearly every day of our lives. But somehow previously it all seemed inevitable; there seemed to be a reason, a cause, somehow an explanation. Now, for the first time, we realize that it is all insane, abnormal, inhuman, and inhumane. There is no reason for all this except that the system periodically whips itself up into a state of madness, and the massacres and destructions begin. There are anthems and flags and symbols and medals for actions that if witnessed at another time and place would be considered criminal. If *those countries* that have the power and the money are not themselves directly involved, the killing and destruction continues for decades: witness Afghanistan, Iraq, Syria. If it is *those countries'* homes, *their* children, *their* livelihood, and *their* cities that are being torn apart, then it ends sooner. Women have had little to nothing to do with the decisions that bring us these horrors. But there are those who try to convince the smarter and stronger of us to try to join this scene, to adopt the values, behavior, and beliefs that create and justify these acts.

MEN AND women of goodwill and understanding have warned us against the folly and danger of our ways. As women, we have not used our potential power, first because circumstances would not allow it, then because the cultural and structural systems appropriating and distributing power were in our way. But, most important, because as those responsible for training and educating both our male and female children, we pass on to them the nuances of the same patriarchal culture that we were taught by our mothers. We are as much a product of the culture that shapes our lives and our values as the men. The patriarchal culture is not limited to gender relations but also includes the

ambition, aggression, and acquisitiveness that governs the world we have created. This also explains why we have accepted our role in life not as a member
of the majority of the population of the earth that embodies and includes all
minorities but in effect as another oppressed minority.

But now that our planet is in danger of becoming inhospitable because of
our destructive climate policies or the unbridled production of armaments
capable of destroying the earth and its people many times over, we women
must take the responsibility of exerting the power of our numbers to encourage peaceful interaction and major change in the entire unfair, unsafe, and
unsustainable conditions of life that the people of the earth experience. The
first thing we need to accept is that there is no savior except ourselves, and
we cannot save our children and grandchildren simply by accepting our fate,
feeling helpless, or struggling in the silos that some of us have chosen, focusing
on our specific oppression and the injustice our group experiences.

Science, technology, and intellect tell us that we have little time. We are
closer to destroying ourselves and our planet than we have ever been. Sensible
and rational people go about their daily lives with a false sense of security,
mostly worrying about mundane issues, while placing in power systems that
can destroy the planet by accident or by the whim of unbalanced dictators.

We all—women *and* men—must not accept the behavior that has brought
us to where we are. We must adjust our vision to our goals and be the example
by walking the talk. Anger, violence, and intolerance will not bring us peace,
inclusion, and tolerance. Neither will victimhood make women strong role
models. What has been done to women has been unjust and unfair, but that
does not justify our behaving in the same way. That we have not been heard
does not justify our refusing to hear others. Women, who constitute more
than half of the world's population, have not been respected or allowed to
participate and have been oppressed and abused. But changing that culture
and that reality requires that we do not replicate it.

Women must work with men to change the culture of institutions and the
workplace, across communities and societies from local to global. Women
must also share with men what we have learned from centuries of caregiv-
ing, consensus building, negotiation, managing young and old in families and
communities, articulating our emotions, and communicating our thoughts
and feelings. Women must also learn from men all that the privilege of their
gender in the patriarchal culture has nurtured in them and has allowed them
to practice for centuries: their boldness, decisiveness, and belief in themselves.

One lesson I learned early was that the structure of human relations around
the world has taken shape in the family with father—the patriarch—at the top

of the authority pyramid, and that all other institutions replicated that structure. Laws, civic and political organizations, religious institutions, supported by arts and literature, have strengthened and sustained that system. The patriarchal culture shaped in the family has been predominant throughout the world and throughout history until science and technology helped us begin to search for other ways of life based on the possibility of changing the relationship between men and women. Cultures around the world have changed to accommodate this major revamping of human relations, though at different speeds in different parts of the world. As has been said, "All people are not contemporary, though we do live on the same planet at the same time."

Today, systems of social organization rely on culturally defined hierarchies. While dismantling only one or some of the hierarchies could change the balance of power between men and women in many situations, it would not fundamentally change the way people relate to one another or the criteria for their choices and actions. We all—men and women—must replace traditional, patriarchal command structures with inclusive, participatory, and egalitarian decision-making and leadership. These changes need to occur at every level, from the family unit to the highest echelons of human authority, in order to create a social order that is responsive to the needs of all people, irrespective of gender or other distinctions. We must move beyond the historical definitions of equality and work together to create a new vision of human relations and to make that vision real. This new vision is what I hope I have touched on in this book, namely my understanding that to realize a just and peaceful world, and above all, a rational world, we need to change the architecture of human relations, which is based primarily on the culture of patriarchy and the structures that support it. To do that we must think and behave in new ways. We cannot replicate patriarchal leadership styles that encourage us to retain the existing models of competition, aggression, consumerism, greed, and unbridled ambition.

As I look back on my life within the women's movement, from my childhood in Iran to growing up in the United States, to my return to Iran to bring about change by helping build a vibrant women's movement, I am deeply conscious not only of the strategies that brought about the successes but also of the dimensions of the enormous backlash that brought the only theocratic government in history to one of the most modern developing nations in the Middle East and which spread quickly to a huge part of the world. As I followed my passion and experience, working in exile in the United States, I have used the lessons of my experience in Iran and shared them with my colleagues around the world, mindful of how to use those lessons with better results.

I look forward to a day, not too far in the future, when the evolving architecture of human relations will support and create the fundamentals of equal rights, human security, and well-being for *everyone* across the world. I am exuberant and profoundly confident that the younger generation of women and men will continue the effort with new ideas and expedite it with energy and determination and—most important—with humility, unity, and harmony.

Acknowledgments

L OOKING BACK AT THE narrative of my life's work with and for women, I am taken aback at how few of those who have been a part of it I have named or described in this work. I see their faces, hear their voices, and can remember the sound of their laughter and at times the muffled cries of discontent as they met challenges—and I recall how they appeared, were distanced by events, and often reappeared in my life and work. I marvel at what these women accomplished under difficult circumstances, when the law, the words of God, human values, the beauty of art, and the impact of culture were all used against them. I salute them and feel a deep gratitude for their courage and perseverance. The whole narrative of this book is about them and how they taught me, supported me, and made me feel "I am not alone" but also, more important, helped me realize "We can do it!"

I bow to the Iranian women who used the possibilities of the historical moment with amazing creativity, intelligence, and unity and built a national women's organization that applied the experience of their predecessors and the opportunities of a changing and modernizing world to develop a model of civic activism and internal democratic decision-making that I later brought to my colleagues and partners at the Women's Learning Partnership (WLP). WLP partners have gone on to adapt and use this model in thirty languages in sixty countries in four regions of the world with exceptional results. I acknowledge my debt to the hundreds of thousands of these amazing women with awe and gratitude.

My immediate family—brought up in the East and the West, who love the arts and literature of both worlds, have picked up the humor and joy of life that are expressed differently in each part of the world but that end in similar, humane results. The women of my family have been mentioned, some at length, but the men have not had much space in this narrative. They should have, if nothing else for their unusually "feminist" spirit, invariably treating women as true allies and partners. I am deeply indebted to my husband, Gholam; my son, Babak; my brother, Hamid; my nephew, Nema; and my grandson, Kiyan Alexander. I appreciate their generous help and support.

The WLP team has been helpful and enthusiastic about this project, and I thank them all, especially our executive director, Allison Horowski, who is replicating my youthful life by taking the huge responsibility of managing WLP while taking care of her new, wonderful baby, Leo, and moving to a new house.

Nanette Pyne, my longtime friend and ally, has been irreplaceable as critic, researcher, and all-around adviser.

I thank Cate Hodorowicz, my editor at the University of North Carolina Press, who has been ceaselessly kind and supportive, and the UNC Press team, for their proficient handling of this book.

Notes

CHAPTER 1

1. Short for *Shahzadeh*, meaning "princess."

2. The chador, the Iranian version of the veil, is a semicircle of fabric that women hold closed at the front.

3. *Khanom* is a Persian honorific and term of respect for a woman.

CHAPTER 3

1. Tahereh Saffarzadeh, "Love Poem," in *The Red Umbrella* (Iowa City, Iowa: Windhover, 1969), 20.

2. The call to prayer.

3. Tahereh Saffarzadeh, "Fath Kamel Nist" ("Victory Is Not Complete"), 1962–63, in Tahereh Saffarzadeh, *Tanin dar delta* (*Echo in Delta*) (Tehran: Amir Kabir, 1970), 94–96.

CHAPTER 4

1. Prince Sadr-ul-din Agha Khan was the brother of Karim Agha Khan, the head of the Ismaili sect of Islam. Sadr-ul-din was much respected in the international diplomatic community.

2. Zamzam is the name of the well within the Masjid al-Haram in Mecca.

CHAPTER 5

1. In 1966, 17.42 percent of the Iranian female population (over the age of six) was literate; the male literacy rate was 39.19 percent (over the age of six).

2. Unfortunately, "guardianship" laws like this one are still in force in many Muslim countries.

3. The toman was Iran's official currency until 1932, when it was replaced by the rial. However, many Iranians still use "toman" to refer to the equivalent of ten rials.

4. During our WOI team's travels to all provinces of Iran, women stressed the importance and priority of "economic independence"—and that required literacy- and skills-building classes, followed by jobs—both of which required childcare. This became a priority for me when I was appointed to the cabinet, as I remembered not only the stories we heard from workers on our WOI trips but also my days at University in Colorado, when I carried my toddler on my back from the library to the grocery store and back to my apartment every day. The WOI centers and branches were built around these ideas. We noticed later in our conversations with our Western guests, people we met on our trips to China, Russia, and other communist countries, as well as those in capitalist states like India, Iraq, Pakistan, and the United States, that the needs there were the same as for our women, but in no country was this issue properly and comfortably addressed.

5. Much of the information presented here about the WOI comes from three of my essays: "An Introduction to the Women's Organization of Iran" (Bethesda, Md.: Foundation for Iranian Studies), http://www.fis-iran.org/en/women/organization/introduction; "The Women's Organization of Iran: Evolutionary Politics and Revolutionary Change," in *Women in Iran from 1800 to the Islamic Republic,* ed. Lois Beck and Guity Nashat (Champaign: University of Illinois Press, 2004), 107–35; and "Women's Human Rights in Iran: From Global Declarations to Local Implementation," in *Women and Girls Rising: Progress and Resistance around the World,* ed. Ellen Chesler and Terry McGovern (New York: Routledge, 2016), 129–43.

6. David Heer, "Abortion, Contraception, and Population Policy in the Soviet Union," *Demography* 2 (1965): 531–39.

CHAPTER 6

1. *Lectures by Helvi Sipilä, Betty Friedan, and Germaine Greer* (Tehran: WOI, 1975), 14.

2. Germaine Greer, "The Betty I Knew," *Guardian,* February 7, 2006, https://www.theguardian.com/world/2006/feb/07/gender.bookscomment.

3. Betty Friedan, "The Feminist Empress of Iran," *Ladies' Home Journal,* June 1975, 102.

4. INSTRAW is the leading UN institute devoted to research, training, and knowledge management to achieve gender equality and women's empowerment.

5. Friedan, "Feminist Empress of Iran," 104.

CHAPTER 7

1. This and the following quotes are from Molly Haskell, "Feminism Is a Mirage in the Shah's Iran," *Village Voice*, June 21, 1976.

2. Haskell.

3. Haskell.

4. See Afkhami, "The Women's Organization of Iran: Evolutionary Politics and Revolutionary Change," in *Women in Iran from 1800 to the Islamic Republic*, ed. Lois Beck and Guity Nashat (Champaign: University of Illinois Press, 2004), 107–35.

5. The Group of Seventy-Seven was established in 1967 to promote economic cooperation and greater influence in world affairs among developing countries. Originally consisting of 77 nonaligned nations, the organization now has 134 member nations, primarily in Africa, Asia, and Latin America.

CHAPTER 8

1. Oral history interview with Elizabeth Reid, http://fis-iran.org/en/oralhistory.

2. The WOI High Council consisted of several cabinet members who met with Princess Ashraf and me twice a year to discuss women's issues. This led to the creation of the formal ministerial meeting, headed by the prime minister, provided for in Iran's National Plan of Action.

3. In March 1975, while I was in New York, immersed in the work of the Consultative Committee for the UN Mexico City conference, we heard news that the Shah had launched the Rastakhiz, or national awakening, and that in the process the two major political parties had been disbanded. Back in Iran, I was asked to represent women on the committee that was tasked with working out the outline and structure of the emerging movement. The committee was headed by Prime Minister Hoveyda, and I was intrigued by the discussions and saw possibilities for carving out a place for increasing women's political role and visibility. Though as a movement Rastakhiz was received with enthusiasm, its concept remained politically vague.

CHAPTER 9

1. The program was a global initiative of the Shah, for which he was given the title of Aryamehr (Light of the Aryans) by the ministers of education. The committee, launched in 1965, had as its mandate spreading education and permanently eradicating illiteracy in Iran. See Comité National pour le Programme Mondial d'Alphabétisation (Iran), "Programme d'alphabétisation en Iran (Literacy Campaign in Iran)," September 1970, https://files.eric.ed.gov/fulltext/ED048552.pdf.

2. Devoted to bringing the standards of opera in Iran up to international standards, Monir Vakili produced and hosted a music series on the National Iranian Television, created an opera film festival, and established the Academy of Voice in Iran.

CHAPTER 10

1. Jimmy Carter, "Tehran, Iran: Toasts of the President and the Shah at a State Dinner," December 31, 1977, American Presidency Project, https://www.presidency.ucsb.edu/documents/tehran-iran-toasts-the-president-and-the-shah-state-dinner.

2. See Yarden Mariuma, "Taqiyya as Polemic, Law and Knowledge: Following an Islamic Legal Term through the Worlds of Islamic Scholars, Ethnographers, Polemicists and Military Men," *Muslim World* 104, no. 1–2 (2014): 89–108.

3. Mahnaz Afkhami, "Iran's National Plan of Action: Ideology, Structure, Implementation" (Tehran: Manuscript prepared for publication for the Center for Research, WOI, 1978).

4. By this time Rastakhiz had evolved into one political party encompassing all of the people—a politically absurd concept that satisfied neither the Left nor the Right.

5. Article 20 of the constitution adopted after the Islamic Revolution proclaims equality for men and women. However, the constitution also mandates adhering to Shari'a law, according to which women inherit half of what a man would, and a woman's death is compensated at half that of a man's. After the Revolution, veiling was made compulsory, cosmetics were banned, women were banned from acting as judges, contraception was banned, and women were banned from various professions and fields of study.

6. After a two-year interim location in New York, INSTRAW moved to the Dominican Republic, which was not well positioned to help the center grow to its full potential. Nevertheless, INSTRAW remains to this day an important arm of the United Nations' work on women. By 1976 the ESCAP center had moved to Thailand and lost its independent function as a regional research and training center for women.

CHAPTER 12

1. See "Young Praises Islam as 'Vibrant' and Calls the Ayatollah 'a Saint,'" *New York Times*, February 8, 1979, https://timesmachine.nytimes.com/timesmachine/1979/02/08/issue.html; Raymond Tanter, "How Not to Negotiate with Rogue Regimes," *Foreign Policy*, January 6, 2015, https://foreignpolicy.com/2015/01/06/how-not-to-negotiate-with-rogue-regimes; Terence Smith, "Kennedy Chided by the Leaders of Both Parties," *New York Times*, December 4, 1979, https://www.nytimes.com/1979/12/04/archives/kennedy-chided-by-the-leaders-of-both-parties-remarks-on-shah.html.

2. Forough Farokhzad, "Fath-e bagh" ("Conquering the Garden"), 1960–61, in the author's possession.

3. Elizabeth Mason, foreword to *The Oral History Collection of the Foundation for Iranian Studies*, ed. Gholam Reza Afkhami and Seyyed Vali Reza Nasr (Bethesda, Md.: Foundation for Iranian Studies, 1991). Vali Nasr would become dean of the

Johns Hopkins School of Advanced International Studies. Gholam Reza prepared and published thirteen volumes based on the oral histories, titled *A Series in Iran's Economic and Social Development, 1941–1978.*

CHAPTER 13

1. A detailed version of my sister's story can be found in Azar Salamat, "Of Chance and Choice," in *Women in Exile,* ed. Mahnaz Afkhami (Charlottesville: University of Virginia Press, 1994), 78–99. Pseudonyms are used throughout that chapter, which is based on hours of oral interviews with my sister.

2. The Revolutionary Guards were called "brothers" by their supporters.

CHAPTER 14

1. The first global conference to focus exclusively on human rights was the International Conference on Human Rights held in Tehran, in April and May 1968, to mark the twentieth anniversary of the Universal Declaration of Human Rights.

2. His daughters continue to document the human rights abuses committed by the Islamic Republic and memorialize its victims through the Abdorrahman Boroumand Foundation for the Promotion of Human Rights and Democracy in Iran, an NGO that promotes human rights awareness through education and the dissemination of information as a necessary basis for the eventual establishment of a stable democracy in Iran.

3. For a riveting account documenting these murders and the subsequent trial, read Roya Hakakian, *Assassins of the Turquoise Palace* (New York: Grove, 2012).

4. Vienna Declaration and Programme of Action, adopted by the World Conference on Human Rights in Vienna on June 25, 1993; see https://www.ohchr.org/en /professionalinterest/pages/vienna.aspx.

5. Robin Morgan, ed., *Sisterhood Is Global: The International Women's Movement Anthology* (New York: Feminist Press at CUNY, 1996), 813–14.

CHAPTER 15

1. Mahnaz Afkhami and Haleh Vaziri, *Claiming Our Rights: A Manual for Women's Human Rights Education in Muslim Societies* (Bethesda, Md.: Sisterhood Is Global Institute, 1998).

2. Although *Claiming Our Rights* was first designed for use in Muslim-majority societies, the concept and methodology are adaptable to other ethnic and religious groups.

3. Sunder, professor of law at the University of California, Davis, called the manual "a radical new conception of human rights. While traditional legal understanding of 'the right to religion' favor leaders' views over the rights of dissenters and actively

affirms the right of leaders to impose their views on members, the *Manual* views freedom of religion and choice as an individual right to participate in the group and to shape one's own religion—not just as an individual right to belong or to leave." She went on to say, "The twenty-first century public is acquiring a New Enlightenment from the real-world activists of the transnational human rights movement [who] are doing the hard work of reimagining the present and future." Madhavi Sunder, "Piercing the Veil," *Yale Law Journal* 112, no. 6 (2003): 1453.

4. Kelly J. Shannon notes that *Claiming Our Rights* was "a tremendous success," that with it, "SIGI thus established itself as an influential transnational organization just as the Taliban seized power," and that after its publication SIGI "put itself in a position to lobby policymakers just as the U.S. government was deciding how to deal with the Taliban." Shannon, *U.S. Foreign Policy and Muslim Women's Human Rights* (Philadelphia: University of Pennsylvania Press, 2018), 133.

CHAPTER 16

1. Pourzand was convicted and sentenced to eleven years' imprisonment and a flogging of seventy-four lashes. While in Evin Prison, he suffered a severe heart attack and was ultimately transferred to house arrest. In 2011, he committed suicide by jumping from the balcony of his Tehran apartment.

CHAPTER 17

1. The Bible: Mark 12:17 and John 18:36.

2. The coauthor and author of several WLP publications, Ann Eisenberg was the assistant director of the Jacob Blaustein Institute for the Advancement of Human Rights in New York City and became the associate director of programs and publications at SIGI. She continues to assist WLP on development of its learning tools and with strategic planning. Rakhee Goyal went on to coordinate culture-specific human rights education and gender violence projects in South Asia and the Middle East at SIGI and later became the executive director of WLP.

CHAPTER 18

1. The Cosmos Club is a private social club on Embassy Row in Washington, D.C., for individuals distinguished in science, literature, the arts, a learned profession, or public service.

2. See Women's Learning Partnership, "Mission, Vision, and Guiding Principles," accessed January 14, 2021, https://learningpartnership.org/who-we-are/mission -vision-and-guiding-principles for a description of the Partnership's core values, objectives, and practices.

3. See Women's Learning Partnership, *Cultural Boundaries and Cyber Spaces: Women's Voices on Empowerment, Leadership, and Technology,* video, 2000, https://learningpartnership.org/resource/cultural-boundaries-and-cyber-spaces-womens-voices-empowerment-leadership-and-technology.

4. Women's Learning Partnership, *Leading to Choices: A Leadership Training Handbook for Women* (Bethesda, Md.: WLP, 2001), 30, https://learningpartnership.org/sites/default/files/resources/pdfs/English%20LTC%20Manual.pdf.

5. Oxfam International is a major international confederation of independent charitable organizations focusing on alleviating global poverty.

CHAPTER 19

1. For example, US Attorney General John Ashcroft said "the attacks of September 11 drew a bright line of demarcation between the civil and the savage." Attorney General John Ashcroft, Testimony before the House Committee on the Judiciary, September 24, 2001, https://irp.fas.org/congress/2001_hr/h092401_ashcroft.html. The Bush administration also described "terrorists" as "hateful," "treacherous," "barbarous," "mad," "twisted," "perverted," "without faith," "parasitical," "inhuman," and "evil." Richard Jackson, *Writing the War on Terrorism: Language, Politics and Counter-terrorism* (Manchester: Manchester University Press, 2005), 8, 62–75.

2. The four days of live, interactive radio webcast discussions of international women leaders' reactions to the September 11 terrorist attacks were titled "In the Aftermath of Terror: Women Leaders Discuss Peace, Justice, & Conflict Resolution in a Globalized World." See https://learningpartnership.org/events/aftermath-terror-women-leaders-discuss-peace-justice-conflict-resolution-globalized-world.

3. The program was called "Faith & Freedom: Women from the Three Abrahamic Religions Talk About Terror, War, and Peace." See https://learningpartnership.org/events/faith-freedom-women-from-three-abrahamic-religions-talk-about-terror-war-and-peace.

4. Dwight D. Eisenhower, "Transcript of President Dwight D. Eisenhower's Farewell Address (1961)," https://www.ourdocuments.gov/doc.php?flash=true&doc=90&page=transcript.

5. For example, the FBI's annual hate crimes statistics reports document the average numbers of anti-Islamic offenses at 31 per year before 2001, a figure that leaped to 546 in 2001. Federal Bureau of Investigation, Uniform Crime Reporting, "Crime in the United States 2001," accessed January 14, 2021, https://ucr.fbi.gov/crime-in-the-u.s/2001.

6. Interestingly, given the definition of *democracy* as holding elections, the Islamic Republic, for instance, was sometimes considered "democratic," although no secular candidate was ever allowed to stand for office and all candidates were preselected based on their religious credentials.

7. See Pew Global Attitudes Project, *How Global Publics View: War in Iraq, Democracy, Islam and Governance, Globalization*, Views of a Changing World 2003 (Washington, D.C.: Pew Research Center for the People and the Press, 2003), https://www.pewresearch.org/global/2003/06/03/views-of-a-changing-world-2003/.

CHAPTER 20

1. Women's Learning Partnership, *Guide to Equality in the Family in the Maghreb* (Bethesda, Md.: WLP Translation Series, 2005) (authorized translation of *Dalil pour l'égalité dans la famille au Maghreb*, Collective 95 Maghreb-Égalité, 2003).

2. This was formerly the impressive mansion of a Baha'i industrialist who founded one of Iran's first television stations.

3. This transcript of the conversation is based on the notes I took directly after this meeting.

4. Women's Learning Partnership, *Iranian Women's One Million Signatures Campaign for Equality: The Inside Story* (Bethesda, Md.: WLP Translation Series, 2009), https://learningpartnership.org/resource/iranian-womens-one-million-signatures-campaign-for-equality-inside-story-translation-1.

5. Ijtihad, for instance, could make a case against explaining polygamy by arguing that "When the Quran says 'a man can marry up to four wives,' the intention is that all four should be treated equally; and since no man can treat four wives equally, it actually means a man should not take four wives." What is needed is more than that. Religious leaders need to persuade their followers that in today's world with the changed life circumstances, polygamy, like slavery, is incompatible with human dignity and must be banned. Some have sought to make this argument, but it will only really prevail in the current context if justification for change is change in life conditions and cultures as ijtihad was meant to do. Polygamy should be banned not because "no man can treat four wives equally" but because the consciousness of individual rights and the context of relationships makes the practice abhorrent. "The ardent advocates of reinterpretation talk as if the limitation of women's rights in Shari'a law is a simple misunderstanding—a problem of communication!" one of our partners sardonically exclaimed!

6. The World Movement for Democracy is a thought leader and a platform for building practical synergies among democracy activists around the world on particular challenges. The organization organizes several initiatives to respond to pressing global issues. See World Movement for Democracy, "Join the Movement," accessed January 14, 2021, https://www.movedemocracy.org/.

7. Edna St. Vincent Millay, "Figs from Thistles: First Fig," *Poetry* 12, no. 3 (1918): 130.

CHAPTER 21

1. See the video recording on the Women's Learning Partnership website, https:// learningpartnership.org/resource/lifelines-2001-literature-human-rights-video.

2. See Women's UN Report Network, "Introducing the Women, Faith, and Development Alliance," March 17, 2008, https://wunrn.com/2008/03/women-faith -development-alliance/.

3. Religions for Peace is an international coalition of representatives from the world's religions dedicated to promoting peace founded in 1970. See Religions for Peace, home page, accessed January 14, 2021, www.rfp.org.

4. Azza Karam has served in a variety of posts over the years, all of which make her appointment as secretary general of RfP appropriate and hold promise for great collaboration with other NGOs.

5. Asma Khader and her group at SIGI/Jordan also developed the Young Women's Learning Partnership, an initiative that has taken place annually beginning in 2008, with eighteen-to-twenty-four-year-old men and women from all provinces of Jordan and eventually across the Middle East and North Africa. The initiative includes a manual that provides creative and collaborative workshop sessions on leadership skills for youth (Women's Learning Partnership, *Yes I Can: Leadership for Teens*, 2011, https://learningpartnership.org/resource/yes-i-can-leadership-for-teens-manual -english), which has been published in Arabic, English, French, Turkish, and Urdu; and trainings focusing on using social media and information technology to advocate for and advance equality, human rights, and democracy.

Index